Race and Epistemologies of Ignorance

SUNY series, Philosophy and Race

Ronald Bernasconi and T. Denean Sharpley-Whiting, editors

Race and Epistemologies of Ignorance

EDITED BY

Shannon Sullivan
and
Nancy Tuana

State University of New York Press

Published by
State University of New York Press, Albany

For information, contact State University of New York Press, Albany, NY
www.sunypress.edu

Production by Diane Ganeles
Marketing by Anne M. Valentine

Cover art: Remedios Varo (Spain 1908–Mexico 1963) "Spiral Transit" 1962 Oil on Masonite

Library of Congress Cataloging-in-Publication Data

Race and epistemologies of ignorance / edited by Shannon Sullivan, Nancy Tuana.
        p. cm — (SUNY series, philosophy and race)
    Includes bibliographical references and index.
    ISBN-13: 978-0-7914-7101-2 (hardcover : alk. paper)
    ISBN-13: 978-0-7914-7102-9 (pbk. : alk. paper)
   1. Race relations.   2. Social epistemology.   I. Sullivan, Shannon, 1967–   II. Tuana,
Nancy.

HT1521.R234 2007
305.8—dc22
                                                                        2006021972

10 9 8 7 6 5 4 3 2 1

CONTENTS

Introduction

Shannon Sullivan and Nancy Tuana

Epistemology and ignorance—how could two such different things go together? Given that epistemology is the study of how one knows and ignorance is a condition of not knowing, epistemology would seem to have
nothing to do with ignorance. At best, it might appear that the two concepts are related in that epistemology studies the operations of knowledge with the goal of eliminating ignorance. But in either case,
epistemology and ignorance seem diametrically opposed. What, then,
might be an epistemology of ignorance, and what possible connections
might it have to issues of race?

The epistemology of ignorance is an examination of the complex
phenomena of ignorance, which has as its aim identifying different
forms of ignorance, examining how they are produced and sustained,
and what role they play in knowledge practices. The authors in this volume examine the value of applying an epistemology of ignorance to issues of race, racism, and white privilege. Ignorance often is thought of as
a gap in knowledge, as an epistemic oversight that easily could be remedied once it has been noticed. It can seem to be an accidental by-product
of the limited time and resources that human beings have to investigate
and understand their world. While this type of ignorance does exist, it is
not the only kind. Sometimes what we do not know is not a mere gap in
knowledge, the accidental result of an epistemological oversight. Especially in the case of racial oppression, a lack of knowledge or an unlearning of something previously known often is actively produced for
purposes of domination and exploitation. At times this takes the form of
those in the center refusing to allow the marginalized to know: witness
the nineteenth-century prohibition against black slaves' literacy. Other
times it can take the form of the center's own ignorance of injustice, cru-
elty, and suffering, such as contemporary white people's obliviousness to
racism and white domination. Sometimes these "unknowledges" are consciously produced, while at other times they are unconsciously generated

1

and supported. In both cases, our authors examine instances where they work to support white privilege and supremacy.

But ignorance is not only a tool of oppression wielded by the powerful. It also can be a strategy for the survival of the victimized and oppressed, as in the case of black slaves' feigned ignorance of many details of their white masters' lives. This survival strategy also can take the form of the oppressed combating their oppression by unlearning the oppressor's knowledge, which has been both passively absorbed and actively forced upon them. Ignorance can be used against itself. It can be an important tool for the oppressed to wield against their oppressors, including their production of ignorance to dominate and exploit.

As this volume attests, tracing what is not known and the politics of such ignorance should be a key element of epistemological and social and political analyses, for it has the potential to reveal the role of power in the construction of what is known and provide a lens for the political values at work in our knowledge practices. Although racial oppression has been investigated as an unjust practice, few have fully examined the ways in which such practices of oppression are linked to our conceptions and productions of knowledge. Even less attention has been paid to the epistemically complex processes of the production and maintenance of ignorance. As the underside of knowledge, ignorance warrants careful examination, and nowhere is this truer than in the case of race and racism.

An exception to the neglect of racialized ignorance can be found in the work of Charles Mills who, in his book *The Racial Contract* (1997), argues that "[o]n matters related to race, the Racial Contract prescribes for its signatories an inverted epistemology, an epistemology of ignorance, a particular pattern of localized and global cognitive dysfunctions (which are psychologically and socially functional), producing the ironic outcome that whites will in general be unable to understand the world they themselves have made" (1997, 18). For Mills, the epistemology of ignorance is part of a white supremacist state in which the human race is racially divided into full persons and subpersons. Even though—or, more accurately, precisely because—they tend not to understand the racist world in which they live, white people are able to fully benefit from its racial hierarchies, ontologies, and economies.

Another exception to the neglect of racialized ignorance can be found in the work of Marilyn Frye. In *The Politics of Reality* (1983), Frye similarly explains that "ignorance is not something simple: it is not a simple lack, absence or emptiness, and it is not a passive state. Ignorance of this sort—the determined ignorance most white Americans have of American Indian tribes and clans, the ostrichlike ignorance most white Americans have of the histories of Asian peoples in this country, the impoverishing ignorance most white Americans have of Black language—

ignorance of these sorts is a complex result of many acts and many neg-
ligences" (1983, 118). Frye demonstrates how white ignorance often is an
active force in the lives of those, such as feminists, who think of themselves as anti-racist. Far from accidental, the ignorance of the racially
privileged often is deliberately cultivated by them, an act made easier by
a vast array of institutional systems supporting white people's obliviousness of the worlds of people of color.

Although they do not focus on race, other exceptions to the neglect
of manufactured ignorance can be found in the fields of history and science studies. Robert Proctor's (1996) examination of the "cancer wars"
in the United States argued that political factors have negatively im-
pacted cancer research, deliberately creating confusion and uncertainty
about the carcinogenic risk of products such as tobacco, meat, and as-
bestos. Influenced by the work of Proctor, Mills, and Frye, Nancy Tuana
(2004) examined the value of an epistemology of ignorance for a better
understanding of the ways in which sexism informs the science of female
sexuality. Invoking the idea of "agnotology," or the study of what is unknown, Londa Schiebinger (2004) examined the sexual politics behind
the creation of ignorance of abortifacients in Europe. Given Proctor's,
Tuana's, and Schiebinger's focus on ignorance as a culturally and politically induced product, their work on the role of ignorance in science
complements the application of epistemologies of ignorance to racialized ignorance introduced by Frye and Mills and developed here.[1]

Building on previous work on the epistemologies of ignorance and
working out of continental, analytic, and pragmatist traditions, the thirteen authors in this volume critically examine practices of not knowing
that are linked to and often support racism. Part I, "Theorizing Ignorance," explores some of the theoretical complexities of racialized ignorance. Charles W. Mills begins with "White Ignorance," in which he
elaborates on one of the key themes of his book *The Racial Contract*. Linked
with white supremacy, white ignorance includes both false belief and the
absence of true belief about people of color, supporting a delusion of
white racial superiority that can afflict white and nonwhite people alike.
White ignorance operates with a particular kind of social cognition that
distorts reality. For example, the lens with which white people (and others
suffering from white ignorance) perceive the world is shaped by white supremacy, causing them to mis-see whites as civilized superiors and nonwhites as inferior "savages." White ignorance also impacts social and
individual memory, erasing both the achievements of people of color and
the atrocities of white people. A collective amnesia about the past is the result, which supports hostility toward the testimony and credibility of nonwhite people. By mapping white ignorance in these ways, Mills seeks both
to minimize it and to make possible genuine knowledge about the world.

Mills's work in *The Racial Contract* plays an important role in Linda Martín Alcoff's chapter "Epistemologies of Ignorance: Three Types," which develops a typology of recent arguments for an epistemology of ignorance. Beginning with the feminist philosophy of Lorraine Code, Alcoff explains that the first argument is that ignorance results from humans' situatedness as knowers. Because we are located, partial beings, we cannot know everything. Based on the standpoint theory of Sandra Harding, the second argument further develops the first by connecting ignorance to aspects of group identities. Situatedness is not merely a general feature of human existence. It is shaped by things such as race, which means that the ignorance that results from it also is racially inflected. The third argument is drawn from Mills's work and provides a structural analysis of how oppressive systems generate ignorance. Elaborating on that argument, Alcoff turns to Jurgen Horkheimer and the Frankfurt School, using their critique of rationality under capitalism to show how systemic ignorance is generated. With Horkheimer and Mills, Alcoff concludes that successful analyses of racial and other forms of systemic ignorance must be able to demonstrate alternatives to them and thus cannot afford postmodern refusals of concepts of truth, reason, and reality.

Harvey Cormier implicitly challenges Mills and Alcoff by arguing that an epistemology of ignorance will not help combat white privilege and racial injustice. In "Ever Not Quite: Unfinished Theories, Unfinished Societies, and Pragmatism," Cormier alleges that a dichotomy between appearance and reality lies at the heart of the epistemologies of ignorance. This dichotomy leads to the problem of ideology: if a structure of deceptively egalitarian appearances has been erected on top of a racist reality, then how can a person be sure that her vision of the world is untainted by the reigning ideology? Drawing on the pragmatist philosophies of Richard Rorty, Cornell West, and William James, Cormier urges that we jettison talk of appearance and reality and accept that all truths are a creation of human beings seeking to satisfy their desires and mold the world in particular ways. For Cormier, critical race theorists would be better off asking if certain beliefs help eliminate racism than if they match reality. The problem of white privilege and domination is not one of pervasive ignorance of reality but of the need for political struggle to build an antiracist society.

In her contribution titled "Strategic Ignorance," Alison Bailey shares Cormier's concern that dichotomous thinking limits Mills's epistemology of ignorance. If the Racial Contract operates with an inverted epistemology that uses ignorance to present a falsehood as a truth, then the solution would seem to be a kind of cognitive therapy that allows the truth about white and nonwhite people to be recognized. Bailey argues that while this sort of therapy has a limited role to play in antiracist struggle, it utilizes the same logic of purity that plagues the problem it attempts to solve. A more radical and long-lasting solution to racism and white supremacy can be developed, according to Bailey, with the curdled logic found in the work of María Lugones. Curdled logic draws on the resistance of people of color to highlight agency under oppression. Rather than simply oppose ignorance to knowledge, curdled logic demonstrates how a strategic use of ignorance is made possible through ambiguity, multiplicity, and dissembling. Reading Mills's work through a curdled lens, Bailey proposes an epistemology of ignorance in which oppressed people are not merely victims but also what she refers to as "oppressed<->resisting subjects."

Sarah Lucia Hoagland also draws on Lugones to argue that relationality is crucial to antiracist and feminist struggle. In "Denying Relationality: Epistemology and Ethics and Ignorance," she examines the denial of relationality that is at the heart of practitioners of dominant culture who are ignorant about those whom they oppress. Epistemologies that presuppose autonomy render invisible the relationality that structures subjectivites at both the individual and cultural levels. Recognizing relationality means acknowledging ontological interdependence, which transforms how we think of communicating across and through differences. Rather than exist as distinct categories—woman, man, lesbian, white, Latina, and so on—across which common ground needs to be found, those struggling against oppression are located in concrete geographies that support different worlds of meaning. Engaging in dialogue with Lugones and others having different geographies from her own, Hoagland enacts the complex communication that relationality demands.

Part I concludes with Elizabeth V. Spelman's analysis of some of the strategies deployed in the management of white ignorance. In "Managing Ignorance," Spelman draws on the work of James Baldwin to show how white America avoided inquiry into and knowledge of the horrors of white racism in the decades following the Civil War. White people tend to have a complicated relationship to the reality of black grievances, simultaneously believing that they are false and wanting to believe that they are false (which implies a recognition that they are true), a messy cognitive state that often is avoided by ignoring black grievances altogether. The management of this ignorance can be seen in the reunions of white Confederate and Union soldiers that were meant to repair relationships damaged by the war. The reconciliation of North and South carefully avoided any mention of slavery or race, as if the war were a squabble between two brothers that had nothing to do with the status of black people in the United States. Spelman demonstrates how the cultivated ignorance of the plight of black people and the neglect of racial justice were requirements for white healing to occur.

Part II, "Situating Ignorance," explores some of the geographical, historical, and disciplinary sites in which racial ignorance has operated and often continues to operate. In "Race Problems, Unknown Publics, Paralysis, and Faith," Paul C. Taylor draws on John Dewey and W. E. B. Du Bois to examine the social production of ignorance about race. Taylor describes racial groups as Deweyan publics: populations that collectively experience similar social situations and need to become self-aware to abolish ignorance of their common plight. Applying this radical constructionist view of race to the case of the 2004 coup in Haiti, Taylor confronts both the widespread ignorance about the history of U.S. intervention in Latin America and the Caribbean and his own crisis in faith in public moral deliberation. Personally invested in the welfare of Haiti and thus shaken by the U.S. government's obscurantism about its foreign policy, Taylor challenges the utopian optimism that, he discovers, lies behind his radical constructionism. Urging that belief in the complete elimination of racial and colonialist injustice be replaced by permanent struggle against it, Taylor confronts the existential obstacles that millenarian faith can lay across the path of liberatory activity.

Shannon Sullivan also examines the role that ignorance plays in the relationship between the United States and the Caribbean. In "White Ignorance and Colonial Oppression: Or, Why I Know So Little about Puerto Rico," she explores her relationship as a white person with Puerto Rico. Providing a historical overview of the United States' acquisition of Puerto Rico as a colony and then focusing on the educational system subsequently installed, Sullivan charts how knowledge and ignorance intertwined to transform Puerto Ricans into "Porto Ricans" in the eyes of non-Puerto Rican U.S. citizens. Unlike the allegedly dark and savage Filipinos, "Porto Ricans" were seen as docile colonial subjects capable of Americanization. While the image of "Porto Ricans" thus contributes to the oppression of Puerto Ricans, it also can be a site for resistance when Puerto Ricans strategically use colonialist ignorance/knowledge to redistribute wealth from the mainland to the island. Challenging white ignorance of Puerto Rico, Sullivan demonstrates how the solution cannot be a simple increase in knowledge, because certain forms of knowledge can support rather than undermine racism and (neo)colonialism.

In "John Dewey, W. E. B. Du Bois, and Alain Locke: A Case Study in White Ignorance and Intellectual Segregation," Frank Margonis continues the discussion begun by Taylor and Cormier about the possible contributions of pragmatism to epistemologies of ignorance. Margonis examines Dewey's neglect of issues of race, which created an absence in his published work that is more than an insignificant gap. Erasing racial violence from the story of the United States' development, Dewey prepared the way for "color-blind" understandings of the nation's international affairs as exercises in democracy. Du Bois and Locke, in contrast, confronted the racial violence of U.S. history and as a result saw World War I as an imperialist war in which white nations were fighting over access to the riches of predominantly nonwhite nations. As Margonis argues, Dewey's erasure of race offers a negative lesson to contemporary pragmatists and other antiracist theorists. Like Dewey, white philosophers today cannot afford to intellectually segregate themselves from philosophers of color. Speaking across and through racial divisions is the most potent weapon against epistemologies of ignorance that support white domination.

Lucius T. Outlaw (Jr.) also voices his concern about the current state of American philosophy in "Social Ordering and the Systematic Production of Ignorance." Focusing on practices of education, Outlaw explains how schools have been a primary site for the production and distribution of white ignorance of other races. From the nineteenth century onward, schools have been institutions of "Americanization," a process of teaching a hierarchical racial ontology in which white people dominate all others. According to Outlaw, the academic field of philosophy participates in this process just as much as other fields and levels of schooling. Philosophers in the United States can be—and often are—completely ignorant of figures and issues that fall outside of a white, male canon. This is particularly problematic given that today's Ph.D. candidates in philosophy will be teaching an increasing number of nonwhite undergraduate students. In response, Outlaw calls for a transformation of knowledge production in academic philosophy that will eliminate its present (mis)education into ignorance.

Lorraine Code further explores the relationship between ignorance and racialized colonialism in "The Power of Ignorance." Juxtaposing George Eliot's 1876 novel *Daniel Deronda* and James Mill's 1817 *The History of British India*, Code diagnoses some of the modes of ignorance that shaped the English-speaking white Western world in the nineteenth century. Although one work is fiction and the other history, together they expose patterns of privilege and ignorance at both the personal and global level. The female protagonist of the novel, Gwendolen Harlech, is ignorant of her ignorance of the lives of the poor and lower classes, while Mill celebrates his ignorance of colonized India. Both texts show how ignorance helps reify sexual, racial, and colonial hierarchies. The class and colonial-racial forms of ignorance in these works are coconstitutive with gender-based ignorance: Harlech's cosseted privilege is in part a result of the patriarchal world in which she lives, and the country of India is feminized by Mill as a compliant subject to a paternalistic colonizer. Connecting these modalities of ignorance to Michele Le Doueff's work on the maintenance of epistemic hierarchies in European history, Code develops an ecology of ignorance that focuses on the human subjects that embody and live not-knowing.

In "On Needing Not to Know and Forgetting What One Never Knew: The Epistemology of Ignorance in Fanon's Critique of Sartre," Robert Bernasconi explores the significance of Franz Fanon's claim that "the European knows and does not know" in the context of Jean-Paul Sartre's essay on negritude, "Black Orpheus." When Sartre depicts negritude as a temporary moment in the dialectical movement to a raceless society, he undermines Fanon's attempts to affirm his blackness. From Fanon's perspective, Sartre's criticism of negritude is not necessarily wrong, but it is a piece of knowledge of which Fanon needed to remain ignorant in his fight against white supremacy. By claiming to know more than black people about their own situation of racial struggle, Sartre failed to acknowledge both his own racial location and the ignorance that accompanied it. As Bernasconi argues, Sartre's efforts to support antiracist work were undermined by his blind spots. Although well intentioned, they serve as a warning to white people who think their knowledge is sufficient to eliminate racism.

Stephanie Malia Fullerton closes the volume by challenging the belief commonly held by philosophers that science has disproved the existence of distinct races and that ignorance of this fact is what impedes the fight against racism. In "On the Absence of Biology in Philosophical Considerations of Race," Fullerton explains that while physical anthropology and population genetics have shown that no fixed, innate biological differences separate people into different races, they also have demonstrated that genetic differences correlate with geography and map onto racial categories. Focusing on Kwame Anthony Appiah's eliminitivist philosophy, Fullerton explains how biology wrongly has been written out of many philosophical accounts of race, creating a problematic ignorance of both race's biological dimensions and the current state of the biological sciences. Cautioning that biology should not be left at the door of critical race theory, Fullerton encourages philosophers to acknowledge the complex bio-social relation between genetic inheritance and phenotype, culture, and history that gives rise to racial identity and meaning.

Many more topics and issues are related to racialized ignorance that deserve investigation, and we hope these thirteen chapters will inspire further work on them. Some of the discipline-based topics include problems of ignorance in Western philosophy as found in the work of Nietzsche (truth as necessary error), Heidegger (truth as simultaneous disclosure and concealment), Plato (epistemology as anamnesis), Descartes (ignorance and the evil deceiver), Rawls (the veil of ignorance), and many others; and the epistemology of ignorance vis-à-vis the long-standing philosophical tradition of skepticism. The operation of racialized ignorance in recent geopolitical events warrants exploration, especially in the case of genocide in the Sudan, the wars in Afghanistan and Iraq, the slaughter in

Rwanda and Burundi, and the September 11, 2001, attacks. The role that race- and class-based ignorance has played in recent natural disasters, such as Hurricane Katrina, also deserves attention. Finally, some of the broad questions that might guide future work on race and epistemology of ignorance include the following: To what extent are we obliged to know all that there is to know, or is allegedly knowable? Are there degrees of culpability for incurred ignorance? Are all epistemic subjects under the same obligations to know the same things? Are there term limits on certain forms of ignorance, and are some forms of ignorance more grievous than others, and if so, what are the criteria for differentiation? While these topics and questions are not comprehensive, we present them as a "wish list" for additional research in the blossoming field of the epistemology of ignorance.[2]

* * *

This book grew out of the 2004 Penn State Rock Ethics Institute Conference, "Ethics and Epistemologies of Ignorance." This conference was cosponsored by the Penn State Africana Research Center, the Department of Philosophy, and the Women's Studies Program. The conference, in turn, had its roots in a National Endowment for the Humanities (NEH) Summer Seminar on Feminist Epistemologies that we codirected in 2003. Fifteen gifted scholars, Rita Alfonso, Lisa Diedrich, Carla Fehr, Mary Margaret Fonow, Heidi Grasswick, Catherine Hundleby, Debra Jackson, Marianne Janack, Nancy McHugh, Patricia Moore, L. Ryan Musgrave, Mariana Ortega, Mary Solberg, Alice Sowaal, and Penny Weiss, participated in the intense five-week seminar, exploring connections between ethics, politics, and epistemology and culminating in a focus on ignorance. Their work, and our work as directors of the seminar, was augmented by four visiting scholars: Linda Martín Alcoff, Lorraine Code, Lynn Hankinson Nelson, and Charlene Haddock Seigfried. The NEH scholars and visiting scholars contributed to the enormous success of the multidisciplinary conference, which explored the ethical, political, and epistemological implications of the conscious and unconscious production of ignorance as it impacts practices of domination, exploitation, and oppression. Many scholars who participated in the first NEH Summer Seminar on Feminist Epistemologies directed by Nancy Tuana in 1996 came to the conference, as well as over sixty participants. The topic sparked a great deal of interest, dialogue, and exciting new work, more of which can be found in a guest-edited issue of the feminist philosophy journal *Hypatia* on Feminist Epistemologies of Ignorance (Tuana and Sullivan, 2006). The second NEH Summer Seminar and the "Ethics and Epistemologies of Ignorance" conference gave birth to a new scholarly organization called FEMMSS—Feminist Epistemologies, Metaphysics, Methodologies, and Science Studies—which had its inaugural meeting at the University of Washington in 2004. We would like to thank all of the feminist and race theory scholars who supported the conference and the development of FEMMSS, including Linda Martín Alcoff, Susan Babbitt, Robert Bernasconi, Peg Brand, Tina Chanter, Lorraine Code, Harvey Cormier, Penelope Deutscher, Carla Fehr, Mary Margaret Fonow, Marilyn Frye, Heidi Grasswick, Sandra Harding, Lisa Heldke, Sarah Lucia Hoagland, Catherine Hundleby, Debra Jackson, Marianne Janack, María Lugones, Nancy McHugh, Charles Mills, Patricia Moore, L. Ryan Musgrave, Lynn Hankinson Nelson, Mariana Ortega, Lucius T. Outlaw Jr., Naomi Scheman, Alice Sowaal, Elizabeth V. Spelman, Gail Weiss, and Penny Weiss. We also would like to thank the National Endowment for the Humanities; Penn State University's Rock Ethics Institute, the Africana Research Center, the Philosophy Department, and the Women's Studies Program, as well as the NEH Summer Seminar participants and the conference speakers and attendees for their support of and excited involvement in the blossoming field of epistemologies of ignorance. Finally, we cannot thank enough Kathy Rumbaugh and Barb Edwards for all of the hard work they both put into the conference and the preparation of this anthology. Without the support of all of these people and institutions, this volume would not have been possible.

Notes

1. For additional work related to the epistemologies of ignorance, especially in connection to race, see Sullivan (2006).

2. Thanks to two anonymous reviewers for help with these lists of topics and questions.

References

Frye, Marilyn. 1983. *The Politics of Reality: Essays in Feminist Theory*. Freedom, CA: Crossing Press.

Mills, Charles. 1997. *The Racial Contract*. Ithaca, NY: Cornell University Press.

Proctor, Robert N. 1996. *Cancer Wars: How Politics Shapes What We Know and Don't Know about Cancer*. New York: HarperCollins.

Schiebinger, Londa. 2004. "Feminist History of Colonial Science." *Hypatia* 19 (1): 233–54.

Sullivan, Shannon. 2006. *Revealing Whiteness: The Unconscious Habits of Racial Privilege*. Bloomington: Indiana University Press.

Tuana, Nancy. 2004. "Coming to Understand: Orgasm and the Epistemology of Ignorance." *Hypatia* 19 (1): 194–232.

Tuana, Nancy, and Shannon Sullivan, eds. 2006. Special Issue on Feminist Epistemologies of Ignorance. *Hypatia* 21 (3).

PART I

Theorizing Ignorance

CHAPTER 1

White Ignorance

Charles W. Mills

White ignorance . . .
It's a big subject. How much time do you have?
It's not enough.
Ignorance is usually thought of as the passive obverse to knowledge,
*   the darkness retreating before the spread of Enlightenment.*
But . . .
Imagine an ignorance that resists.
Imagine an ignorance that fights back.
Imagine an ignorance militant, aggressive, not to be intimidated,
*   an ignorance that is active, dynamic, that refuses to go quietly—*
*   not at all confined to the illiterate and uneducated but propagated*
*   at the highest levels of the land, indeed presenting itself unblushingly*
*   as* knowledge.

I

Classically individualist, indeed sometimes—self-parodically—to the verge
of solipsism, blithely indifferent to the possible cognitive consequences of
class, racial, or gender situatedness (or, perhaps more accurately, taking a
propertied white male standpoint as given), modern mainstream Anglo-
American epistemology was for hundreds of years from its Cartesian origins profoundly inimical terrain for the development of any concept of
structural group-based miscognition. The paradigm exemplars of phenomena likely to foster mistaken belief—optical illusions, hallucinations,
phantom limbs, dreams—were by their very banality universal to the
human condition and the epistemic remedies prescribed—for example,
rejecting all but the indubitable—correspondingly abstract and general.

13

Nineteenth-century Marxism, with its theoretical insistence on locating the individual agent and the individual cognizer in group (basically class) structures of domination, and its concepts of ideology, fetishism, societal "appearance," and divergent group (basically class) perspectives on the social order, offered a potential corrective to this epistemological individualism. But to the extent that there was a mainstream twentieth-century appropriation of these ideas, in the form of *Wissenssoziologie*, the sociology of knowledge, it drew its genealogy from Karl Mannheim rather than Karl Marx, was frequently (despite terminological hedges such as Mannheim's "relationism") relativistic, and was in any case confined to sociology (Curtis and Petras 1970). So though some figures, such as Max Scheler and Mannheim himself, explicitly argued for the epistemological implications of their work, these claims were not engaged with by philosophers in the analytic tradition. A seemingly straightforward and clear-cut division of conceptual and disciplinary labor was presumed: descriptive issues of recording and explaining what and why people actually believed could be delegated to sociology, but evaluative issues of articulating cognitive norms would be reserved for (individualist) epistemology, which was philosophical territory.

But though mainstream philosophy and analytic epistemology continued to develop in splendid isolation for many decades, W. V. Quine's naturalizing of epistemology would initiate a sequence of events with unsuspectedly subversive long-term theoretical repercussions for the field (Quine 1969b; Kornblith 1994b). If articulating the norms for *ideal* cognition required taking into account (in some way) the practices of *actual* cognition, if the prescriptive needed to pay attention (in some way) to the descriptive, then on what principled basis could cognitive realities of a *supra*-individual kind continue to be excluded from the ambit of epistemology? For it then meant that the cognitive agent needed to be located in her specificity—as a member of certain social groups, within a given social milieu, in a society at a particular time period. Whatever Quine's own sympathies (or lack thereof), his work had opened Pandora's box. A naturalized epistemology had, perforce, also to be a socialized epistemology; this was "a straightforward extension of the naturalistic approach" (Kornblith 1994a, 93). What had originally been a specifically Marxist concept, "standpoint theory," was adopted and developed to its most sophisticated form in the work of feminist theorists (Harding 2004), and it became possible for books with titles such as *Social Epistemology* (Fuller 2002) and *Socializing Epistemology* (Schmitt 1994) and journals called *Social Epistemology* to be published and seen (at least by some) as a legitimate part of philosophy. The Marxist challenge thrown down a century before could now finally be taken up.

Obviously, then, for those interested in pursuing such questions this is a far more welcoming environment than that of a few decades ago. Nonetheless, I think it is obvious that the *potential* of these developments for transforming mainstream epistemology is far from being fully realized. And at least one major reason for this failure is that the conceptions of society in the literature too often presuppose a degree of consent and inclusion that does not exist outside the imagination of mainstream scholars—in a sense, a societal population essentially generated by simple iteration of that originally solitary Cartesian cognizer. As Linda Martín Alcoff has ironically observed, the "society" about which these philosophers are writing often seems to be composed exclusively of white males (Alcoff 1996, 2, n. 1), so that one wonders how it reproduces itself. The Marxist critique is seemingly discredited, the feminist critique is marginalized, and the racial critique does not even exist. The concepts of domination, hegemony, ideology, mystification, exploitation, and so on that are part of the lingua franca of radicals find little or no place here. In particular, the analysis of the implications for social cognition of the legacy of white supremacy has barely been initiated. The sole reference to race that I could find in the Schmitt (1994) collection, for example, was a single cautious sentence by Philip Kitcher (1994, 125), which I here reproduce in full: "Membership of a particular ethnic group within a particular society may interfere with one's ability to acquire true beliefs about the distribution of characteristics that are believed to be important to human worth (witness the history of nineteenth-century craniometry)."

I sketch out in this chapter some of the features and the dynamic of what I see as a particularly pervasive—though hardly theorized—form of ignorance, what could be called white ignorance, linked to white supremacy. (This chapter is thus an elaboration of one of the key themes of my 1997 book, *The Racial Contract* [Mills 1997].) The idea of group-based cognitive handicap is not an alien one to the radical tradition, if not normally couched in terms of "ignorance." Indeed, it is, on the contrary, a straightforward corollary of standpoint theory: if one group is privileged, after all, it must be by comparison with another group that is handicapped. In addition, the term has for me the virtue of signaling my theoretical sympathies with what I know will seem to many a deplorably old-fashioned, "conservative," realist, intellectual framework, one in which *truth, falsity, facts, reality*, and so forth are not enclosed with ironic scare quotes. The phrase "white ignorance" implies the possibility of a contrasting "knowledge," a contrast that would be lost if all claims to truth were equally spurious, or just a matter of competing discourses. In the same way *The Racial Contract* was not meant as a trashing of contractarianism, as such, but rather the demystification of a contractarianism that ignored racial subordination, so similarly, mapping an epistemology of ignorance is for me a preliminary to reformulating an epistemology that will give us genuine knowledge.

The metatheoretical approach I find most congenial is that recently outlined by Alvin Goldman in his book *Knowledge in a Social World* (Goldman 1999; see also Kornblith 1994a; Kitcher 1994). Goldman describes his project as "an essay in social veritistic epistemology," oriented "toward truth determination," as against contemporary poststructuralist or Kuhn-Feyerabend-Bloor-Barnes-inspired approaches that relativize truth (5). So though the focus is social rather than individual, the traditional concerns and assumptions of mainstream epistemology have been retained:

> Traditional epistemology, especially in the Cartesian tradition, was highly individualistic, focusing on mental operations of cognitive agents in isolation or abstraction from other persons. . . . [This] individual epistemology needs a social counterpart: *social epistemology.* . . . In what respects is social epistemology social? First, it focuses on social paths or routes to knowledge. That is, considering believers taken one at a time, it looks at the many routes to belief that feature interactions with other agents, as contrasted with private or asocial routes to belief acquisition. . . . Second, social epistemology does not restrict itself to believers taken singly. It often focuses on some sort of group entity . . . and examines the spread of information or misinformation across that group's membership. Rather than concentrate on a single knower, as did Cartesian epistemology, it addresses the distribution of knowledge or error within the larger social cluster. . . . Veritistic epistemology (whether individual or social) is concerned with the production of knowledge, where knowledge is here understood in the "weak" sense of *true belief.* More precisely, it is concerned with both knowledge and its contraries: *error* (false belief) and *ignorance* (the absence of true belief). The main question for veritistic epistemology is: Which practices have a comparatively favorable impact on knowledge as contrasted with error and ignorance? Individual veritistic epistemology asks this question for nonsocial practices; social veritistic epistemology asks it for social practices. (Goldman 1999, 4–5, emphasis in original)

Unlike Goldman, I will use *ignorance* to cover both false belief and the absence of true belief. But with this minor terminological variation, this is basically the project I am trying to undertake: looking at the "spread of misinformation," the "distribution of error" (including the possibility of "massive error" [Kornblith 1994a, 97]), within the "larger social cluster," the "group entity," of whites, and the "social practices" (some "wholly pernicious" [Kornblith 1994a, 97]) that encourage it. Goldman makes glancing reference to some of the feminist and race literature (there is a grand total of a single index entry for *racism*), but in general the implications of systemic social oppression for his project are not addressed. The picture of "society" he is working with is one that—with perhaps a few unfortunate exceptions—is inclusive and harmonious. Thus his account offers the equivalent in social epistemology of the mainstream theorizing in political science that frames American sexism and racism as "anomalies": U.S. political culture is conceptualized as *essentially* egalitarian and inclusive, with the long actual history of systemic gender and racial subordination being relegated to the status of a minor "deviation" from the norm (Smith 1997). Obviously such a starting point crucially handicaps any realistic social epistemology, since in effect it turns things upside down. Sexism and racism, patriarchy and white supremacy, have not been the *exception* but the *norm.* So though his book is valuable in terms of conceptual clarification, and some illuminating discussions of particular topics, the basic framework is flawed insofar as it marginalizes domination and its consequences. A less naïve understanding of how society actually works requires drawing on the radical tradition of social theory, in which various factors he does not consider play a crucial role in obstructing the mission of veritistic epistemology.

II

Let me turn now to race. As I pointed out in an article more than fifteen years ago (Mills 1998), and as has unfortunately hardly changed since then, there is no academic philosophical literature on racial epistemology that remotely compares in volume to that on gender epistemology. (Race and gender are not, of course, mutually exclusive, but usually in gender theory it is the perspective of white women that is explored.) However, one needs to distinguish academic from lay treatments. I would suggest that "white ignorance" has, whether centrally or secondarily, been a theme of many of the classic fictional and nonfictional works of the African American experience, and also that of other people of color. In his introduction to a collection of black writers' perspectives on whiteness, David Roediger (1998) underlines the fundamental epistemic *asymmetry* between typical white views of blacks and typical black views of whites: these are not cognizers linked by a reciprocal ignorance but rather groups whose respective privilege and subordination tend to produce self-deception, bad faith, evasion, and misrepresentation, on the one hand, and more veridical perceptions, on the other hand. Thus he cites James Weldon Johnson's remark "colored people of this country know and understand the white people better than the white people know and understand them" (5). Often for their very survival, blacks have been forced to become lay anthropologists, studying the strange culture, customs, and mind-set of the "white tribe" that has such frightening power over them, that in certain time periods can even determine their life or death on a whim. (In particular circumstances, then, white ignorance may need to be actively *encouraged*, thus the black American folk poem, "Got one mind for white folks to see/Another for what I know is me," or, in James Baldwin's brutally candid assessment, "I have spent most of my life, after all, watching white people and outwitting them, so that I might survive" [Baldwin 1993, 217].) What people of color quickly come to see—in a sense, the primary epistemic principle of the racialized social epistemology of which they are the object—is that they are not seen at all. Thus the "central metaphor" of W. E. B. Du Bois's *The Souls of Black Folk* is the image of the "veil" (Gibson 1989, xi), and the black American cognitive equivalent of the shocking moment of Cartesian realization of the uncertainty of everything one had taken to be knowledge is the moment when, for Du Bois, as a child in New England, "It dawned upon me with a certain suddenness that I was different from the others; or like, mayhap, in heart and life and longing, but shut out from their [white] world by a vast veil" (Du Bois 1989, 4).

Similarly, Ralph Ellison's classic *Invisible Man* (1995), generally regarded as the most important twentieth-century novel of the black experience, is arguably, in key respects—while a multidimensional and multilayered work of great depth and complexity, not to be reduced to a single theme—an *epistemological* novel. For what it recounts is the protagonist's quest to determine what norms of belief are the right ones in a crazy looking-glass world where he is an invisible man "simply because [white] people refuse to see me. . . . When they approach me they see only my surroundings, themselves, or figments of their imagination—indeed, everything and anything except me." And this systematic misperception is not, of course, due to biology, the intrinsic properties of his epidermis or physical deficiencies in the white eye but rather to "the construction of their inner eyes, those eyes with which they look through their physical eyes upon reality" (3). The images of light and darkness, sight and blindness, that run through the novel, from the blindfolded black fighters in the grotesque battle royal at the start to the climactic discovery that the Brotherhood's (read: American Communist Party) leader has a glass eye, repeatedly raise, in context after context, the question of how one can demarcate what is genuine from only apparent insight, real from only apparent truth, even in the worldview of those whose historical materialist "science" supposedly gave them "super vision."

Nor is it only black writers who have explored the theme of white ignorance. One of the consequences of the development of critical white studies has been a renewed appreciation of the pioneering work of Herman Melville, with *Moby Dick* (2000) now being read by some critics as an early nineteenth-century indictment of the national obsession with white-

ness, Ahab's pathological determination to pursue the white whale regardless of its imperilment of his multiracial crew. But it is in the 1856
short novel *Benito Cereno* (1986)—used as the source of one of the two
epigraphs to *Invisible Man* by Ellison—that one finds the most focused investigation of the unnerving possibilities of white blindness. Boarding a
slave ship—the *San Dominick*, a reference to the Haitian Revolution—
which, unknown to the protagonist, Amasa Delano, has been taken over
by its human cargo, with the white crew being held hostage, Delano has
all around him the evidence for black insurrection, from the terror in
the eyes of the nominal white captain, the eponymous Benito Cereno, as
his black barber Babo puts the razor to his throat, to the Africans clash-
ing their hatchets ominously in the background. But so unthinkable is
the idea that the inferior blacks could have accomplished such a thing
that Delano searches for every possible alternative explanation for the
seemingly strange behavior of the imprisoned whites, no matter how far-
fetched. In Eric Sundquist's summary (1993):

> Melville's account of the "enchantment" of Delano, then, is also a means
> to examine the mystifications by which slavery was maintained. . . .
> Minstrelsy—in effect, the complete show of the tale's action staged for
> Delano—is a product, as it were, of his mind, of his willingness to accept
> Babo's Sambo-like performance. . . . Paradoxically, Delano watches Babo's
> performance without ever seeing it. . . . Delano participates in a continued
> act of suppressed revolt against belief in the appearances presented to
> him . . . [a] self-regulation by racist assumptions and blind "innocence."
> (151–55, 171)

The white delusion of racial superiority insulates itself against refuta-
tion. Correspondingly, on the positive epistemic side, the route to black
knowledge is the self-conscious recognition of white ignorance (including
its black-faced manifestation in black consciousness itself). Du Bois's
(1989) famous and oft-cited figure of "double consciousness" has been variously interpreted, but certainly one plausible way of reading it is as a prescription for a critical cognitive distancing from "a world which yields [the
Negro] no true self-consciousness, but only lets him see himself through
the revelation of the other world," a "sense of always looking at one's self
through the eyes of others" (5). The attainment of "second sight" requires
an understanding of what it is about whites and the white situation that
motivates them to view blacks erroneously. One learns to see through identifying white blindness and avoiding the pitfalls of putting on these specta-
cles for one's own vision.

This subject is by no means unexplored in white and black texts, but
as noted, because of the whiteness of philosophy, very little has been
done here. (One exception is Lewis Gordon's [1995] work on bad faith,

which is obviously relevant to this subject, though not itself set in a formal epistemological framework.) In this chapter, accordingly, I gesture
toward some useful directions for mapping white ignorance and developing, accordingly, epistemic criteria for minimizing it.

III

What I want to pin down, then, is the idea of an ignorance, a non-knowing, that is not contingent, but in which race—white racism and/or white
racial domination and their ramifications—plays a crucial causal role.
Let me begin by trying to clarify and demarcate more precisely the phenomenon I am addressing, as well as answering some possible objections.
To begin with, *white ignorance* as a cognitive phenomenon has to be
clearly historicized. I am taking for granted the truth of some variant of
social constructivism, which denies that race is biological. So the causality in the mechanisms for generating and sustaining white ignorance on
the macro level is social-structural rather than physico-biological, though
it will of course operate through the physico-biological. Assuming that
the growing consensus in critical race theory is correct—that race in general, and whiteness in particular, is a product of the modern period
(Fredrickson 2002)—then you could not have had white ignorance in
this technical, term-of-art sense in, say, the ancient world, because whites
did not exist then. Certainly people existed who by today's standards
would be counted as white, but they would not have been so categorized
at the time, either by themselves or others, so there would have been no
whiteness to play a causal role in their knowing or non-knowing. Moreover, even in the modern period, whiteness would not have been univer-
sally, instantly, and homogeneously instantiated; there would have been
(to borrow an image from another field of study) "uneven development"
in the processes of racialization in different countries at different times.
Indeed, even in the United States, in a sense the paradigm white supremacist state, Matthew Frye Jacobson (1998) argues for a periodization
of whiteness into different epochs, with some European ethnic groups
only becoming fully white at a comparatively late stage.

   Second, one would obviously need to distinguish what I am calling
white ignorance from general patterns of ignorance prevalent among
people who are white but in whose doxastic states race has played no determining role. For example, at all times (such as right now) there will be
many facts about the natural and social worlds on which people, including white people, have no opinion, or a mistaken opinion, but race is not
directly or indirectly responsible, for instance, the number of planets 200
years ago, the exact temperature in the earth's crust twenty miles down
right now, the precise income distribution in the United States, and so

forth. But we would not want to call this white ignorance, even when it is shared by whites, because race has not been responsible for these non-knowings, but other factors.

Third (complicating the foregoing), it needs to be realized that once indirect causation and diminishing degrees of influence are admitted, it will sometimes be very difficult to adjudicate when specific kinds of non-knowing are appropriately categorizable as white ignorance or not. Recourse to counterfactuals of greater or lesser distance from the actual situation may be necessary ("what they should and would have known if . . ."), whose evaluation may be too complex to be resolvable. Suppose, for example, that a particular true scientific generalization about human beings, P, would be easily discoverable in a society were it not for widespread white racism, and that with additional research in the appropriate areas, P could be shown to have further implications, Q, and beyond that, R. Or, suppose that the practical application of P in medicine would have had as a spin-off empirical findings p_1, p_2, p_3. Should these related principles and factual findings all be included as examples of white ignorance as well? How far onward up the chain? And so forth. So it will be easy to think up all kinds of tricky cases where it will be hard to make the determination. But the existence of such problematic cases at the borders does not undermine the import of more central cases.

Fourth, the racialized causality I am invoking needs to be expansive enough to include both straightforward racist motivation and more impersonal social-structural causation, which may be operative even if the cognizer in question is not racist. It is necessary to distinguish the two not merely as a logical point, because they are analytically separable, but because in empirical reality they may often be found independently of each other. You can have white racism, in particular white cognizers, in the sense of the existence of prejudicial beliefs about people of color without (at that time and place) white domination of those people of color having been established; and you can also have white domination of people of color at a particular time and place without all white cognizers at that time and place being racist. But in both cases, racialized causality can give rise to what I am calling white ignorance, straightforwardly for a racist cognizer, but also indirectly for a nonracist cognizer who may form mistaken beliefs (e.g., that after the abolition of slavery in the United States, blacks generally had opportunities equal to whites) because of the social suppression of the pertinent knowledge, though without prejudice himself. So white ignorance need not always be based on bad faith. Obviously from the point of view of a social epistemology, especially after the transition from de jure to de facto white supremacy, it is precisely this kind of white ignorance that is most important.

Fifth, the "white" in "white ignorance" does not mean that it has to be confined *to* white people. Indeed, as the earlier Du Bois discussion emphasized, it will often be shared by nonwhites to a greater or lesser extent because of the power relations and patterns of ideological hegemony involved. (This is a familiar point from the Marxist and feminist traditions—working-class conservatives, "male-identified" women, endorsing right-wing and sexist ideologies against their interests.) Providing that the causal route is appropriate, blacks can manifest white ignorance also.

Sixth, and somewhat different, *white* racial ignorance can produce a doxastic environment in which particular varieties of *black* racial ignorance flourish—so that racial causality is involved—but which one would hesitate to subsume under the category "white ignorance" itself, at least without significant qualification. Think, for example, of "oppositional" African American varieties of biological and theological determinism: whites as melanin deficient and therefore inherently physiologically and psychologically flawed, or whites as "blue-eyed devils" created by the evil scientist Yacub (as in early Black Muslim theology). Insofar as these theories invert claims of white racial superiority, though still accepting racial hierarchy, they would seem to be deserving of a separate category, though obviously they have been shaped by key assumptions of "scientific" and theological white racism.

Seventh, though the examples I have given so far have all been factual ones, I want a concept of white ignorance broad enough to include moral ignorance—not merely ignorance of facts *with* moral implications but moral non-knowings, incorrect judgments about the rights and wrongs of moral situations themselves. For me, the epistemic desideratum is that the naturalizing and socializing of epistemology should have, as a component, the naturalizing and socializing of *moral* epistemology also (Campbell and Hunter 2000) and the study of pervasive social patterns of mistaken *moral* cognition. Thus the idea is that improvements in our cognitive practice should have a practical payoff in heightened sensitivity to social oppression and the attempt to reduce and ultimately eliminate that oppression.

Eighth, it presumably does not need to be emphasized that white ignorance is not the only kind of privileged, group-based ignorance. Male ignorance could be analyzed similarly and clearly has a far more ancient history and arguably a more deep-rooted ancestry in human interrelations, insofar as it goes back thousands of years. I am focusing on white ignorance because, as mentioned, it has been relatively undertheorized in the white academy compared to the work of feminist theorists.

Ninth, speaking generally about white ignorance does not commit one to the claim that it is uniform across the white population. Whites are not a monolith, and if the analysis of white ignorance is to be part of a social epistemology, then the obvious needs to be remembered—that people have other identities beside racial ones, so that whites will be divisible by class, gender, nationality, religion, and so forth, and these factors will modify, by differential socialization and experience, the bodies of belief and the cognitive patterns of the subpopulations concerned. But this is, of course, true for all sociological generalizations, which has never been a reason for abandoning them but of employing them cautiously. White ignorance is not indefeasible (even if it sometimes seems that way!), and some people who are white will, because of their particular histories (and/or the intersection of whiteness with other identities), overcome it and have true beliefs on what their fellow whites get wrong. So white ignorance is best thought of as a cognitive tendency—an inclination, a doxastic disposition—which is not insuperable. If there is a sociology of knowledge, then there should also be a sociology of ignorance.

Tenth, and finally, the point of trying to understand white ignorance is, of course, *normative* and not merely sociological—hence the emphasis on the continuity with classic epistemology—the goal of trying to reduce or eliminate it. In classic individualist epistemology, one seeks not merely to eliminate false belief but to develop an understanding, wariness, and avoidance of the cognitive processes that typically produce false belief. For a social epistemology, where the focus is on supra-individual processes, and the individual's interaction with them, the aim is to understand how certain social structures tend to promote these crucially flawed processes, how to personally extricate oneself from them (insofar as that is possible), and to do one's part in undermining them in the broader cognitive sphere. So the idea is that there are typical ways of going wrong that need to be adverted to in light of the social structure and specific group characteristics, and one has a better chance of getting things right through a self-conscious recognition of their existence, and corresponding self-distancing from them.

IV

Let us turn now to the processes of cognition, individual and social, and the examination of the ways in which race may affect some of their crucial components. As examples, I will look at perception, conception, memory, testimony, and motivational group interest (in a longer treatment, differential group experience should also be included). Separating these various components is difficult because they are all constantly in interaction with one another. For example, when the individual cognizing agent is perceiving, he is doing so with eyes and ears that have been socialized. Perception is also in part conception, the viewing of the world through a particular conceptual grid. Inference from perception involves the overt or tacit appeal to memory, which will be not merely individual but social. As such, it will be founded on testimony and ultimately on the perceptions and conceptions of others. The background knowledge that will guide inference and judgment, eliminating (putatively) absurd alternatives and narrowing down a set of plausible contenders, will also be shaped by testimony, or the lack thereof, and will itself be embedded in various conceptual frameworks and require perception and memory to access. Testimony will have been recorded, requiring again perception, conception, and memory; it will have been integrated into a framework and narrative and from the start will have involved the selection of certain voices as against others, selection in and selection out (if these others have been allowed to speak in the first place). At all levels, interests may shape cognition, influencing what and how we see, what we and society choose to remember, whose testimony is solicited and whose is not, and which facts and frameworks are sought out and accepted. Thus at any given stage it is obvious that an interaction of great complexity is involved, in which multiple factors will be affecting one another in intricate feedback loops of various kinds. So an analytic separation of elements for conceptual isolation and clarification will necessarily be artificial, and in a sense each element so extracted bears a ghostly trail of all the others in its wake.

Start with perception. A central theme of the epistemology of the past few decades has been the discrediting of the idea of a raw perceptual "given," completely unmediated by concepts. Perceptions are in general simultaneously conceptions, if only at a very low level. Moreover, the social dimension of epistemology is obviously most salient here, since individuals do not in general make up these categories themselves but inherit them from their cultural milieu. "The influence of social factors begins at birth, for language is not reinvented by each individual in social isolation, nor could it be. Because language acquisition is socially mediated, the concepts we acquire are themselves socially mediated from the very beginning" (Kornblith 1994a, 97). But this means that the conceptual array with which the cognizer approaches the world needs itself to be scrutinized for its adequacy to the world, for how well it maps the reality it claims to be describing. In addition, it is not a matter of monadic predicates, reciprocally isolated from one another, but concepts linked by interlocking assumptions and background belief sets into certain complexes of ideation that by their very nature tend to put a certain interpretation on the world. So in most cases the concepts will not be neutral but oriented toward a certain understanding, embedded in subtheories and larger theories about how things work.

In the orthodox left tradition, this set of issues is handled through the category "ideology"; in more recent radical theory, through Foucault's "discourses." But whatever one's larger metatheoretical sympathies, whatever approach one thinks best for investigating these ideational matters, such concerns obviously need to be part of a social epistemology. For if the society is one structured by relations of domination and subordination (as of course most societies in human history have been), then in certain areas this conceptual apparatus is likely going to be shaped and inflected in various ways by the biases of the ruling group(s). So crucial concepts may well be misleading in their inner makeup and their external relation to a larger doxastic architecture. Moreover, what cognitive psychology has revealed is that rather than continually challenging conceptual adequacy by the test of disconfirming empirical data, we tend to do the opposite—to interpret the data through the grid of the concepts in such a way that seemingly disconfirming, or at least problematic, perceptions are filtered out or marginalized. In other words, one will tend to find the confirmation in the world whether it is there or not.

Now apply this to race: consider the epistemic principle of what has come to be called "white normativity," the centering of the Euro and later Euro-American reference group as constitutive norm. Ethnocentrism is, of course, a negative cognitive tendency common to all peoples, not just Europeans. But with Europe's gradual rise to global domination, the European variant becomes entrenched as an overarching, virtually unassailable framework, a conviction of exceptionalism and superiority that seems vindicated by the facts, and thenceforth, circularly, shaping perception of the facts. We rule the world because we are superior; we are superior because we rule the world. In his pioneering 1950s' essays against Eurocentrism, world historian Marshall G. S. Hodgson (1993b) invokes Saul Steinberg's famous March 29, 1976, *New Yorker* cover cartoon depiction of the "View of the World from 9th Avenue," the bizarrely foreshortened view of the United States afforded from the Upper East Side and argues that the standard geographical representations of Europe by Europeans, as in the Mercator projection world map, are not really that radically different:

> It would be a significant story in itself to trace how modern Westerners have managed to preserve some of the most characteristic features of their ethnocentric medieval image of the world. Recast in modern scientific and scholarly language, the image is still with us. . . . The point of any ethnocentric world image is to divide the world into moieties, ourselves and the others, ourselves forming the more important of the two. . . . We divide the world into what we call "continents." . . . Why is

> Europe one of the continents but not India? . . . Europe is still ranked as
> one of the "continents" because our cultural ancestors lived there. By
> making it a "continent," we give it a rank disproportionate to its natural
> size, as a subordinate part of no larger unit, but in itself one of the major
> component parts of the world. . . . (I call such a world map the "Jim
> Crow projection" because it shows Europe as larger than Africa.) . . .
> [Mercator] confirms our predispositions. (3–5)

This geographical misrepresentation and regional inflation have
gone in tandem with a corresponding historical misrepresentation and
inflation. Criticizing the standard historical categories of Western historians, Hodgson suggests that "the very terms we allow ourselves to use foster distortion." The "convenient result" is that Europe, an originally
peripheral region of what Hodgson calls the "Afro-Eurasian historical
complex," is lifted out of its context and elevated into a self-creating entity unto itself, "an independent division of the whole world, with a history that need not be integrated with that of the rest of mankind save on
the terms posed by European history itself" (9).

From this fatally skewed optic, of course, stem all those theories of
innate European superiority to the rest of the world that are still with us
today but in modified and subtler versions. Whiteness is originally coexten-
sive with full humanity, so that the nonwhite Other is grasped through a historic array of concepts whose common denominator is their subjects'
location on a lower ontological and moral rung.

Consider, for example, the category of the "savage" and its conceptual role in the justification of imperialism. As Francis Jennings (1976)
points out, the word was "created for the purposes of conquest rather
than the purposes of knowledge." "Savagery" and "civilization" were "rec-
iprocals" and were "both independent of any necessary correlation with
empirical reality." The conceptual outcome was a "conjoined myth" that
"greatly distorted [white] Americans' perceptions of reality," necessarily
involving "the suppression of facts" (12, 10). In effect,

> the Englishman devised the savage's form to fit his function. The word
> *savage* thus underwent considerable alteration of meaning as different
> colonists pursued their varied ends. One aspect of the term remained
> constant, however: the savage was always inferior to civilized men. . . .
> The constant of Indian inferiority implied the rejection of his hu-
> manity and determined the limits permitted for his participation in
> the mixing of cultures. The savage was prey, cattle, pet, or vermin—he
> was never citizen. Upholders of the myth denied that either savage
> tyranny or savage anarchy could rightfully be called government, and
> therefore there could be no justification for Indian resistance to
> European invasion. (59)

When Thomas Jefferson excoriates the "merciless Indian Savages" in the Declaration of Independence, then, neither he nor his readers will experience any cognitive dissonance with the earlier claims about the equality of all "men," since savages are not "men" in the full sense. Locked in a different temporality, incapable of self-regulation by morality and law, they are humanoid but not human. To speak of the "equality" of the savage would then be oxymoronic, since one's very location in these categories is an indication of one's inequality. Even a cognizer with no antipathy or prejudice toward Native Americans will be cognitively disabled trying to establish truths about them insofar as such a category and its associated presuppositions will tend to force his conclusions in a certain direction, will constrain what he can objectively see. One will experience a strain, a cognitive tension between possible egalitarian findings and overarching category, insofar as "savage" already has embedded in it a narrative, a set of assumptions about innate inferiority, which will preclude certain possibilities. "Savages" tend to do certain things and to be unable to do others; these go with the conceptual territory. Thus the term itself encourages if not quite logically determines particular conclusions. Concepts orient us to the world, and it is a rare individual who can resist this inherited orientation. Once established in the social mind-set, its influence is difficult to escape, since it is not a matter of seeing the phenomenon with the concept discretely attached but rather of seeing things *through* the concept itself. In the classic period of European expansionism, it then becomes possible to speak with no sense of absurdity of "empty" lands that are actually teeming with millions of people, of "discovering" countries whose inhabitants already exist, because the nonwhite Other is so located in the guiding conceptual array that different rules apply. Even seemingly straightforward empirical perception will be affected—the myth of a nation of hunters in contradiction to widespread Native American agriculture that saved the English colonists' lives, the myth of stateless savages in contradiction to forms of government from which the white Founders arguably learned, the myth of a pristine wilderness in contradiction to a humanized landscape transformed by thousands of years of labor (Jennings 1976). In all of these cases, *the concept is driving the perception, with whites aprioristically intent on denying what is before them.* So if Kant famously said that perceptions without concepts are blind, then here it is the blindness of the concept itself that is blocking vision.

Originally, then, foundational concepts of racialized difference, and their ramifications in all sociopolitical spheres, preclude a veridical perception of nonwhites and serve as a categorical barrier against their equitable moral treatment. The transition away from old-fashioned racism of this kind has not, however, put an end to white normativity but subtly transformed its character. If previously whites were color demarcated as biologically and/or culturally unequal and superior, now through a strategic "color blindness" they are assimilated as putative equals to the status and situation of nonwhites on terms that negate the need for measures to repair the inequities of the past. So white normativity manifests itself in a white refusal to recognize the long history of structural discrimination that has left whites with the differential resources they have today, and all of its consequent advantages in negotiating opportunity structures. If originally whiteness was race, then now it is racelessness, an equal status and a common history in which all have shared, with white privilege being conceptually erased. Woody Doane (2003) suggests that

> "Color-blind" ideology plays an important role in the maintenance of white hegemony. . . . Because whites tend not to see themselves in racial terms and not to recognize the existence of the advantages that whites enjoy in American society, this promotes a worldview that emphasizes *individualistic* explanations for social and economic achievement, as if the individualism of white privilege was a universal attribute. Whites also exhibit a general inability to perceive the persistence of discrimination and the effects of more subtle forms of institutional discrimination. In the context of color-blind racial ideology, whites are more likely to see the opportunity structure as open and institutions as impartial or objective in their functioning. . . . this combination supports an interpretative framework in which whites' explanations for inequality focus upon the cultural characteristics (e.g., motivation, values) of subordinate groups. . . . Politically, this blaming of subordinate groups for their lower economic position serves to neutralize demands for antidiscrimination initiatives or for a redistribution of resources. (13–14, emphasis in original)

Indeed, the real racists are the *blacks* who continue to insist on the importance of race. In both cases white normativity underpins white privilege, in the first case by justifying differential treatment by race and in the second case by justifying formally equal treatment by race that—in its denial of the cumulative effects of past differential treatment—is tantamount to continuing it.

What makes such denial possible, of course, is the management of memory. (Thus as earlier emphasized it is important to appreciate the *interconnectedness* of all of these components of knowing or non-knowing: this concept is viable in the white mind because of the denial of crucial facts.) Memory is not a subject one usually finds in epistemology texts, but for social epistemology it is obviously pivotal. French sociologist Maurice Halbwachs (1992) was one of the pioneers of the concept of a collective, social memory, which provided the framework for individual memories. But if we need to understand collective memory, we also need to understand collective amnesia. Indeed, they go together insofar as memory is necessarily selective—out of the infinite sequence of events, some trivial, some momentous, we extract what we see as the crucial ones and organize them into an overall narrative. Social memory is then inscribed in text-books, generated and regenerated in ceremonies and official holidays, concretized in statues, parks, and monuments. John Locke famously suggested memory as the crucial criterion for personal identity, and social memory plays a parallel role in social identity. Historian John Gillis (1994b, 3) argues that "the notion of identity depends on the idea of memory, and vice versa. . . . [But] memories and identities are not fixed things, but representations or constructions of reality. . . . '[M]emory work' is . . . embedded in complex class, gender, and power relations that determine what is remembered (or forgotten), by whom, and for what end. If memory has its politics, so too does identity." As the individual re-presses unhappy or embarrassing memories that may also reveal a great deal about his identity, about who he is, so in all societies, especially those structured by domination, the socially recollecting "we" will be divided, and the selection will be guided by different identities, with one group suppressing precisely what another wishes to commemorate. Thus there will be both official and counter-memory, with conflicting judgments about what is important in the past and what is unimportant, what happened and does matter, what happened and does not matter, and what did not happen at all. So applying this to race, there will obviously be an intimate relationship between white identity, white memory, and white amnesia, especially about nonwhite victims.

Hitler is supposed to have reassured his generals, apprehensive about the launching of World War II, by asking them: "Who now remembers the Armenians?" Because the Third Reich lost, the genocide of the Jews (though far less the Romani) is remembered. But who now remembers the Hereros, the Nama, the Beothuks, the Tasmanians, the Pequots? (For that matter, who does remember the Armenians, except the Armenians themselves?) Who remembers the Congolese? In Adam Hochschild's (1998, ch. 19) chilling book on King Leopold II's regime of rubber and extermi-nation, which resulted in the deaths of 10 million people in the Belgian Congo, the final chapter is titled "The Great Forgetting." Through the sys-tematic destruction of state archives in Brussels—"the furnaces burned for eight days"—and the deliberate noncommemoration of the African vic-tims—"in none of the [Brussels Royal Museum of Central Africa's] twenty large exhibition galleries is there the slightest hint that millions of Con-golese met unnatural deaths"—a "deliberate forgetting" as an "active deed" was achieved (293–95), a purging of official memory so thorough and effi-cient that a Belgian ambassador to West Africa in the 1970s was astonished by the "slander" on his country in a Liberian newspaper's passing reference to the genocide: "I learned that there had been this huge campaign, in the international press, from 1900 to 1910; millions of people had died, but we Belgians knew absolutely nothing about it" (297).[1] Similarly, and closer to home, James Loewen's (1996) critical study of the silences and misrepresentations of standard American history textbooks points out that "The Indian-white wars that dominated our history from 1622 to 1815 and were of considerable importance until 1890 have disappeared from our national memory," encouraging a "feel-good history for whites": "By downplaying Indian wars, textbooks help us forget that we wrested the continent from Native Americans" (133). In the case of blacks, the "forgetting" takes the form of whitewashing the atrocities of slavery—the "magnolia myth" of paternalistic white aristocrats and happy, singing darkies that dominated American textbooks as late as the 1950s—and minimizing the extent to which "the peculiar institution" was not a sectional problem but shaped the national economy, polity, and psychology (137–70). Du Bois refers to "the deliberately educated ignorance of white schools" (1995, 459) and devotes the climactic chapter of his massive *Black Reconstruction in America* (1998) to the documentation of the sanitization of the history of slavery, the Civil War, and Reconstruction by white Southern historians.

Moreover, the misrepresentations of national textbooks have their counterpart in monuments and statuary: social memory made marble and concrete, national mnemonics of the landscape itself. In his study of Civil War monuments, Kirk Savage (1994, 130–31) argues that "Monuments served to anchor collective remembering," fostering "a shared and standardized program of memory," so that "local memory earned credibility by its assimilation to a visible national memory." The postbellum decision to rehabilitate Robert E. Lee, commander in chief of the Confederate Army, thereby "eras[ing] his status as traitor," signified a national white reconciliation that required the repudiation of an alternative black memory:

> The commemoration of Lee rested on a suppression of black memory, black truth. . . . [U.S. statesman Charles Francis] Adams could not justify a monument to Lee without denying the postwar reality of racial injustice and its congruence with the Confederate cause. "Sectional reconciliation" of this kind was founded on the nonconciliation of African Americans, and on their exclusion from the legitimate arenas of cultural representation. Black Americans did not have their own monuments, despite the critical role they had played in swinging the balance of power—both moral and military—to the North. . . . The commemoration of the Civil War in physical memorials is ultimately a story of systematic cultural repression. . . . Public monuments . . . impose a permanent memory on the very landscape within which we order our lives. Inasmuch as the monuments make credible particular collectivities, they must erase others. (134–35, 143)

At the level of symbolism and national self-representation, then, the denial of the extent of Native American and black victimization buttresses the airbrushed white narrative of discovery, settlement, and building of a shining city on the hill. But the editing of white memory has more concrete and practical consequences also: as earlier emphasized it enables a self-representation in which differential white privilege, and the need to correct for it, does not exist. In other words, the mystification of the past underwrites a mystification of the present. The erasure of the history of Jim Crow makes it possible to represent the playing field as historically level, so that current black poverty just proves blacks' unwillingness to work. As individual memory is assisted through a larger social memory, so individual amnesia is then assisted by a larger collective amnesia. In his research on the continuing, indeed deepening, gap between white and black Americans, Thomas Shapiro (2004, 75–76) remarks on how often white interviewees seemed to "forget" what they had just told him about the extensive parental assistance they received, claiming instead that they had worked for it: "[X's] memory seems accurate as she catalogues all sorts of parental wealthfare with matching dollar figures. . . . However, as soon as the conversation turns to how she and her husband acquired assets like their home, cars, and savings account, her attitude changes dramatically. . . . The [Xs] describe themselves as self-made, conveniently forgetting that they inherited much of what they own." Thus the "taken-for-granted sense of [white] entitlement" erases the fact that "*transformative assets,*" "inherited wealth lifting a family beyond their own achievements," have been crucial to their white success (76, 10, emphasis in original) and that blacks do not in general have such advantages because of the history of discrimination against them. Thomas McCarthy (2002, 2004) points out the importance of a politics of memory for closing the "peculiar gap between academic historical scholarship and public historical consciousness that marks our own situation" (2002, 641) and emphasizes that the eventual achievement of racial justice can only be accomplished through a systematic national re-education on the historic extent of black racial subordination in the United States and how it continues to shape our racial fates differentially today.

But forgetting, whether individual or social, will not even be necessary if there is nothing to remember in the first place. C. A. J. Coady's (1994) now classic book on testimony has made it irrefutably clear how dependent we are on others for so much of what we know, and is thus crucial to the elaboration of a social epistemology. Yet if one group, or a specific group, of potential witnesses is discredited in advance as being epistemically suspect, then testimony from the group will tend to be dismissed or never solicited to begin with. Kant's (1960, 113, emphasis in original) infamous line about a "Negro carpenter's" views has often been quoted, but never stales: "And it might be, that there were something in this which perhaps deserved to be considered; but in short, this fellow was *quite black* from head to foot, a clear proof that what he said was stupid." Nonwhite inferiority necessarily has cognitive ramifications, undermining nonwhite claims to knowledge that are not backed up by European epistemic authority. In an 1840 letter, Daniel Butrick, a missionary to the Cherokees, gives a long list of the reasons "how whites try and fail to find out what Indians know because they refuse to recognize the humanity or intelligence of Native peoples," the result being "that such persons may spend all their days among the Indians and yet die as ignorant of their true character almost as if they had never been born" (Konkle 2004, 90, 92). During slavery, blacks were generally denied the right to testify against whites, because they were not seen as credible witnesses, so when the only (willing) witnesses to white crimes were black, these crimes would not be brought to light. At one point in German South-West Africa, white settlers demanded "that in court only the testimony of seven African witnesses could outweigh evidence presented by a single white person" (Cocker 1998, 317). Similarly, slave narratives often had to have white authenticators, for example, white abolitionists, with the racially based epistemic authority to write a preface or appear on stage with the author to confirm that what this worthy Negro said was indeed true.

Moreover, in many cases, even if witnesses would have been given some kind of grudging hearing, they were terrorized into silence by the fear of white retaliation. A black woman recalls the world of Jim Crow and the dangers of describing it for what it was: "My problems started when I began to comment on what I saw. . . . I insisted on being accurate. But the world I was born into didn't want that. Indeed, its very survival depended on not knowing, not seeing—and certainly, not saying anything at all about what it was really like" (cited in Litwack [1998, 34]). If black testimony could be aprioristically rejected because it was likely to be false, it could also be aprioristically rejected because it was likely to be true. Testimony about white atrocities—lynchings, police killings, race riots—would often have to be passed down through segregated informational channels, black to black, too explosive to be allowed exposure to white cognition. The memory of the 1921 Tulsa race riot, the worst American race riot of the twentieth century, with a possible death toll of 300 people, was kept alive for decades in the black community long after whites had erased it from the official record. Ed Wheeler, a white researcher trying in 1970 to locate documentation on the riot, found that the official Tulsa records had mysteriously vanished, and he was only able, with great difficulty, to persuade black survivors to come forward with their photographs of the event: "The blacks allowed Wheeler to take the pictures only if he promised not to reveal their names, and they all spoke only on the condition of anonymity. Though fifty years had passed, they still feared retribution if they spoke out" (Hirsch 2002, 201).

Even when such fears are not a factor, and blacks do feel free to speak, the epistemic presumption against their credibility remains in a way that it does not for white witnesses. Black countertestimony against white mythology has always existed but would originally have been handicapped by the lack of material and cultural capital investment available for its production—oral testimony from illiterate slaves, ephemeral pamphlets with small print runs, and self-published works such as those by autodidact J. A. Rogers (1985), laboriously documenting the achievements of men and women of color to contest the white lie of black inferiority. But even when propagated in more respectable venues—for example, the Negro scholarly journals founded in the early twentieth century— they were epistemically ghettoized by the Jim Crow intellectual practices of the white academy. As Stephen Steinberg (1995) points out, the United States and its white social sciences have "played ostrich" on the issues of race and racial division (ix), so that—in Du Bois's famous image of blacks in a cave trying desperately to communicate to white passersby, before gradually realizing that they are silenced behind the updated version of the veil, "some thick sheet of invisible but horribly tangible plate glass"—"[black critics] of whatever political stripe . . . were simply met with a deaf ear." The testimony of Negro scholars saying the wrong thing (almost an analytic statement!) would not be registered. "[T]he marginalization of black voices in academia was facilitated by an 'invisible but horribly tangible' color line that relegated all but a few black scholars to teach in black colleges far removed from the academic mainstream" (51). Consider, for example, an anthropology founded on the "obvious" truth of racial hierarchy. Or a sociology failing to confront the central social fact of structural white domination. Or a history sanitizing the record of aboriginal conquest and black exploitation. Or a political science representing racism as an anomaly to a basically inclusive and egalitarian polity. Or, finally—in our own discipline—a political philosophy thriving for thirty years and supposedly dedicated to the elucidation of justice that makes next to no mention of the centrality of racial *injustice* to the "basic structure" of the United States and assumes instead that it will be more theoretically appropriate to start from the "ideal theory" assumption that society is the product of a mutually agreed upon, nonexploitative enterprise to divide benefits and burdens in an equitable way—and that this is somehow going to illuminate the distinctive moral problems of a society based on exploitative white settlement. In whatever discipline that is affected by race, the "testimony" of the black perspective and its distinctive conceptual and theoretical insights will tend to be whited out. Whites will cite other whites in a closed circuit of epistemic authority that reproduces white delusions.

Finally, the dynamic role of *white group interests* needs to be recognized and acknowledged as a central causal factor in generating and sustaining white ignorance. Cognitive psychologists standardly distinguish between "cold" and "hot" mechanisms of cognitive distortion, those attributable to intrinsic processing difficulties and those involving motivational factors, and in analytic philosophy of mind and philosophical psychology there is a large and well-established body of work on self-deception and motivated irrationality, though located within an individualistic framework (McLaughlin and Rorty 1988; Mele 2001). So claiming a link between interest and cognition is not at all unheard of in this field. But because of its framing individualism, and of course the aprioristic exclusion in any case of the realities of *white* group domination, the generalization to racial interests has not been carried out.

What needs to be done, I suggest, is to extrapolate some of this literature to a social context—one informed by the realities of race. Because of its marginalization of social oppression, the existing social epistemology literature tends to ignore or downplay such factors. In contrast, in the left tradition this was precisely the classic thesis: (class) domination and exploitation were the foundation of the social order, and as such they produced not merely material differentials of wealth in the economic sphere but deleterious cognitive consequences in the ideational sphere. Marxism's particular analysis of exploitation, resting as it does on the labor theory of value, has proven to be fatally vulnerable. But obviously this does not negate the value of the concept itself, suitably refurbished,[2] nor undercut the prima facie plausibility of the claim that if exploitative socioeconomic relations are indeed foundational to the social order, then this is likely to have a fundamental shaping effect on social ideation. In other words, one can detach from a class framework a Marxist "materialist" claim about the interaction between exploitation, group interest, and social cognition and apply it with far more plausibility within a race framework. I have argued elsewhere that *racial exploitation* (as determined by conventional liberal standards) has usually been quite clear and unequivocal (think of Native American expropriation, African slavery, Jim Crow), requiring—unlike exploitation in the technical Marxist sense—no elaborate theoretical apparatus to discern, and that it can easily be shown to have been central to U.S. history (Mills 2004). So vested white group interest in the racial status quo—the "wages of whiteness" in David Roediger's (1999) adaptation of

Du Bois's famous phrase from *Black Reconstruction* (1998)—needs to be recognized as a major factor in encouraging white cognitive distortions of various kinds.

Nor is such "motivated irrationality" confined to the period of overt racism and de jure segregation. Recent attitudinal research by Donald Kinder and Lynn Sanders on public policy matters linked to race reveals "a deep and perhaps widening racial divide [that] makes the discovery of commonality and agreement between the races a dim prospect," and central to the shaping of white opinion, it turns out, is their perception of their group interests: "the threats blacks appear to pose to whites' collective well-being, not their personal welfare" (Kinder and Sanders 1996, 33, 85). Race is the primary social division in the United States, these two political scientists conclude, and whites generally see black interests as opposed to their own. Inevitably, then, this will affect white social cognition—the concepts favored (e.g., today's "color blindness"), the refusal to perceive systemic discrimination, the convenient amnesia about the past and its legacy in the present, and the hostility to black testimony on continuing white privilege and the need to eliminate it to achieve racial justice. As emphasized at the start, then, these analytically distinguishable cognitive components are in reality all interlocked with and reciprocally determining one another, jointly contributing to the blindness of the white eye.

In his wonderfully titled *States of Denial*, Stanley Cohen (2001) argues that "[w]hole societies may slip into collective modes of denial":

> Besides collective denials of the past (such as brutalities against indigenous peoples), people may be encouraged to act as if they don't know about the present. Whole societies are based on forms of cruelty, discrimination, repression or exclusion which are "known" about but never openly acknowledged. . . . Indeed, distortions and self-delusions are most often synchronized. . . . Whole societies have mentioned and unmentionable rules about what should not be openly talked about. You are subject to a rule about obeying these rules, but bound also by a meta-rule which dictates that you deny your knowledge of the original rule. (10–11, 45)

White ignorance has been able to flourish all of these years because a white epistemology of ignorance has safeguarded it against the dangers of an illuminating blackness or redness, protecting those who for "racial" reasons have needed not to know. Only by starting to break these rules and meta-rules can we begin the long process that will lead to the eventual overcoming of this white darkness and the achievement of an enlightenment that is genuinely multiracial.

Notes

1. However, Hochschild's book initiated a debate in Belgium that has now led to a Royal Museum of Central Africa show on the issue: "Memory of Congo: The Colonial Era." Belgian historians dispute his figures and reject the charge of genocide. See the *New York Times*, February 9, 2005, B3.

2. See Ruth J. Sample (2003) for a recent Kantian updating of the concept and an argument for bringing it back to the center of our concerns.

References

Alcoff, Linda Martín. 1996. *Real Knowing: New Versions of the Coherence Theory.* Ithaca, NY: Cornell University Press.

Baldwin, James. 1993 [1961]. *Nobody Knows My Name: More Notes of a Native Son.* New York: Vintage International.

Campbell, Richmond, and Bruce Hunter, eds. 2000. *Moral Epistemology Naturalized. Canadian Journal of Philosophy* (supp.) 26. Calgary, AB: University of Calgary Press.

Coady, C. A. J. 1994 [1992]. *Testimony: A Philosophical Study.* Oxford: Clarendon Press.

Cocker, Mark. 1998. *Rivers of Blood, Rivers of Gold: Europe's Conflict with Tribal Peoples.* London: Jonathan Cape.

Cohen, Stanley. 2001. *States of Denial: Knowing about Atrocities and Suffering.* Malden, MA: Polity Press.

Curtis, James E., and John W. Petras, eds. 1970. *The Sociology of Knowledge: A Reader.* New York: Praeger.

Doane, Ashley W., and Eduardo Bonilla-Silva, eds. 2003. *White Out: The Continuing Significance of Racism.* New York: Routledge.

Doane, Woody. 2003. "Rethinking Whiteness Studies." In Doane and Bonilla-Silva (2003), 3–18.

Du Bois, W. E. B. 1989 [1903]. *The Souls of Black Folk.* New York: Penguin Books.

———. 1995 [1920]. "The Souls of White Folk." In *W. E. B. Du Bois: A Reader*, ed. David Levering Lewis, 453–65. New York: Henry Holt.

———. 1998 [1935]. *Black Reconstruction in America, 1860–1880.* New York: The Free Press.

Ellison, Ralph. 1995 [1952]. *Invisible Man.* New York: Vintage Books.

Fredrickson, George M. 2002. *Racism: A Short History.* Princeton, NJ: Princeton University Press.

Fuller, Steve. 2002. *Social Epistemology.* 2nd ed. Orig. ed. 1988. Bloomington: University of Indiana Press.

Gibson, Donald B. 1989. "Introduction." In Du Bois (1989), vii–xxxv.

Gillis, John R., ed. 1994a. *Commemorations: The Politics of National Identity.* Princeton, NJ: Princeton University Press.

———. 1994b. "Memory and Identity: The History of a Relationship." In Gillis (1994a), 3–24.

Goldman, Alvin I. 1999. *Knowledge in a Social World.* New York: Oxford University Press.

Gordon, Lewis R. 1995. *Bad Faith and Antiblack Racism.* Atlantic Highlands, NJ: Humanities Press.

Halbwachs, Maurice. 1992. *On Collective Memory.* Edited and translated by Lewis A. Coser. Chicago: University of Chicago Press.

Harding, Sandra, ed. 2004. *The Feminist Standpoint Theory Reader: Intellectual and Political Controversies.* New York: Routledge.

Hirsch, James S. 2002. *Riot and Remembrance: The Tulsa Race War and Its Legacy.* New York: Houghton Mifflin.

Hochschild, Adam. 1998. *King Leopold's Ghost: A Story of Greed, Terror, and Heroism in Colonial Africa.* New York: Houghton Mifflin.

Hodgson, Marshall G. S. 1993a. *Rethinking World History: Essays on Europe, Islam, and World History.* Edited by Edmund Burke III. New York: Cambridge University Press.

————. 1993b. "The Interrelations of Societies in History." In Hodgson (1993a), 3–28.

Jacobson, Matthew Frye. 1998. *Whiteness of a Different Color: European Immigrants and the Alchemy of Race.* Cambridge, MA: Harvard University Press.

Jennings, Francis. 1976 [1975]. *The Invasion of America: Indians, Colonialism, and the Cant of Conquest.* New York: W.W. Norton.

Kant, Immanuel. 1960. *Observations on the Feeling of the Beautiful and Sublime.* Translated by John T. Goldthwait. Berkeley and Los Angeles: University of California Press.

Kinder, Donald R., and Lynn M. Sanders. 1996. *Divided by Color: Racial Politics and Democratic Ideals.* Chicago: University of Chicago Press.

Kitcher, Philip. 1994. "Contrasting Conceptions of Social Epistemology." In Schmitt (1994), 111–34.

Konkle, Maureen. 2004. *Writing Indian Nations: Native Intellectuals and the Politics of Historiography, 1827–1863.* Chapel Hill: University of North Carolina Press.

Kornblith, Hilary. 1994a. "A Conservative Approach to Social Epistemology." In Schmitt (1994), 93–110.

————, ed. 1994b. *Naturalizing Epistemology.* 2nd ed. Orig. ed. 1985. Cambridge: MIT Press.

Litwack, Leon F. 1998. *Trouble in Mind: Black Southerners in the Age of Jim Crow.* New York: Alfred A. Knopf.

Loewen, James W. 1996 [1995]. *Lies My Teacher Told Me: Everything Your American History Textbook Got Wrong.* New York: Touchstone/Simon & Schuster.

McCarthy, Thomas. 2002. "*Vergangenheitsbewältigung* in the USA: On the Politics of the Memory of Slavery, Part I." *Political Theory* 30: 623–48.

————. 2004. "Coming to Terms with Our Past: On the Morality and Politics of Reparations for Slavery, Part II." *Political Theory* 32: 750–72.

McLaughlin, Brian P., and Amelie Oksenberg Rorty, eds. 1988. *Perspectives on Self-Deception.* Berkeley and Los Angeles: University of California Press.

Mele, Alfred R. 2001. *Self-Deception Unmasked.* Princeton, NJ: Princeton University Press.

Melville, Herman. 1986. "Benito Cereno." In *Billy Budd, Sailor and Other Stories,* 159–258. New York: Viking Penguin.

————. 2000. *Moby Dick, or, The Whale.* New York: Modern Library.

Mills, Charles W. 1997. *The Racial Contract*. Ithaca, NY: Cornell University Press.
———. 1998 [1988]. "Alternative Epistemologies." In *Epistemology: The Big Questions*, ed. Linda Martín Alcoff, 392–410. Malden, MA: Blackwell.
———. 2004. "Racial Exploitation and the Wages of Whiteness." In *What White Looks Like: African American Philosophers on the Whiteness Question*, ed. George Yancy, 25–54. New York: Routledge.
Quine, W. V. O. 1969a. *Ontological Relativity and Other Essays*. New York: Columbia University Press.
———. 1969b. "Epistemology Naturalized." In Quine (1969a), 69–90.
Roediger, David R., ed. 1998. *Black on White: Black Writers on What It Means To Be White*. New York: Schocken Books.
———. 1999. *The Wages of Whiteness: Race and the Making of the American Working Class*. Rev. ed. Orig. ed. 1991. New York: Verso.
Rogers, J. A. 1985 [1952]. *100 Amazing Facts about the Negro with Complete Proof: A Short Cut to the World History of the Negro*. St. Petersburg, FL: Helga M. Rogers.
Sample, Ruth J. 2003. *Exploitation: What It Is and Why It's Wrong*. Lanham, MD: Rowman & Littlefield.
Savage, Kirk. 1994. "The Politics of Memory: Black Emancipation and the Civil War Monument." In Gillis (1994a), 127–49.
Schmitt, Frederick F., ed. 1994. *Socializing Epistemology: The Social Dimensions of Knowledge*. Lanham, MD: Rowman & Littlefield.
Shapiro, Thomas M. 2004. *The Hidden Cost of Being African American: How Wealth Perpetuates Inequality*. New York: Oxford University Press.
Smith, Rogers M. 1997. *Civic Ideals: Conflicting Visions of Citizenship in U.S. History*. New Haven, CT: Yale University Press.
Steinberg, Stephen. 1995. *Turning Back: The Retreat from Racial Justice in American Thought and Policy*. Boston: Beacon Press.
Sundquist, Eric J. 1993. *To Wake the Nations: Race in the Making of American Literature*. Cambridge, MA: Belknap Press.

CHAPTER 2

Epistemologies of Ignorance
Three Types

Linda Martín Alcoff

Ignorance is of increasing concern. The public discourse of anti-intellectualism poses ignorance as a positive alternative and antidote to elitism, and polls of the U.S. population, one of the most elite populations in the world, reveal alarming ignorance about world geography and history as well as current events. The problem is not explainable by a lack of access to resources for knowledge and information, nor is it a problem that decreases with the advantages of class. It is, or appears to be, a willful ignorance.

As this chapter will endeavor to demonstrate, the study and analysis of ignorance poses some special epistemological questions beyond the expected sociological and educational ones, questions having to do with how we understand the intersection between cognitive norms, structural privilege, and situated identities. Is the normative project of epistemology sufficiently well formulated to take up the challenge that a widespread and growing ignorance poses? Perhaps the pursuit of ever more fine-tuned reliable belief-forming practices should give way for work that explores the range of epistemically unreliable but socially functional belief-forming practices. Work in this area has already begun in feminist epistemology, social epistemology, sociological studies of the sciences, and also in the traditions of critical rationality in German social theory and other traditions, such as subaltern and postcolonial studies, that have developed critiques of dominant Western rationalities.

Even in mainstream epistemology, the topic of ignorance as a species of bad epistemic practice is not new, but what is new is the idea of explaining ignorance not as a feature of *neglectful* epistemic practice but as a *substantive* epistemic practice in itself. The idea of an epistemology of

39

ignorance attempts to explain and account for the fact that such substantive practices of ignorance—willful ignorance, for example, and socially acceptable but faulty justificatory practices—are structural. This is
to say that there are identities and social locations and modes of belief
formation, all produced by structural social conditions of a variety of
sorts, that are in some cases epistemically disadvantaged or defective.
Here, social epistemology intersects in a more intense way than usual
with social and political theory.

In this chapter, I develop a typology of the recent arguments for epistemologies of ignorance and compare and contrast them. I then push the
analysis of ignorance further by relating it to a previous generation's discussion about structural ignorance, that is, from the work of Max Horkheimer and the Frankfurt School. Horkheimer's analysis helps us see, I
shall argue, that ignorance is a problem relating not just to justificatory
practices but also to ontologies of truth.

Three broad arguments can be made for epistemologies of ignorance. The first, drawn mainly out of Lorraine Code's work, is an argument that ignorance follows from the general fact of our situatedness as
knowers. The second argument, drawn mainly from Sandra Harding's
work, relates ignorance to specific aspects of group identities. The third
argument, drawn from Charles Mills's work, develops a structural analysis of the ways in which oppressive systems produce ignorance as one of
their effects. These three arguments are not by any means incompatible:
one could develop an account that combined all three (and I suspect
Code, Harding, and Mills would agree). But taken *by themselves*, each argument has different ideas about the nature of the problem of epistemic
ignorance and the nature of possible solutions, as I shall try to show.

I

The idea of our general situatedness as knowers is developed best in the
work of Lorraine Code, who famously and effectively argued against "S
knows that p" epistemologies for mistakenly assuming that all S's are fungible or interchangeable. Such epistemologies share the assumption that
any person in an identical situation with identical access to perceptual
data will form the same conclusions if she or he is performing epistemic
operations in a responsible way. This assumption may work well for simple claims such as "The sun is shining" but cannot be generalized to
more complex beliefs such as "Silvio is trustworthy," or "The defendant is
guilty," or "The job applicant is well qualified." These sorts of beliefs involve complicated processes of judgment that will bring the knower's
specific history of experience to bear. Given the nonfungible nature of
knowers, then, Code argued that we need to develop a "geography of the

epistemic terrain . . . a population geography that develops qualitative analyses of subjective positions and identities and the sociopolitical structures that produce them. Because differing social positions generate variable constructions of reality and afford different perspectives on the world . . . these analyses derive from a recognition that knowers are always *somewhere*—and at once limited and enabled by the specificities of their locations" (Code 1993, 39).

The fact that judgment is sometimes correlated to social position does not yield relativist conclusions, because judgments from any location must still be subject to challenge and verification. But it indicates that we should expand our account of how justification operates and hence our ability to develop more realistic ideas about how to provide normative checks on what are now considered best practices. Thus, as she succinctly put it, "objectivity requires taking subjectivity into account" (Code 1995, 44).

This argument works, then, from the epistemically substantive differences between situations to show that epistemic advantages and disadvantages are not the same for all. Some situations are in positions of ignorance, even though the knowers in those situations may have identical access to the relevant facts. For example, I may be attending an operation as a support person for the patient and have access to all of the same monitoring devices seen by the medical attendants, but my ability to understand the meaning of what the monitoring devices are reporting is not equal to trained professionals. I am not interchangeable with them as a knower in this context, and I am in fact ignorant in regard to some important elements required for judgment about the health and well-being of the patient. Code's argument is simply that in many such instances some knowers are ignorant vis-à-vis others, just as a layperson in an operating room is clearly ignorant vis-à-vis the medical experts. Thus we need to do a qualitative analysis of the epistemic implications of various subject positions rather than assume that all S's are epistemically equivalent.

The operating room case is a relatively uncontroversial example, but it can be used to indicate that an adequate conception of epistemic situation should include two claims. First, *most* knowledge is the product of judgment calls rather than deductive argument or simple perceptual reports. The doctors and I both have the necessary perceptual access to the monitoring equipment in the operating room, but an adequate judgment of the patient's condition will require more than a simple reading off of numbers, given its dependence on an understanding of the patient's current health and a knowledge and an acceptance of certain medical theories. Doctors' medical expertise cannot be analogized to an increased ability (increased over my own) to read the data off the screen but involves more complex epistemic operations of judgment. Second, any given individual who is called upon to make a judgment call will rely on her or his own specific experiences. These experiences are sometimes correlated to the individual's social location or social identity, habits of perceptual attention, what Ian Hacking calls "styles of reasoning," and also with the individual's own interests—interests that are fluid and open to interpretation but that have some objective elements in regard to the conditions of the knower's material reality. Thus an adequate concept of epistemic situatedness must involve much more than the knower's position in time and space and must include individual factors about her or his history and experience. We recognize the variability in medical judgment when we accept the practice of "getting a second opinion": this acknowledges the complexity of analysis required for diagnosis and treatment recommendations, and the fact that judgment is not reducible to algorithmic procedures.

Because it builds from a *general* condition of all knowers—that is, their situatedness—this kind of argument provides a general case about epistemic situatedness that potentially applies to every knower. We can summarize this argument by the following four premises:

1. All knowers are situated in time and space, with specific experiences, social locations, modes of perceptual practices and habits, styles of reasoning, and sets of interests that are fluid and open to interpretation but that have some objective elements in regard to the conditions of the knower's material reality.
2. This specificity of situatedness is relevant, at least in some cases, to the ways that a knower will make judgment calls about issues of coherence, consistency, relevance, plausibility, and credibility.
3. From this it follows that knowers are not, in fact, fungible or interchangeable.
4. Further, it must also follow that knowers are not all "epistemically equal." As Code said, knowers are at once limited *and* enabled by the specificities of their locations.

If we use this type of argument, then how would one develop the "geography of the epistemic terrain" for which Code calls? I suggest that from the fact of our general situatedness alone it follows that the epistemic implication of any given epistemic situation is determined by the context of the object of inquiry. That is, the fact that we are all situated does not give us reasons to classify any *given* situation as ignorant in and of itself; rather, a given epistemic situation may be advantaged or disadvantaged, depending on what kind of knowledge we are pursuing, or, in other words, in regard to a specific epistemic objective. As an untrained attendant at an operation, I am in a good position to know whether the patient is still breathing; I am not in a good position to know whether the patient is in danger. Epistemic advantages and disadvantages do not accrue to social locations per se but only to locations as they exist *in relation to* specific kinds of inquiry.

Thus from the fact of our general situatedness it follows that ignorance should be understood as contextual, since it does not accrue to me simply as an individual outside of a particular situation. I may be a trained linguist with the ability to communicate in eight languages, or an excellent seamstress capable of making my own designs from scratch, but insofar as I am attending a medical operation, I am ignorant of the skills needed to fully assess the health of the patient. What is determinative of ignorance is the interplay between my individual epistemic situatedness—my location, experience, perceptual abilities, and so forth, not all of which will be relevant in any given case—and what is called for in reaching conclusions about this particular object of inquiry.

II

Next consider a different kind of argument for epistemic ignorance, one not focused on the general features of every epistemic situation but on the specific features of groups of knowers who share a social location. Sandra Harding has argued that the specific features of women's epistemic situation vis-à-vis men give them an epistemic advantage. She gave eight grounds for the claim that by starting research from women's lives, we can arrive at empirically and theoretically more adequate descriptions and explanations (Harding 1991, 119–33). These grounds build primarily from the systemic ways in which women's lives differ from men's lives: usually being alienated from social power, but rarely alienated from the everyday needs of maintaining material existence. Such arguments are not applicable if we imagine them globally, but they should be applied locally. That is, *within* given specific communities that share other features such as position in the global labor market, for example, or race, ethnicity, and nationality, the patterns that gender differences make generally play out in the ways that Harding and Dorothy Smith and other standpoint theorists have hypothesized. In other words, gender marks a reliable pattern of difference in experience within a culturally specific social group, because the substantive features that characterize any given gender identity will be dependent on cultural practices.

Particularly interesting for the topic of ignorance is Harding's argument that "members of oppressed groups have fewer interests in ignorance about the social order and fewer reasons to invest in maintaining or justifying the status quo than do dominant groups" (1991, 126). Against this claim, one could argue that members of oppressed groups also have specific reasons to maintain their own ignorance about the social order; for example, reasons based on the need to maintain civil relations with other people with whom they may have to work, to avoid the emotional distress of having to acknowledge the full weight of one's oppression or the humiliation of one's family members, and thus reasons that have to do with overall mental health and functional social relations. But such reasons to avoid thinking about social oppression may be outweighed by the need to know the true reality of the social conditions within which one must survive, the need to know who one's potential allies and enemies are, for example. And those who are oppressed within a system are unlike those who benefit from it in having no need to make excuses for its rampant unfairness in order to avoid shame, guilt, or moral consternation. Thus I believe that Harding's claim can be interpreted as the claim that, *on balance*, members of oppressed groups have fewer reasons to fool themselves about this being the best of all possible worlds, and have strong motivations to gain a clear-eyed assessment of their society.

Whether or not one agrees with this particular argument about the situation of the oppressed, one might still assent to the general idea here that social identities can confer motivations, or not, to develop a critical consciousness toward conventional beliefs and values. Such self-interested motivations can of course be overcome, as for example when the facts are too obvious to be ignored, but the point is that in some groups a given justified claim will encounter more obstacles to its fair assessment than in other groups, depending on the social identity of the individuals involved. Many of us who have taught philosophy classes in different kinds of institutions note a difference in how open various groups of students are to critical social theory, or critical race theory, or feminist theory, a difference that is often correlated to students' social identities, albeit in complex ways.

Group identity, certainly as Harding makes the argument, does not confer justification in and of itself, so one might also wonder here whether the epistemic salience of group identity could be overcome by simply instituting good intellectual virtues. In other words, one might think that one should subject all new beliefs to the same rigorous demands for reasons, and if my group identity affects my willingness to do so in some cases then I am simply failing in my epistemic duties. The problem, then, would not be group identity but bad epistemic behavior.

To respond to this, we need to remember that belief formation generally involves judgment calls about relevance, plausibility, coherence, consistency, and credibility. What I already know and believe will have a privileged place in my judgments by affecting my determinations of coherence, consistency, and plausibility, and this is in fact good epistemic practice. Moreover, I cannot reasonably be expected to treat every one of my beliefs as in need of rigorous scrutiny and independent verification; generally, it takes a crisis of some sort for a person to radically question one of her or his basic beliefs or belief sets. This crisis can be as mild as taking an introductory ethics course, or it can be as dramatic as being sent to war. Nevertheless, the law of entropy operates in the realm of belief: we tend toward conserving the beliefs we have until forced to call them into question. Again, this universal tendency is applied to very different sets of beliefs, given that we each start our mature epistemic lives with different sets of epistemic commitments depending on the accidents of our birth. Our judgment calls about coherence and plausibility depend in no small part on what happens to be in our core belief set. Thus the argument for the salience of group identity does not require one to hold that there are no universal epistemic practices, either "best practices" or simply human epistemic tendencies, but simply to hold that our universal tendencies are applied to different epistemic challenges depending, in part, on our group identity.

For example, I recount to a dinner party of academics that someone I know has been arrested and charged with a crime, and roughed up by the police, on trumped-up charges. I say that he was doing nothing to elicit this reaction from the police. I get two different sorts of responses, sympathy and skepticism. One group thinks "he must have done something" to elicit this reaction from the police, while another group nods knowingly, giving at least presumptive credibility to my story. Each group is weighing the plausibility of such a story based on its own knowledge and experience with the police and the criminal justice system. Each group may be performing at least minimally well by a standard of epistemic responsibility, but each comes to different conclusions. Such group differences, as this example illustrates, are often correlated to class and/or race differences. If my story had involved sexual harassment, sexual abuse, or domestic violence, then I might get a different set of responses in which gender played a larger role than class or race.

Group identity makes an epistemically relevant difference, then, not because identity alone can settle questions of justification, or because groups follow different procedures for justifying claims, but simply because groups will sometimes operate with different starting belief sets based on their social location and their group-related experiences, and these starting belief sets will inform their epistemic operations such as judging coherence and plausibility. Essentially, to acknowledge the occasional relevance of group identity on epistemic performance is no different than acknowledging such epistemically relevant differences as medical training or being positioned to be able to see an instrument panel.

The advantage that Harding claims for female gender identity follows from these kinds of considerations. Why is it important to have

women on the Supreme Court or in other law-making governmental
bodies? Because the quality of the discussion about certain matters that
only women are in a position to see the full weight of, such as the significance of pregnancy in a woman's life, will be enriched. Her arguments
could thus be used to suggest that women may raise new questions to
consider in assessing legal judgments regarding pregnancy, for example,
because they will operate from a different set of experiences that may affect how they judge plausibility on a variety of matters. Thus their critical orientation may be different and richer in regard to certain kinds of
gender-related issues, richer in the sense of being based on more direct
and comprehensive knowledge and experience.

In brief, then, we can summarize the argument for the specific relevance of group identity as follows:

1. The first premise repeats the first two parts of the general argument given earlier, that all knowers are situated, and that this situatedness has epistemic implications for knowers' judgment at
   least some of the time.
2. The second premise holds that these situations are correlated in
   at least some important respects to social identity. (Such a claim
   does not require any biological or essentialist assumptions about
   the uniformity of identity but is entirely compatible with a theory
   about the historical and social construction of groups and of
   group identities.)
3. Specifically, the situation of having female gender identity has
   epistemically relevant aspects, including a general marginality
   from social power and a general lack of alienation from everyday
   materiality. Given the significant ways in which gender systems
   organize social life and child socialization, it would only make
   sense that part of what gender systems organize is going to be
   epistemically relevant to how knowers make judgments.
4. Because of its specific aspects, female-gendered location is a re-
   source from which to build a feminist standpoint that can provide new critical questions for inquiry. This is not to say that the
   experience of this identity yields knowledge in and of itself, but
   that it contains resources from which new knowledges can be developed with critical and theoretical reflection, carried out both
   individually and collectively.
5. Male-gendered identity is, conversely, epistemically disadvantaged in its situatedness in regard to certain matters: it has less of
   an outsider perspective on dominant gender-related social scripts
   and forms of power and less of an overall interest in critically
   questioning them.

This argument makes an important addition to the earlier argument from the general situatedness of knowers, specifying the fact that epistemic situations are correlated to group identity, and that specific group identities may confer epistemic advantages or disadvantages. It has the explanatory power to explain the significant differences, some would say significant improvement, in the production of academic knowledge that can be seen as a trend since at least the passage of the G.I. Bill, which began a process of democratizing the U.S. academy and making it accessible to some groups that were previously excluded. Since the 1950s various marginalized groups in U.S. society have been able to engage in academic inquiry in significant numbers, which has spurred the development of many new areas of research and paradigms of inquiry, including social history, ethnic studies, labor studies, and feminist philosophy. Would such new areas of inquiry and knowledge have developed in research departments that remained 95 percent white, male, and upper class?

In terms of developing a "geography of the epistemic terrain," what follows most significantly from Harding's approach is that epistemic advantages and disadvantages accrue to social and group identities per se rather than identities only in relation to a given context of inquiry. This is not to say that women or marginalized peoples will have *absolute* epistemic advantage in having more critical questions in regard to every conceivable line of inquiry, but that the pattern of epistemic positionality created by some identities has the potential for relevance in broad domains of inquiry, perhaps in any inquiry. Thus ignorance is contextual, but there are patterns of ignorance associated with social and group identities.

III

The third type of argument for epistemic ignorance provides an even more explicitly structural account of the nature of oppressive systems. While it shares a commitment to the general account of epistemic situatedness that comes from the two previously discussed arguments, the structural argument has some distinctive features.

The structural argument focuses not on *generally* differentiated experiences and interests, but on the *specific* knowing practices inculcated in a socially dominant group. Where the last argument argued that men, for example, have *less* interest in raising critical questions about male dominance, the structural argument argues that whites have a *positive* interest in "seeing the world wrongly," to paraphrase Mills. Here ignorance is not primarily understood as a *lack*—a lack of motivation or experience as the result of social location—but as a substantive epistemic practice that differentiates the dominant group. As a member of a dominant social group, I might indeed lack an interest in pursuing all of the ramifications of social injustice, or I might lack a marginalized experience from which to critique accepted social conventions. Thus my epistemic practices will be deficient vis-à-vis others because I lack something—motivations, experiences—that they have. However, the structural argument suggests that as a member of a dominant social group, I also may have inculcated a pattern of belief-forming practices that created the effect of systematic ignorance. I may be actively pursuing or supporting a distorted or an otherwise inaccurate account.

Mills writes, ". . . on matters related to race, the Racial Contract prescribes for its signatories an inverted epistemology, an epistemology of ignorance, a particular pattern of localized and global cognitive dysfunctions (which are psychologically and socially functional), producing the ironic outcome that whites will in general be unable to understand the world they themselves have made" (Mills 1997, 18). What might such "localized and global cognitive dysfunctions" be? To answer this question, we might imagine Archie Bunker or some suitable equivalent as the object of epistemological investigation, where the goal is to ascertain how he arrives at his conclusions with such confidence in their validity. If we can generalize from Archie, then we might conjecture that racism produces a pattern of perceptual attentiveness to the world that relegates some significant aspects of it to a murky nether region. Racism can also supply premises—and cast these as unchallengeable premises—that lead to judgments for which otherwise there is insufficient evidence. Thus racism is a type of subjectivity that forms patterns of perceptual attentiveness and supplies belief-influencing premises that result in a distorted or faulty account of reality.

Based on this, we can summarize the structural argument as follows:

1. One of the key features of oppressive societies is that they do not acknowledge themselves as oppressive. Therefore, in any given oppressive society, there is a dominant view about the general nature of the society that represents its particular forms of inequality and exploitation as basically just and fair, or at least the best of all possible worlds.

2. It is very likely, however, that this dominant representation of the unjust society as a just society will have countervailing evidence on a daily basis that is at least potentially visible to everyone in the society.

3. Therefore, cognitive norms of assessment will have to be maintained that allow for this countervailing evidence to be regularly dismissed so that the dominant view can be held stable.

Again, this argument can be differentiated from the previous arguments in that it contends that there exist substantive cognitive norms to explain ignorance rather than merely the *absence* of certain kinds of experience or motivations. It has the explanatory power to explain why it is that most whites in the United States seem to believe that the United States is a form of society based mostly on individual merit, while most nonwhites seem to believe that the United States is a form of society based on a racial contract. The problem that we often encounter is not simply that there is a pattern of difference in doxastic commitment, but that it is very difficult to reach consensus even after extensive discussions, for example, in classrooms.

Mills suggests that "whiteness," which he carefully defines as a political construct rather than simply an ethnic category, brings with it a "cognitive model that precludes self-transparency and genuine understanding of all social realities," that it ensures that whites will live in a "racial fantasyland, [or] a 'consensual hallucination,'" and that the root of all this is the "cognitive and moral economy psychically required for conquest, colonization, and enslavement" (Mills 1997, 18–19). If it is true that most people prefer to think of themselves as moral or at least excusable in their actions, then in unjust societies those in dominant and privileged positions must be able to construct representations of themselves and others to support a fantasyland of moral approbation. Thus such whites might believe that the academy is a meritocracy, that modernity began in Europe and then spread outward, and that global poverty is disconnected from Western wealth. The persistence of such myths in spite of increasing empirical and theoretical counterevidence certainly suggests that the cognitive dysfunctions responsible for myth maintenance are more than a matter of differences in group experiences or expertise. However, Mills's claims about the existence of a white cognitive dysfunction need more explanation, and I will argue in the following section that Horkheimer's critique of the ontologies of Western science can help us fill out the story.

First let me summarize the typologies of ignorance I have developed here by comparing the geography of the epistemic terrain suggested by these three types of arguments for ignorance. The idea of a general epistemic situatedness developed in the first argument renders ignorance contextually dependent on the particular configuration—that is, the fit—between knower and known. The idea that group identity yields variable epistemic dispositions renders ignorance the result of an underprivileged set of experiences and motivations, so to speak. Finally, the idea of a cognitive model to ensure distortions of reality renders ignorance an effect of inculcated practices common to a group. There is a contextualism built into this latter scenario: for Mills, the cognitive dysfunctions associated with whiteness concern issues relevant to racism, not any and every possible area of belief. We can further combine the second and third arguments to reveal an especially troubling result: not only are whites inculcated in some pernicious epistemic practices, but they will have less motivation or ability than others would have to either detect their errors or correct them.

Now there are numerous questions here that invite further analysis. In regard to motivations to critique existing social relations, we clearly need to address the class, ethnicity, and gender heterogeneity among whites, for example, and to think through the relationship between the objective interests of colonialism generally and the objective interests of whites as a group. We would need to consider how a multiplicity of identity alignments might produce conflicting effects on belief formation. If members of dominant groups are responsible for essentially duping themselves about the true nature of their social world, then are there resources in their own experiences from which to draw out the truth? Much more needs to be asked about the susceptibility of nondominant groups to various misrepresentations of reality. These are essentially questions of social psychology, but the structural argument that Mills develops shows that social psychology as well as political analysis will have epistemic implications on real-world practices of justification.

Noting the ways in which cognitive situatedness can be correlated to group identity cannot lead to a replacement of epistemic considerations for identity considerations. The point remains that the problem is in the cognitive norm, not in the identity per se, and so we need to focus on isolating and identifying these dysfunctional norms and understanding how they operate. The remainder of this chapter, then, will focus on a further understanding of such norms.

IV

The Frankfurt School's critique of instrumental rationality will prove especially helpful here, since its project was to do a materialist critical analysis of reason under conditions of capitalism and fascism, where strategic goals of productivity and efficiency circumscribed the practices of reasoning activity. Thus, like Mills, the Frankfurt School made links between the kinds of knowing practices that exist in contemporary society and macro structures of political economy. In effect, it portrays instrumental rationality as a kind of a dysfunctional cognitive norm, functional within very narrow parameters of capital accumulation and the maintenance of ideology but dysfunctional as a reliable, truth-seeking practice. This claim about the dysfunctional status of instrumental rationality later became one of the central issues of disagreement between Habermas, on one side, and Marcuse and Horkheimer, on the other. Habermas argued that instrumental rationality was a legitimate epistemic practice as long as it was not universalized hegemonically as the whole of reason, while Horkheimer and Marcuse argued that the dangers and problems with instrumental rationality did not disappear from simply circumscribing its scope of application. This debate, I suggest, mirrors in some important respects the debate over whether some of the dominant white epistemic practices to which Mills's work calls attention are intellectually virtuous but simply limited by a narrowness of experience, or whether these practices are not sound even in limited application. By referring to cognitive norms that support a "consensual hallucination," I take it that Mills means to take the latter, stronger critical position.

The work of Max Horkheimer is especially relevant to the topic of ignorance. For example, Horkheimer argued against the assumptions of naive empiricism that, "The facts which our senses present to us are socially preformed in two ways: through the *historical character of the object perceived* and through the *historical character of the perceiving organ*" (Horkheimer 1975, 200, emphasis added). This idea that the "perceiving organ" has a *historical* character led to Horkheimer's proposal that the crucial task for critical theorists is to denaturalize both the product and the process of knowledge. He argued, thus, that we need to analyze the *social* production of the "knowing individual as such" (Horkheimer 1975, 199). If we accept the idea that both the object perceived and the perceiving organ are socially and politically preformed, then we might begin to think of ignorance as the result of a historically specific mode of knowing and perceiving.

Horkheimer distinguishes what he calls traditional theory, which is dominant in the academy, from critical theory, which the Frankfurt School hoped to develop through a complex analysis that unites epistemological and political considerations. He analyzed the kind of reason used in traditional theory as an instrumentalized reason focused on means-end calculations, where the question of ends is set apart as beyond rational deliberation. For Horkheimer, this instrumentalized reason is not an aid in truth seeking but actually works to obscure the truth. In order to see how this works, Horkheimer believed that we need to denaturalize both the product and the process of knowing.

First of all, when we describe the world around us we are not simply reporting on a natural creation but on the product of collective human praxis, meaning reflective practical activity.

> . . . human action unconsciously determines not only the subjective side of perception [through, e.g., production of certain kinds of perceptual and measuring tools] but in larger degree the object as well. The sensible

world which a member of industrial society sees about him every day
bears the marks of deliberate work: tenement houses, factories, cotton,
cattle for slaughter, men, and in addition, not only objects such as subway
trains, delivery trucks, autos, and airplanes, but the movements in the
course of which they are perceived. (Horkheimer 1975, 201)

The problem is that these objects are generally defined not as the
product of praxis but as if they were found objects. "The whole perceptible world as present to a member of bourgeois society and as interpreted
within a traditional worldview which is in continuous interaction with
that world, is seen by the perceiver as a sum-total of facts; it is there and
must be accepted" (Horkheimer 1975, 199). Consider how well this idea
might apply to our contemporary, everyday world of racial and gendered
identity, and the associations between race and crime or between race
and poverty. Women's interrupted career paths, Latinos' low scores on
standardized tests, and the disparities in mortality rates between African
American and white men might all be taken as bare facts without need of
sociological explanation. Indeed, in Horkheimer's time, such factors as
these were not the subject of social inquiry, and only became so when the
academy started to become more inclusive.

In Horkheimer's view, the cognitive norms at fault here are deductive and quantitative methods that sideline interpretative analysis in favor
of the amassing of data or facts. Given that perceptible reality, as well as
the mode or process of perception, is in actuality the product of social activity, then empirical description, no matter how detailed, is incapable of
serving by itself as any kind of ultimate foundation or reliable testing
ground for a general or universal account of, for example, human nature
or human social organization (Horkheimer 1975, 201).

Moreover, traditional theory's focus on problem solving is consonant
with the mode of rationality used in capitalism. Traditional theory mimics
capitalism's focus on product accumulation and quantitative increases in
its assumption that the sheer accumulation of facts is an intrinsic epistemic good (no matter how trivial or irrelevant). The result is the pro-
mulgation of a mode of naturalism in the social sciences that aims only at
prediction and uses tools restricted almost entirely to quantification. Explanation, hermeneutic interpretation, and even normative argument are
denigrated as useless speculations because they have no firm foundation
in the deductions of what are taken as bare, incontrovertible facts.

But for Horkheimer the root of the problem here is not simply the
kind of mistake found in Moritz Schlick's early work, which tried to excise
interpretation and normativity from philosophical reason proper. In other
words, the root of the problem is not so much in positivism itself, as in the
social context within which positivism was developed and nurtured. Thus,

the real root of the problem is in the *structural* context within which reason finds itself located. The actual structural context in which organized and collective rationality pursues knowledge is not, and increasingly less so, a kind of Socratic utopia where, as Ben Okri describes it, universities might be "places where people sat and meditated and absorbed knowledge from the silence . . . [where] research was a permanent activity, and all were researchers and appliers of the fruits of the research . . . [where] the purpose [is] to discover the hidden unified law of all things, to deepen the spirit, to make more profound the sensitivities of the individual to the universe, and to become more creative" (quoted in Mohanty 2003, 169). As Chandra Talpade Mohanty points out in her analysis of corporatized academies, Okri's description seems today impossibly utopian. Open spaces for the development of critical and creative reason are rapidly shrinking as universities themselves become corporatized, "digital diploma mills" instrumentalized by a war economy engaged in global imperial projects. What flourishes best in such a location, under the banner of reason, are pragmatic debates over the most efficient means for database surveillance systems, and not what might assist anybody in truly understanding social reality or in changing it.

But neither understanding nor change is really the goal in these sites of inquiry. Horkheimer says:

> Theory in the traditional sense based on Descartes as it exists above all in the areas of academic science organizes experience on the basis of statements of a problem in a manner which devotes itself to *the reproduction of life within contemporary society*. (quoted in Frisby 1972, 107, emphasis added)

Horkheimer suggests that the result of this social production of the knowing individual is a "liquidation of the subject" by which he means not the death of the subject, as in postmodernism, but the atrophied ability to resist or critique. As Georg Lohmann points out in his commentary on Horkheimer, all that remains from the social production of the knowing individual "is the individual who must submit to reality, who must accommodate himself in order to maintain himself" (Lohmann 1993, 394). This is because the reduction of reason to the calculation of means, and the foreclosure of any interpretation, analysis, and critique of ends themselves, results necessarily in a loss of a sense of meaningful ends. The actual ends to which we must accommodate our lives then have no perceptible justification. This demoralizes the critical faculty even in its atrophied state. Horkheimer describes this as a process of "self-preservation without the self" (Lohmann 1993, 393). White ignorance, then, may be a species of this loss of critical rationality.

To the extent that Horkheimer's arguments are based on the idea of the theory-dependent nature of observation, or the theory ladenness of facts, we might be led to think that our sophisticated contemporary philosophies of science that generally reject the possibility of out-of-theory experiences have nothing to learn from Horkheimer. But why, then, does ignorance still abound? Positivist characterizations of data have lost ground ever since Quine's "Two Dogmas" (1951), and it is now widely acknowledged that pragmatic considerations are critical in theory choice. Yet I would argue that what has not been considered in the mainstream epistemology and philosophy of science discussions—even in the new field of social epistemology—is Horkheimer's idea that the way pragmatic considerations play out in theory choice in the sciences involves the market, and that an epistemology of the social sciences must analyze the latter's position within a society in which the market has achieved near hegemony. That is, there is little attention paid in the philosophy of the sciences to the structural economic organization of society, its reigning paradigms, and the coherence between these paradigms and scientific methodology. Traditional epistemology has no space for the incorporation of this level of reflexivity, relegating such concerns to the sociology of knowledge. Horkheimer's critical theory, in contrast to traditional theory, views such "sociological" concerns as being intrinsic to any epistemological assessment of current knowledge.

The project of critical theory, then, is to bring to consciousness the link between the social production of knowledge and the social production of society, and thus to show that the production of knowledge is the product of conscious activity (even when it is not self-conscious about this fact) rather than activity that operates merely in the sphere of nature or that is wholly determined. In other words, knowledge, no less than "subway trains and tenement houses," reflects the current condition of human praxis.

This view of the social-structural context for the production of historical modes of perception that result in ignorance is a claim about truth. Any claim that charges ignorance must have access to the alternative to ignorance, must judge ignorance on the basis of some standard, and thus make a claim of improved reference and reliability. Reference, in Horkheimer's view, is a complex operation because, like Adorno, he believed we must factor in not only a reference to the actual but also a reference to the possible. When we acknowledge, in other words, that our best empirical descriptions refer not to found objects but to products of human praxis, then we must acknowledge that we can, in effect, through a new praxis, choose the descriptions that we will make in the future. Thus we have to acknowledge the realm of the possible at work in our very description, and this in turn opens us up to a new kind of responsibility for the knowledge we have. The idea of joining both truth, as the alternative to ignorance, and responsibility is combined in Horkheimer's concept of objective reason.

Although he takes a relatively contemporary view on the indistinguishability of fact and value, in characterizing the knowledge that critical theory seeks Horkheimer takes a position on the relation between politics and knowledge that is startlingly unlike what we might expect today from the postmodernists: He vehemently criticizes the use of pragmatic criteria and defends a notion of objective reason, which is surprising given the importance that he attaches to the political context of knowledge. In the postmodern view, it is the objectivists who would foreclose the argument for a democratic epistemology by making political and sociological considerations essentially irrelevant to truth seeking.

In contrast, in *Eclipse of Reason*, Horkheimer relies on what he calls "objective reason" to critique the "subjective reason" that would legitimate pragmatic criteria in theory choice and belief formation. He charges that the empiricist validation of pragmatic criteria in theory choice has simply opened the door to the colonization of reason, and to rescue reason we must return to rather old-fashioned (by today's standards) concerns about objective truth.

> The philosophical systems of objective reason implied the conviction that an all-embracing or fundamental structure of being could be discovered *and a conception of human destination derived from it*. They understood science, when worthy of this name, as an implementation of such reflection or speculation. They were opposed to any epistemology that would reduce the objective basis of our insight to a chaos of uncoordinated data, and identify our scientific work as the mere organization, classification, or computation of such data. (Horkheimer 1947, 12, emphasis added)

Horkheimer thus positively contrasts a notion of science as providing the grounds for normative social theory (deriving a conception of human destination) with a notion that empties science of its ability to provide political direction. Such an impotent characterization of scientific reason is the result of putting science to the service of subjective ends, ends that are themselves placed beyond rational debate and considered incapable of objective justification.

In order to prove its right to be conceived, each thought must have an alibi, must present a record of expediency. Even if its direct use is "theoretical," it is ultimately put to the test by the practical application of the theory in which it functions. Thought must be gauged by something that is not thought, by its effect on production or its impact on social conduct, as art today is being ultimately gauged in every detail by something that is not art, be it box-office or propaganda value (1947, 50–51).

One might well take such a view to be a denial of the constitutive relationship between knowledge and power. Horkheimer here seems to be
arguing that those who would put knowledge to the service of social justice are no better than those who would put it to the service of capitalism.
In both cases, thought is guided by nonthought, or extra-epistemic considerations. However, the objective reason that Horkheimer champions
is not politically neutral, a mere method subject to various political uses
but without a politics of its own. He argues that the political implications
of reason will emerge from following reason beyond pragmatic concerns,
rather than truncating it to a means-ends calculation. Capitalism forecloses rational deliberations over ends, because it well knows that it cannot win that game: its ends are no match for critical reason. Hence,
reason must be restricted in order to preempt the objective truths it
would reveal. Ignorance is the result. The cognitive norms that produce
ignorance as an effect of substantive epistemic practice are those that
naturalize and dehistoricize both the process and product of knowing,
such that no political reflexivity or sociological analysis is thought to be
required or even allowable. If one is simply describing the facts as they
appear, then political questions about knowledge are indeed irrelevant
and even unintelligible. If science is simply the coordination of such naturalized data, then the highest degree of epistemic authority will be con-
ferred on "fantasyland."

V

Horkheimer's critiques of rationality under capitalism can helpfully sup-
plement our understanding of the ways in which knowers are situated,
structured, differentially able to do critique, and sometimes locked into
patterns of ignorance. Horkheimer provides us with a cognitive norm—
a substantive epistemic practice rather than merely a lack—that explains
systemic ignorance. Consider Edward Said's detailed analysis and critique of *Orientalism* as an example here (1978). Said's critique is not at all
that Orientalists were sloppy reasoners, nor that their descriptions were
mostly inaccurate, nor that they were mere ideologues. Rather, Orientalism naturalized its object of study as wholly discrete, stable, and fixed,
providing sharp contrast to the Occident. Orientalism further operated
with dominant Western epistemological ideas that precluded reflexivity
about the situatedness of the knowers. Orientalism conditioned the perceiving organ of knowers to such an extent that these knowers would visit
the countries comprising the "Orient" and have their beliefs confirmed.
Thus they remained ignorant.

I draw two conclusions from the previous arguments. The first is that
an analysis of ignorance as a structural condition should cause us to look

again at postmodern refusals of reference, reason, or truth. To be able to claim a structure of ignorance we must be able to show the alternative, which requires reconstructive projects on reason such as Horkheimer's development of the concept of objective reason. The postmodern eclipse of reason in favor of the strategic participates in the Western eclipse of reason through instrumental rationality. The point of the critique of reason is that we can do better epistemically than these frameworks allow. The second conclusion is that analyzing ignorance will require not only an analysis of the general conditions of epistemic situatedness, the epistemic resources distributed differently across social locations, or the structural contexts that organize and reproduce oppression; to truly understand the cause of the problem of ignorance, we also need to make epistemology reflexively aware and critical of its location within an economic system.

References

Code, Lorraine. 1993. "Taking Subjectivity into Account." In *Feminist Epistemologies*, ed. Linda Alcoff and Elizabeth Potter, 15–48. New York: Routledge.

———. 1995. *Rhetorical Spaces: Essays on Gendered Locations*. New York: Routledge.

Frisby, David. 1972. "The Popper-Adorno Controversy: the Methodological Dispute in German Sociology." *Philosophy of Social Science* 2 (1972): 105–19.

Harding, Sandra. 1991. *Whose Science? Whose Knowledge? Thinking From Women's Lives* Ithaca, NY: Cornell University Press.

Horkheimer, Max. 1947. *Eclipse of Reason*. New York: Continuum International Publishing Group.

———. 1975. *Critical Theory: Selected Essays*. New York: Continuum International Publishing Group.

Lohmann, Georg. 1993. "The Failure of Self-Realization: An Interpretation of Horkheimer's *Eclipse of Reason*." In *On Max Horkheimer: New Perspectives*, ed. Seyla Benhabib, Wolfgang Bonß, and John McCole, 387–412. Cambridge: MIT Press.

Mills, Charles. 1997. *The Racial Contract*. Ithaca, NY: Cornell University Press.

Mohanty, Chandra Talpade. 2003. *Feminism without Borders: Decolonizing Theory, Practicing Solidarity*. Durham, NC: Duke University Press.

Quine, W. V. O. 1951. "Two Dogmas of Empiricism." *Philosophical Review* 60 (January): 20–43.

Said, Edward. 1978. *Orientalism*. New York: Random House.

CHAPTER 3

Ever Not Quite

Unfinished Theories, Unfinished Societies, and Pragmatism

Harvey Cormier

Philosophers since Plato have worked to discover how it is that we know whatever it is we know. Western philosophy, ancient and modern, has taken on the task of finding out how we can look past the way things merely seem to the way they really are. Lately, however, a number of thinkers have argued that the question of how we can *fail* to know certain things, especially things with political consequences, is just as interesting and much more pressing. That question is often taken to go along with the question whether we, or at least some among us, are in fact responsible, and indeed culpable, for creating that very useful ignorance.

It's pretty clear that we live in a world unfortunately full of mendacious, propagandizing politicians and pernicious received "wisdom," but in what follows I shall suggest that the prospects for an interesting and a socially beneficial epistemology of ignorance are not good. I do not think that there are deceptive phenomena and intellectual structures that we can penetrate with an improved philosophical perspective; or, at least, I think it won't pay to think in those terms. The idea of phenomena and structures like these, generated by political realities and concealing those same realities, is perhaps not as ancient as the Western quest for certain knowledge, but it is not a new idea either, and it has had its critics for a while now. I shall call on the familiar criticisms of this idea, and I'll try to suggest a better philosophical alternative than the effort to get past the appearances to the reality.

I

Noam Chomsky, in his 1986 book *Knowledge of Language*, described two different but parallel problems that appear to confront anyone who reflects on human knowledge. One, "Plato's problem," is the problem of figuring out just how it happens that we human beings know as much as we do considering what W. V. Quine used to call "the poverty of the stimulus," or our tiny amount of experience of the world. Our scientific and historical knowledge is vast, and, when it comes to our knowledge of certain abstract formal principles, it seems literally infinite. A human life is a short and narrow thing, and our whole species is new to the earth in geological time. How have we come by so much knowledge, and how do we contain it all? Chomsky saw a connection between Plato's problem and the issue of how it is that we human beings learn to produce an infinite variety of sentences, and he summed up the problem as that of determining "the innate endowment that serves to bridge the gap between experience and knowledge attained" (1986, xxv–xxvi). This is, indeed, one way of reconceiving the traditional task of epistemology that has been handed down from Plato. Chomsky thinks that his theory of innate grammatical structures contributes something to that task.

The second problem, which Chomsky designated "Orwell's problem," is that of understanding just how it is that we know as little as we do about our social and political situations given the overwhelming amount of information we have about them. Chomsky observed that George Orwell "was impressed with the ability of totalitarian systems to instill beliefs that are firmly held and widely accepted although they are completely without foundation and often plainly at variance with obvious facts about the world around us" (1986, xxvii). Neither Orwell nor Chomsky in the 1980s thought that the West had turned totalitarian just yet, but each thought that it could happen here, and each was concerned to identify ways in which Westerners were as vulnerable to state deception as the persons living under fascism and communism. Chomsky thought that Plato's problem was the only profound or intellectually interesting one, but he also thought, in those days of cold war tensions, that broaching Orwell's problem was critical to the survival of the human race.

Chomsky argued that while Westerners were not liable to be dragged off to prison or for psychiatric treatment if they spoke out to challenge tenets of what he called the "state religion," they were just as effectively silenced by the process that Walter Lippmann had described in 1921 as the "manufacture of consent." In that manufacturing process, so-called "responsible" thinkers were brought to prominence by the powerful and the privileged, and only those thinkers were ever heard from in the press or the other mainstream news media. It was possible to get a bit of truth out of the news, especially if one watched for governmental denials; what officials said did not happen was what did happen. But in general, here as in the old Soviet Union, we could tell the old joke that there was no news in *Pravda* and no truth in *Izvestiya*. There was plenty of superficial disagreement between Republicans and Democrats over this or that comparatively trivial issue, but the fundamental social and cultural principles were agreed upon by the plutocrats and militarists behind the scenes, and all real dissent was quietly and efficiently ushered to the margins. As Chomsky saw and still sees things,

> Democracy permits the voice of the people to be heard, and it is the task of the intellectual to ensure that this voice endorses what far-sighted leaders determine to be the right course. Propaganda is to democracy as violence is [to] totalitarianism. The techniques have been honed to a high art, far beyond anything that Orwell dreamt of. The device of feigned dissent, incorporating the doctrines of the state religion and eliminating rational critical discussion, is one of the more subtle means, although simple lying and suppression of fact and other crude techniques are also widely used and highly effective in protecting us from knowledge and understanding of the world in which we live. (1986, 286)

A bleak view indeed; but perhaps not a wholly consistent one. After all, if the information managers and thought controllers are as efficient as all that, then there should not *be* any discernible "Orwell's problem"—at least not any more. But since somehow Orwell and Chomsky have evaded the information managers and come up with their knowledge of the real world, a new puzzle emerges to keep Orwell's problem company: How do the Orwells and Chomskys of the world keep themselves apprised of the "obvious facts" about which all the stooges from Dick Cheney and William Kristol to Al Sharpton and Paul Krugman are keeping mum? The first question to ask of a conspiracy theorist is how she or he survived the conspiracy; here, the conspiracy involves skillfully blinding the mass of citizens to the reality that is right in front of them. Thus Orwell's problem leads to a metaproblem: What source of information has enabled Chomsky and his fellow leftists at the margins to escape being blinded, and how can the unconvinced among us come to share their insights, especially since we can look at what is right in front of all of us and not see what Orwell and Chomsky see?

Chomsky, no Marxist himself, might nevertheless have described Orwell's problem as "Marx's problem." Orwell the anti-Stalinist was no Marxist either, but the Marxist theory of bourgeois capitalism famously involves the same idea of a structure of deceptive appearances that is erected on a base of politico-economic realities and that hides those realities in plain

sight.[1] Moreover, some writers have discovered other problems like this
that cut across Marx's class distinctions. Not only are there "inverted" appearances that hide the domination of the bourgeoisie, there are also
appearances that hide racial and gender domination.

Charles Mills, for example, in his recent book *The Racial Contract*, discovers what amount to historical agreements among whites, and especially white males, to think only of themselves as rational human beings;
blacks and the rest are to be understood as so many "Calibans and Tontos, Man Fridays and Sambos" (1997, 19).[2] We can discern these real-life
accords among whites if we look at the historical record of white self-
descriptions and self-valorizations. (We have to look somewhat selec-
tively, leaving aside anti-racist Enlightenment figures like, say, Herder
and James Beattie, who do not represent the "norm").[3] Though whites
tend more and more to theorize philosophically as if there were no real
races, this is in the end only another way of being more or less intention-
ally taken in by white supremacist ideology; it is a way of keeping that ideology safe from criticism. Contemporary liberal theorists of justice are
Manchurian candidates in reverse. Explicit accords and key silences
about race have turned Western political thought into

> a cognitive and moral economy psychically required for conquest, col-
> onization, and enslavement. And these phenomena are in no way *acci-
> dental*, but *prescribed* by the terms of the Racial Contract, which requires
> a certain schedule of structured blindnesses and opacities in order to
> establish and maintain the white polity. (Mills 1997, 19)[4]

Thus just as Marx's problem is a more specific version of Orwell's, one to
be solved by dealing with the inverted appearances that conceal class
domination, what we might call Mills's problem is another more specific
variant, one to be solved by charting and then dismantling the "structured blindnesses" that hide and maintain white supremacy throughout
the world.

Interestingly, though, just as Orwell's problem leads to the further
question of just how that problem surmounted itself in order to come to
consciousness, it is an old question among Marxists how it happened that
the story of inverted appearances managed to get itself told before the
revolution. The very existence of that story at this moment seems to re-
fute the story. It's that metaproblem again: How have the Marxists
avoided being taken in by ideology, the destructive intellectual product
of the oppressive reality? The story they themselves tell says that they
should not be able to.

Marxist thinkers such as Antonio Gramsci have dealt with this question by biting the bullet and acknowledging that Marxism was itself a

kind of ideology, one that could no more reach a reality beyond appearances than could any other outlook on the world. The problem with the ideology of the bourgeois was not that it failed to reflect the real world of material relations accurately; it was that it inhibited the social progress that would benefit not only workers but everyone in the society.[5]

I will have more to say shortly about ideology and Gramsci's remedy for it, but first let me note one apparent virtue of "Mills's problem": No metaproblem. There would seem to be no problem explaining how it is we know that Mills's problem exists. A racial ideology blinds people to a racial reality—but only some people. Observers such as Mills himself, who are black and encounter that reality every day, are in a position to describe it accurately. Only whites, or at least whites who are signatories to the Racial Contract and not "white renegades" or "race traitors," and maybe running-dog blacks, victims of white miseducation, will be unable to look past the structures of deception. This is presumably why Mills is so confidently anti-"postmodernism." His view "lays claims to truth, objectivity, realism, the description of the world as it actually is, [and] the prescription for a transformation of that world to achieve racial justice" (Mills 1997, 129), and Mills rejects the idea that speakers of different languages and holders of different theories of the world are playing "isolated, mutually unintelligible language games" (ibid.).

However, it is worth emphasizing that, in Mills's view, simply being nonwhite will not make a person conscious of this reality any more than being white will make a person unconscious of it. True, white "renegades" will be unable to refuse the Contract entirely and see things entirely from the nonwhite point of view, since "mere skin color will automatically continue to privilege them" (Mills 1997, 107). But, in general, race will not work straightforwardly as a lens that will either obscure or show us the true reality. Hence, while the same metaproblem that confronts Orwell and Marx may not trouble Mills, Mills will still have to deal with a variant of it. Maybe it will not be hard for a given black person to explain how she and certain other black people have avoided false race consciousness and the white man's epistemological traps; maybe it will be easy for her to see how other blacks got turned into Toms, Oreos, and incognegroes by ideological indoctrination. But there will linger for her, as she explains her knowledge in terms of "reality," the problem of explaining how she can tell *which black people* are the victims of ideology and which are not.

Indeed, this may be the most epistemologically compelling issue connected to Mills's problem. Racial Contract theory suggests that certain blacks, especially educated blacks in the West, will be hard-pressed not to play their own supporting role in the ideology of white domination, this even despite experiencing disadvantages every day under white supremacy. How have some of them—I guess I should say "some of us"—

managed to evade the information managers? Can they really be sure
they have?

Something like this is really the fundamental epistemological problem at the bottom of the other metaproblems. If I and someone else can
be confronted with the same reality but come up with two different theories of what is going on right in front of us, then how can I be sure that
mine is the theory free of "ideology"? And in this context, it is especially
striking that the blacks insisting on the reality of race and racial differences are the ones claiming to have evaded indoctrination. Should they
really be so confident of having escaped the intellectual domination of
the racists?

Maybe this question will seem like just the kind of thing that only either a white ideologue or a miseducated black would ask. Willingness to
waste time on such an abstract debate about relations between theories
and reality may seem "symptomatic rather than diagnostic" of the real-
world race problem, as Mills says of one possible position in this debate,
postmodernist irony concerning meaning and truth (Mills 1997, 129).
After all, the real causes and effects of both deception and racism are
right there in front of us, obvious to any observer, or at least any observer
of color . . . but then, that's just the issue, isn't it? To suppose that reality
answers this question is to *beg* the question, taking for granted what has
to be proven.

This is the general problem of appeals to ideology, screens of
thought behind which reality hides. It is not necessarily an insoluble
problem, even if we use only the means Mills uses to solve the (non-
"meta") problem of why Westerners can't see the world in front of them.
One might in fact have to argue in a circle, but it would not necessarily
be a *vicious* circle; a big enough circle that took enough concrete details
about power relations into account could imaginably explain not only
our blindness to the obvious but also our blindness to our obvious blindness to the obvious. Still, I think that there is a better way of dealing with
the metaproblem than starting to look for appearances that screen off
appearances, the ulterior motives that hide the ulterior motives, and the
ideology that hides the ideology. Instead we can dispense with talk of ideology altogether.

Orwell's, Marx's, and Mills's problems, which together amount to the
problem of how we know so little though we experience so much, and
Plato's problem, the problem of how we know so much though we experience so little, are two sides of the same coin—a coin that once was valuable but now is not really worth that much. I think of the "postmodern"
philosophical view known as pragmatism as preeminently an effort to dissolve Plato's problem rather than solve it, to show that our human capacity for infinite knowledge of laws and rules needs to be questioned more

than it needs to be explained; and I think that once Plato's problem loses its grip on our imagination, Orwell's problem begins to lose its grip too. We human beings do have remarkable capacities for cooperation, mutual understanding, and the making and sharing of intellectual tools, but the pragmatist thinks that we can understand those capacities without reference to any ostensible ability to look past the world of our little experiences and struggles. And once we accept this anti-Platonist point and get out of the habit of trying to look past our life of making up and sharing ideas, we will be less impressed by Chomsky's, Orwell's, Marx's, and Mills's idea that our intellectual life may amount to a big lie that stops us from noticing reality. Of course, that will not entail that our current understanding of the political world, or of anything else, is all just fine; and it certainly will not entail that there is no need for big changes in the way the races, classes, and genders are related politically. But the grounds for criticism of that understanding and of the world will have to change to healthier and more (small *r*) realistic grounds, grounds that have more to do with what human beings want out of life than with what there just *is* in the world of "obvious fact."

II

Let me begin describing and promoting the pragmatic alternative by noting a conflict among pragmatists. Cornel West and Richard Rorty have engaged in a dispute about what pragmatism is for and how much social good it can do. I think this dispute reflects something like the difference between Mills's view and that of the anti-ideological "postmodernist." I think that Rorty's understanding of pragmatism can be criticized, but I also think that he makes a crucial point against West. And I think that if we see this point, we will also see the main problem with things like Mills's story of the Racial Contract.

In his 1989 treatment of the American pragmatists, *The American Evasion of Philosophy*, Cornel West argued that the diverse views of Ralph Waldo Emerson, William James, Charles Peirce, W. V. Quine, Richard Rorty, and Roberto Unger can all be usefully understood to compose a politically important American philosophical tradition, a unified movement that not only breaks free of the foundationalist epistemology of past European philosophy but also points the way to a radically democratic future. Rorty, in a mixed but mainly positive review, approved of West's critical hopefulness, especially by comparison with the despair typical of Foucauldian academic leftists, but he also noted a "basic tension" in the book between "the pragmatist as professor and as prophet— the pragmatist as cleaning up rubbish left over from the past and the pragmatist as the dreamer who first glimpses the concrete outlines of a better future" (Rorty 1991, 70–78). Rorty prefers the former of these pictures of pragmatism, West the latter.

Rorty's main philosophical goal is to get both himself and other merely academic thinkers out of the way so that "prophets" and "strong poets" can get on with their work in human society. Feminist thinkers like Marilyn Frye change what is imaginable in the relations between women and men; conscientious political figures such as Walter Reuther used political clout to benefit the worst-off workers; and artists like James Baldwin raise unheard voices and describe unappreciated desires.[6] Rather than looking for absolute truths or goods or evils to use as intellectual foundations, these figures start where they are, with their distinctive sets of pains, pleasures, and desires. They imagine better concrete futures for themselves, and they and their ideas work to bring those futures into being. And Rorty thinks that these intellectual and practical experimenters make better social architects than academic philosophers like him. Despite accusations of positivism and relativism, Rorty persists in championing the idea that human beings like these need the freedom to try out their evolving ideas more than they need to be penned in by universalistic thinking.

West agrees with some of this, but he admires the early pragmatists more than Rorty, his friend and former teacher. The paleo-pragmatists had Emersonian vision; they were not looking outside philosophy for prophets to serve. They had a picture of humanity as a special kind of self-aware force of nature. This picture entailed a way of life, namely, activist radical democracy featuring religious freedom and other kinds of social liberty. We can and do remake the natural and social world, and indeed we might say that this is what we are by nature: the remakers. In a world of adapting organisms, we adapt the fastest, and something has gone wrong when we stop adapting. We cannot live, we can't be what we are, if we cling to the static ideals of the past, including the political ideals.

The point of this philosophy, to adapt the old line from Marx's "Theses on Feuerbach," was not to know the world but to change it so that it will fit our powers and needs. Even in present-day America, the wealthy home of pragmatism, there are still people who are battered down by social circumstances and who therefore cannot act on their ideals and change as the world changes. West therefore proposes a "prophetic pragmatism" that will recover the old detranscendentalized spiritualism, looking at our human needs and demanding social remedies.

By contrast with this visionary program, Rorty's merely trash-clearing version of pragmatism looks, in Rorty's own words, "dwarfish" (Rorty 1991, 74). It is part of a mere exchange among professors, and West complains that "[Rorty's] project . . . remains polemical (principally against other professional academics) and hence barren" (West 1989, 207). Rorty agrees with this assessment, and he says that his only excuse is that he does not think that philosophy professors typically make good prophets. He says that his own merely handy pathway-clearing pragmatism is

> neutral between alternative prophecies, and thus neutral between democrats and fascists. Pragmatism plus Nietzschean prophecy was as handy for Mussolini as pragmatism plus Emersonian prophecy was for Woodrow Wilson and the two Roosevelts. If pragmatism is taken in this, the professorial sense, then the term "prophetic pragmatism" will sound as odd as "charismatic trash removal." (Rorty 1991, 75)

Rorty thinks that the old Emersonian pragmatists could still play a useful role outside academe in their time because there were giants in the earth in those days; forces for stasis and against progressive change had religious, moral, and political arguments on their side, and the pragmatists had the useful public role of offering counterarguments. But now, as Rorty puts it,

> We have nobody worthy of the name "rightist intellectual" who needs to be confuted. Nowadays nobody even bothers to back up opposition to liberal reforms with argument. People merely say that taxes are too high, that their brother-in-law would have had a better job had it not been for his company's affirmative action program, and that it is time for the poor and the weak to start looking after themselves. (Rorty 1991, 76)

In Europe and its other former colonies, there survives among radicals a tradition of taking philosophy seriously and looking to it as a guide; but here in America, philosophy, because of its own renunciation of a public role and willed focus on the justification of science, has a tiny audience and not much that is of political value to offer it. Therefore, says Rorty, the only useful role for a pragmatist like him now is the micro-role of holding the intellectual door for the visionary feminist thinkers, politicians, and artists who might hope to spread their visions.

This seems to me appealingly deferential on the part of such an imposing intellectual figure, but wrong. I think that Rorty is underestimating the value of his own work. The greatest value of the old pragmatism was not support for progressivism and opposition to conservatism. The old *pragmatists* were progressives, but they did not tie their accounts of truth and meaning tightly to their politics. They knew that the fiery revolutionary doctrine of one century is likely to be the tired old dogma of the next century, or that of the century after the next at the latest. They wanted therefore to be able to crack the crust of convention *no matter what the convention was.* Or, better, they wanted a philosophical theory of thought and truth that recognized *and developed* the individual thinker's ability to break through any conventions there might be.

Perhaps Rorty describes this project in belittling terms because he senses a risk that things could get just a little too "philosophical" in the traditional sense, too transcendent and ahistorical, if we start in appreciating the not merely local value of negative, convention-smashing pragmatism. He and West both praise pragmatism because it pays attention to the concrete details of human life rather than to eternal abstractions, and the idea that pragmatism tells us anything of general value, even anything negative, may seem to make pragmatism just another traditional attempt to speak eternal truth. However, while pragmatism is indeed an attempt to help particular people with concrete, local problems, it is not an attempt to help any *particular* particular people with any particular concrete problems. The value of pragmatism is not tied to its moment at the end of the nineteenth century, though it is tied to particular moments in real people's lives.

West also senses the danger of a lapse into traditionalism, and he wants to protect his own pragmatism from it. Look closer at what he has to say about the old Emersonian pragmatists he admires. He does express lots of admiration for those figures, but he concludes his discussion of each pragmatist with a consideration, typically in quite harsh terms, of just how each fell short of achieving his own goal of spreading intellectual and political power. (Sometimes the criticisms are so harsh that the praise begins to seem insincere.) For example, West says that "not one [of the original pragmatists] viewed racism as contributing greatly to the impediments for both individuality and democracy" (West 1989, 147). West bitterly accuses pragmatists such as James, who spent his philosophical energies arguing that the truth was what worked in life, of "pandering to middle-class pieties" (West 1989, 66) and of blindness to

> the plight of the wretched of the earth, namely, the majority of humanity who own no property or wealth, participate in no democratic arrangements, and whose individualities are crushed by hard labor and harsh living conditions. (West 1989, 147–48)

Someone like James was principally concerned with the abstract abilities of individuals, in particular their ability to generate hypotheses freely and innovatively and to "verify" them in their lives of experience. This meant that, paradoxically, James's concern with the individual and individual freedom localized his thought so much that it lost its grip on the real world of particular human struggles. The old pragmatists tried to break free of the tradition, but eventually they fell back into the old abstraction and indifference.[7]

Even the part of pragmatism that is of most interest to today's academicians, its theory of truth, is, in the end, an effort to argue for the idea that *individuals* are and should be free. When James argues that the truth is what works, he is trying not so much to define truth as to argue that it is *not* a grand ideal out beyond our particular little lives of joy and heartbreak. It is instead a tool we innovate into existence, a device to help us live with satisfaction our floundering lives of experience. Grasping the truth is not discovering an infinite, preexisting abstraction; indeed, "grasping" is the wrong metaphor. "Making" is a better one. There is no truth apart from the particular *things that actually are true*, and those particular things are the hypotheses, theories, ideas, claims, faiths, and beliefs we particular individuals *make* as we try to make sense of an open-ended, changing world. Our best thinking, our true thinking, is not the result of our beliefs' meeting the constraint of a preexistent abstract ideal—not even an abstract ideal like accurate representation of the world and its objects. Instead, as Rorty argues in books such as his 1982 *Consequences of Pragmatism*, it is a free creation in response to particular, and changing, wants and needs.

However, says West, if we tell that story and stop, we have produced a naïve and trivial pragmatism that does not really take on the world of action. It is hard to think creatively and share good ideas if you are in dire economic straits, or if you are being unjustly imprisoned, or if other people just don't listen to people who look like you. And even the Emersonian pragmatists of the past failed to face these hard realities. They were, by and large, middle-class white males, and while they were good at illustrating the problems that faced persons like them, they were less good at looking past their own little intellectual headaches to the larger political reality. James in particular advocated a kind of coherentism, an attachment to the body of prior beliefs as a test of truth, and he neglected the possibility that the truth is radically different from what has been said and thought before (West 1989, 65). West's sophisticated neopragmatists will stop treating people simply as believers and language users with particular small problems to solve in a piecemeal way. They will look past all of the middle-class microproblems to the vast, dark world of institutions limiting creative thought and speech.

West is not trying to make a metaphysical point here, and indeed he is trying as hard as he can to "evade" transcendental philosophizing and keep focused on the real-life, everyday world of action and experience. But in the end he himself lapses into something practically indistinguishable from this kind of metaphysical theory. He sets out to pay attention to the particular details of life as we know it, and he winds up looking past them into a world independent of our knowledge. Moreover, he does so in much the way Marx, Orwell, and Mills do. None of these thinkers intend to argue that there is a metaphysically real social world and that the thoughts we come up with in life are a lot of mere appearances that may have nothing to do with that world, but they all wind up thinking in epistemological terms that entail something practically indistinguishable from that metaphysical claim.

In West's way of looking at things, ultra-individualism has made James and Rorty miss a chance to comment on the middle ontological level of particular groups and subgroups of people. That sociopolitical level is by far the most important. That is where the dirty work is done; that's where groups work their deeds of domination, intellectual as well as political, on other groups. And West thinks that Rorty, even more than James or Dewey, lets progressivism down by failing to call attention to these groups as some of them subjugate others. If Rorty really wanted to do the most important work of the old pragmatism, which was the same as the work of left politics, then he would worry less about language and truth in the abstract and more about who can speak and who can't in America. (Here West prefigures Mills and his challenge to liberal political theory.)

However, West's call for the return of what was once valuable in pragmatism is misguided. Even nineteenth-century pragmatism had pretty much the same political neutrality Rorty depreciates in his own door-holding philosophical approach. And far from being a shortcoming, this is pragmatism's best philosophical virtue. Other virtuous intellectual things can also be done, such as the criticism of present and past injustices, but to criticize the pragmatists for failing to do those things in their philosophy is to misrepresent what they were trying to do and what they in fact accomplished.

The old pragmatism was "Emersonian," but one important thing to remember is how apolitical, and even antipolitical, Emerson sometimes sounds. "Are they *my* poor?" he notoriously asks in "Self-Reliance," his essay in praise of individualistic thought (West 1989, 37). (Note that this is a question, not a denial.) "What I must do is all that concerns me," he says, "not what the people think" (38). He looks forward to the day in which he can tell an "angry bigot" who is also an abolitionist to be honest and abandon his "incredible tenderness for black folk a thousand miles off" (36). Emerson may be the great philosopher of democracy, but sometimes he sounds just as indifferent to the general social welfare as Nietzsche—and it may also be important to keep in mind that Emerson was a large influence on Nietzsche.[8] Thus when Rorty demonstrates the neutrality of road-clearing pragmatism by pointing out that it could be used by either an Emersonian or a Nietzschean "prophet," this is misleading, to say the least.

For both Emerson and Nietzsche, politics and justice have to wait until there are beings suitable for political life. We human beings live in always changing times, and we have to *become* what we are—individual beings capable of going our own way and leaving behind dead, established codes—if we are to live in a changing world. We have to give up being mere unreflective products of society, even products of those crucial political subsegments of human society such as nations, races, classes, and genders, before we can be suitable participants in society.[9]

We live in a world that is, for an Emersonian like James, forever insusceptible of being summed up completely. James says that "Ever not quite' has to be said of the best attempts made anywhere in the universe at attaining all-inclusiveness" (James 1977, 145). Not even radical political thinkers have the last word to say about the way things are. Neither classes, races, genders, nations, the universe as a whole, nor even individuals(!) constitute an external reality demanding to be recognized. (Any of them may *be* the external reality, but none of them, as such, can demand to be recognized.) New times and new perspectives will always call for new names and claims—not by presenting us with new realities but by giving us new desires, interests, and goals. ("Us"? Who are "we"? That is for us to decide, curiously enough; the world, apart from us and our thinking, cannot *decide* anything.) And James's nineteenth-century pragmatism, with its depiction of names and truths as tools that free individuals create to serve their interests, is above all part of an Emersonian effort to keep us human agents struggling to fashion and refashion ourselves and our ever-evolving world, or to build *a world in which we can be responsible*—a world that really is *our* world, our home. James wants us to see that *even the truth*, or the sum of all of our true theories, hypotheses, and beliefs, is a product of our struggle as individuals to satisfy our desires and make a home for ourselves. And this goes even for the truth about politics and society.

The project of truth-, world-, and self-making that the pragmatists are trying to jump-start is at bottom a matter of the choices and interests of individuals in localities, and this means that it does lack some of the world-historical sweep, drama, and grandeur that the descendents of Marx look for in their philosophical understandings of things. Throughout The *American Evasion of Philosophy*, West makes it clear that he admires the kind of romantic, world-transforming urge that he finds in both Emerson and Marx (West 1989, 10–11). Gramsci complained disdainfully that the Rotary Club was about the best thing that had come out of the pragmatic movement (Gramsci 1971, 373). But though the project of being what we are is one that we must begin alone or in small groups, we can elect to join like-minded individuals to do battle— intellectual, political, or even military battle, if need be—with individuals of different minds, or with others who have not become what they are and who are still just social products. We don't have to stay alone, and we won't if we can share our ideas.

As part of the groups that we choose to help create—Rotary Clubs, maybe (they actually do a lot of good internationally), but also university faculties, hospital staffs and administrations, disaster-relief organizations, groups of volunteers in public schools, labor unions, political parties, army regiments, nations, nonbiological "races," and, perhaps someday, if we're lucky, even the "human race"—we individuals can make large changes in the world. Human society can act as an amplifier for individuals' efforts, and with some cooperation a Martin Luther King, a Henry Ford, or a Josef Stalin can leave quite a footprint—for better or worse. But as the pragmatist tries to make her own mark on the world, she will not ever see herself as peeking over inaccurate representations at the dark power relations that are sweeping her along. The words and thoughts of particular, unique persons give them power in the world— that is why they bother to generate them—and the world is therefore not a thing independent of those thoughts. We do not live behind a screen, or even in a Quinian-Neurathian boat, of true or false appearances. We live right there in the world, and we have better and worse thought-tools to use in shaping that world. And starting to think of ourselves in this way will help us take advantage of that world-shaping power.

This is the real political meaning of both Emerson's and James's prophetic exhortations. Emerson and James do not tell us about beings with a given social nature requiring democracy, nor are they only advising us of the evils of conservatism. They are *provoking* us, stirring us out of our socially induced torpor, so that we will *make ourselves* into political beings and then do specific moral and political things. They advocate in their philosophy no *specific* specific practices, and James's worries about truth may therefore seem to be no more than a lot of socially indifferent proto-professionalism; but James is in fact enjoining us individuals, whoever we may be and whenever we may exist, to try to be more than just a part of the whole, to be real entities in our own right and to act in our own behalf. He is not ignoring social groupings; he is trying to provoke us to *create and contribute* to those groups and to the world as a whole, to make our specific differences there, thus helping to create both ourselves and a world that will be *our* world.

And Rorty is carrying on James's provocation without quite appreciating it. Where both West and Rorty himself see a tedious struggle for the minds of a few professors, James would see part of the pragmatic battle to keep individual minds open, active, and free in a changing world. Rorty has expressed bewilderment concerning the worldwide popularity of his own work; he cannot figure out why his book *Contingency, Irony, and Solidarity*, which advocates no specific political or moral positions, and which Rorty sees as an effort to talk to a few professional philosophers about a lot of dusty issues, was translated into Bulgarian (Rorty 1995, 56–71). The answer is that the pragmatists, including Rorty, may not offer eternal truth about truth, but they do offer an eternal challenge. They have become the best-known and most successful philosophical figures in American history by challenging their readers, even readers in very different places and times—even in Bulgaria!—to think for themselves and thus become fit for life in democracy,

III

Neither Plato's problem nor Orwell's will trouble us much on the way to this kind of democracy of individuals. Once we take on the task of building truths as we go rather than grasping them, the appearance-reality distinction, on which both of these problems depend, begins to seem not only dubious but—much more important—trivial. ("False" is important, but "unimportant" is more important.) We begin to feel that there are only less useful claims and more useful ones. We will inevitably hold the less useful ones from time to time, but we will dispose of them when we find ones that work better. Many of today's "objective truths" will become tomorrow's "mere appearances" when more helpful beliefs turn up, and the same thing will happen the day after tomorrow.

Even some of that infinite knowledge of the world beyond our limited experience—Euclid's parallel postulate, for one standard example—will amount to no more than rules that seemed good to follow for a while, ways of talking and acting that seemed as if they would pay off forever but did not. And after this happens enough, we will realize, to adapt an idea from both T. H. Green and Jesus in the Gospel of Mark, that the rules of thought are made for us, not we for the rules of thought. We will cease looking for the innate endowment that makes it possible for us to look into a ready-made infinite. What's more, the flip side of this problem, our ignorance of the world that is present to our experience, will begin to seem less compelling as well, since the very ideas of "experience" and "the world" that figure in this formulation will begin to make less sense. After we realize that no one has access to a world beyond all of those deceptive appearances, the issues of what structures of deception are hiding that world from us will not seem urgent. Neither will the meta-issue of how certain persons, or perhaps certain persons of color, managed to see through those structures.

After we have these pragmatic insights, we will not see anything particularly promising about an epistemology of ignorance. We are all ignorant of many things, even "obvious facts," thanks to misperceptions, unquestioned preconceptions, common misconceptions, everyday irrationalities, limited experience, crippling neuroses, white lies and black, half-truths, propaganda, convenient self-deception . . . the usual suspects. No systematic study will reveal the structures of our foolishness. The ignorant people of the world include even people such as Chomsky, Marx,

Orwell, and Mills, who have new, different, and potentially helpful ideas about how we should describe our societies and our histories. No one's ideas, not even those of Chomsky or Mills, are warranted by their closeness to the really objective reality.

This is not, of course, to say that we should just think whatever we like. Chomsky may well be right to argue that we should be more skeptical of the mainstream media, and Mills may be right to argue that we should be skeptical of blithe appeals to universality in political philosophy. Maybe it is true that there is not so much difference between Republicans and Democrats as we might think, and it may be true that, under present circumstances, political philosophy would benefit if it paid more attention to the ways in which persons of color, women, and the poor have historically been judged to be of substandard rationality. Criticism is possible according to a pragmatic outlook, and neither believers in radical new theories nor believers in moribund old ones are trapped in their own discrete language games. The ideas traded in criticism and debate, especially the true ideas we did not have before, can give us *power*. They are useful tools, which is why we want them and why we trade them. If a novel reconception of mainstream politics or human rationality actually makes life, thought, and the world better, then that reconception will be true, or it will at least have the only kind of truth we are interested in getting. But it remains to be seen whose new ideas actually improve things. Maybe it remains eternally to be seen, so that no philosophical closing of these questions by appeal to what is already real and present will ever be possible.

Emersonian philosophy of a Jamesian-Rortian type, far from trapping us in our old ways of thinking, is in fact designed to encourage us to take an experimental, let's-try-this-on approach to new ideas. It does this by showing us what we have to gain by getting things right, and it even takes some of the sting away from the very idea of getting things wrong. Getting things wrong, being ignorant, is not a matter of betraying logical, material, or racial reality; getting things wrong on the way to getting things right is just what we do as we try to make things better, we makers and remakers of ourselves and the world.

Notes

1. The Marxist literature on this topic is almost unsurveyably vast. A brief introduction is found in the article "Base and Superstructure" in Larrain 1983a: 42–45. See also Plekhanov 1992, Eagleton 1991, and Larrain 1983b.

2. See also Mills 1998 and 2003.

3. "Norm" is, of course, ambiguous, and it might seem evident that in the most philosophically pertinent sense of the term, this claim is false, or at least debatable.

However, Mills 1997: 91–134 is devoted to explaining why a "naturalistic" account of norms like this, one that understands ideals in terms of statistical realities, is best.

4. Emphasis in the original.

5. I discuss Gramsci's idea that Marxism is an ideology, and the consequences of that idea for politics and (especially pragmatic) philosophy, at Cormier 2000: 155–80.

6. Rorty offers in "Feminism and Pragmatism" a nice statement of his program for getting philosophy out of the way. See Rorty 1998: 202–27.

7. See Cormier 2000, ch. 6, for the details of James's views as West criticizes them.

8. Nietzsche cites Emerson more than once. See, for example, Nietzsche 1983: 193.

9. Compare this reading of Emerson's basic outlook with the one found in Cavell 1990 *passim*.

References

Cavell, Stanley. 1990. *Conditions Handsome and Unhandsome: The Constitution of Emersonian Perfectionism*. Chicago: Chicago University Press.

Chomsky, Noam. 1986. *Knowledge of Language*. Westport, CT: Praeger.

Cormier, Harvey. 2000. *The Truth Is What Works: William James, Pragmatism, and the Seed of Death*. Lanham, MD: Rowman & Littlefield.

Eagleton, Terry. 1991. *Ideology: An Introduction*. London: Verso.

Emerson, Ralph Waldo. 1951 [1836–60]. *Emerson's Essays*. New York: Harper & Row.

Gramsci, Antonio. 1971 [1929–35]. *Selections from the Prison Notebooks*. Translated and edited by Quentin Hoare and Geoffrey Nowell Smith. New York: International Publishers.

James, William. 1977 [1909]. *A Pluralistic Universe*. Cambridge, MA: Harvard University Press.

Knobe, Joshua. 1995. "A Talent for Bricolage: An Interview with Richard Rorty." *The Dualist* 2: 56–71.

Larrain, Jorge. 1983a. "Base and Superstructure." In *A Dictionary of Marxist Thought*, ed. Tom Bottomore, Lawrence Harris, Victor G. Kiernan, and Ralph Miliband. Cambridge, MA: Harvard University Press.

———. 1983b. *Marxism and Ideology*. London: Hutchinson.

Mills, Charles. 1997. *The Racial Contract*. Ithaca, NY: Cornell University Press.

———. 1998. *Blackness Visible*. Ithaca, NY: Cornell University Press.

———. 2003. *From Class to Race: Essays in White Marxism and Black Radicalism*. Lanham, MD: Rowman & Littlefield.

Nietzsche, Friedrich. 1983 [1873–76]. *Untimely Meditations*. Cambridge: Cambridge University Press.

Plekhanov, Georgi. 1992 [1908]. *Fundamental Problems of Marxism*. New York: International.

Rorty, Richard. 1982. *Consequences of Pragmatism*. Minneapolis: University of Minnesota Press.

————. 1991. "The Professor and the Prophet." *Transition* 52: 70–78.

————. 1998. *Truth and Progress: Philosophical Papers, Volume 3*. Cambridge: Cambridge University Press.

West, Cornel. 1989. *The American Evasion of Philosophy: A Genealogy of Pragmatism*. Madison: University of Wisconsin Press.

CHAPTER 4

Strategic Ignorance

Alison Bailey

[W]hite prejudice completely reverses the truth! It was the slaves and
their children who had to be devious, subtle and complicated. Masters
and their children kind of had to be simple people. If you can *make* people do things, you don't have to persuade them or trick them into doing
what you want them to do. (Carolyn Chase, in Gwaltney 1993, 53, emphasis in original)

[W]hile the movements and productions of ignorance often parallel
and track particular knowledge practices, we cannot assume that their
logic is similar to the knowledges they shadow. (Tuana 2004, 196)

In ordinary language the word "ignorance" suggests a deficiency of information. Ignorant would-be knowers are uninformed or have incomplete
understandings of a given phenomenon. On this view ignorance is theorized as an *accidental* omission or a gap in understanding that can be cor-
rected by an effort to move toward certainty by finding the missing
information or running the experiment again. An important aspect of
feminist epistemology in general and of the epistemologies of ignorance
in particular is the realization that ignorance is often an active social production. So often what people know is shaped by their social location.
From positions of dominance ignorance can take the form of those in the
center either refusing to allow those at the margins to know, or of actively
erasing indigenous knowledges. More subtle examples of socially constructed ignorance include epistemic blank spots that make privileged
knowers oblivious to systemic injustices. But what I find most interesting
are the ways expressions of ignorance can be wielded strategically by
groups living under oppression as a way of gaining information, sabotag-
ing work, avoiding or delaying harm, and preserving a sense of self.

In this chapter I explore strategic expressions of ignorance against the background of Charles W. Mills's account of epistemologies of ignorance in *The Racial Contract* (1997), with two interrelated goals. I want to show how Mills's discussion is restricted by his decision to frame ignorance within the language and logic of social contract theory. And I want to explain why María Lugones's work on purity is useful in reframing ignorance in ways that both expand our understandings of ignorance and reveal its strategic uses. I begin with Mills's account of the Racial Contract and explain how it prescribes for its signatories an epistemology of ignorance, which Mills characterizes as an *inverted* epistemology. I briefly outline his program for undoing white ignorance and indicate that retooling white ignorance is more complex than his characterization suggests. Making this argument requires an abrupt shift from the white-created frameworks of social contract theory to Lugones's system of thinking rooted in the lives of people of color. So the next section outlines Lugones's distinction between the logic of purity and the logic of curdling and explains its usefulness in addressing ignorance. With both accounts firmly in place the third section demonstrates how the Racial Contract produces at least two expressions of ignorance and explains how the logic of purity underlying the Contract shapes each expression in ways that limit possibilities for resistance. I do not mean to suggest that the social contract theory's love of purity invalidates Mills's work, only that this framework limits prospects for long-term change by neglecting the relationship between white ignorance and nonwhite resistance. The final sections explain how people of color use ignorance strategically to their advantage and argue that examining ignorance through a curdled lens not only makes strategic ignorance visible but also points to alternatives for retooling white ignorance.

Mills's Racial Contract and the Epistemology of Ignorance

In *The Racial Contract* Charles Mills uses the conceptual apparatus of the social contract tradition to reveal the cartography of white supremacy as a global political system. Contract talk, he says, is the "lingua franca of our times," and as such it can provide us with a "powerful set of lenses" for looking at society and government in ways that reveal the inner workings of white supremacy (1997, 3). His comparison points to a visible gap between the imagined nonracial normative ideals of the social contract tradition and white people's real treatment of people of color as part of the process of nation building. The social contract of Western political theory is not "a contract between everybody ('we the people')," he argues, "but between just the people who count, the people who are really people ('we the white people'). So it's a Racial Contract" (1997, 3).[1]

The Racial Contract has two dimensions. As a theory, the "Racial Contract" (in quotations) provides political philosophers with an alternative model for critiquing the state: one that makes race the center of political discussion by foregrounding the racial dimensions of the polity. The "Contract" acts as a "rhetorical trope and theoretical method for understanding the inner logic of *racial* domination and how it structures the polities of the West and elsewhere" (1997, 7). The "Contract" is a conceptual bridge between mainstream (white) idealized philosophical definitions of rights, justice, and the good society, on the one hand, and African American, indigenous, and Third World nonidealized political accounts of imperialism, colonialism, and globalization, on the other. The theoretical use of the "Racial Contract" is contrasted with another use of the Racial Contract (without quotations), which refers directly to the historically documented economic, political, and social formation of polities along racial lines. There are countless Racial Contracts, and they are continually rewritten as racial boundaries shift.

The social contract has political, moral, and epistemological dimensions. Politically, it is an account of the origins of government and citizens' obligations to the state. The contract' grounds moral codes and authors the laws that regulate human behavior. The social contract also has an overlooked epistemic dimension: there are socially enforced cognitive norms to which the signatories must adhere. The Racial Contract mirrors these three dimensions with attention to racial formation. Politically, the Racial Contract establishes a society by transforming raceless populations in a state of nature into "white" citizens and "Black," "Native," or "Colored" subpersons. But Mills's most interesting argument—and my primary focus here—explores how the Racial Contract tacitly presupposes a color-coded epistemological, moral, and judicial contract that reflects white dominance and prejudice. That is, the Racial Contract is partially held in place by an implicit consensus about cognitive norms: it concerns what counts as a correct interpretation of the world, and what actions are right and legal in it. Signatories to the Contract must be socialized into epistemic communities. Agreement with the officially sanctioned reality allows some to be contractually granted full cognitive membership in the (white) epistemic polity. If you follow the official epistemic regulations, then you are in! Diverge from the epistemic gold standard and you will be regarded with suspicion at the least and dismissed as crazy at the most. Yet the officially sanctioned view of reality is not an *actual* reality. It is imagined. As Mills explains:

To a significant extent, then, white signatories will live in an invented delusional world, a racial fantasyland, a "consensual hallucination," . . . There will be white mythologies, invented Orients, invented Africas, invented Americas, with correspondingly fabricated populations, countries that never were, inhabited by people who never were—Calibans and Tontos, Man Fridays and Sambos—but who attain a virtual reality through their existence in travelers' tales, folk myth, popular highbrow fiction, colonial reports, scholarly theory and Hollywood cinema living in the white imagination and imposed on their alarmed real-life counterparts. (1997, 18–19)

Implicit agreement to misrepresent the world is coupled with constant cultural pressure to accept these counterfeit images as real currency. Mills's list brings to mind Samuel Morton's scientific attempt to correlate race and skull size with intelligence, minstrel shows, John Ford westerns, Amos n' Andy, and U.S. government representations of Asians as vermin.[2] These images are not accidental; they are prescribed by the Racial Contract. Members of the racial polity must learn to see the world wrongly, but with the assurance that their mistaken ways of making sense of events count as accurate explanations. This is especially true for whites. "[O]n matters related to race, the Racial Contract prescribes for its signatories an *inverted epistemology*, an *epistemology of ignorance*, a particular pattern of localized and global cognitive dysfunctions (which are psychologically and socially functional), producing the ironic outcome that whites will in general be unable to understand the world they themselves have created" (Mills 1997, 18, emphasis added).

White ignorance is the axis around which white Americans construct our political identity.[3] This steady parade of misrepresentations generates a racialized moral psychology in which white perception and conception, memory, experience, and testimony are shaped by a willful and habitual inversion of reality (Mills 2004). The white eye is socialized to see lynchings and racialized torture as entertainment worthy of picnics and postcard reproductions.[4] Whites are taught to see indigenous land as vacant, women of color as sexually available, and Indian schools as charitable. More recently, the American press has described September 11 as the worst enemy attack ever perpetuated on American soil while remaining willfully ignorant of the Trail of Tears or the 1886 U.S. invasion of Mexico's territories north of the Rio Grande. As a political system white supremacy requires that everyday experiences and interactions uphold racial ignorance by resisting corrective information, and that inconsistencies be explained as only momentary slips from contractual ideals.

If the inverted epistemology at the heart of the Racial Contract helps maintain white supremacy, then how should whites go about tearing up the Racial Contract, undoing white ignorance? Mills suggests a twin-pronged solution: a historical revisionist project and a program of cognitive reform. The historical project is offered as a corrective to empirical ignorance fostered by whitewashed versions of history. It is supposed to reveal the contradictions between lofty contractual ideals and their unbalanced application along racial lines. But pointing to the disturbing truths of the past is not enough; we must also understand the racialized moral psychology that favors pleasing falsehoods over displeasing truths (1997, 98). The reason whites were consistently able to act wrongly while thinking they were acting rightly is, in part, "a problem of cognition and of white moral cognitive dysfunction. As such, it can potentially be studied by the new research program of cognitive science" (1997, 94–95). If cognitive science can reveal dysfunctional thought patterns, then perhaps it can also offer strategies for correcting them.[5] Mills does not give readers much detail here and, to be fair, this is not his project. However, the Harvard Implicit Association Test (IAT) offers an example of what I think he has in mind. During the Racial IAT, subjects are asked to quickly sort words and faces into categories. "Concept names" (e.g., "glorious," "wonderful," "evil," and "failure") are paired with black, white, and ambiguous faces. Quick responses to these pairings reveal subjects' implicit attitudes. From there it is a short step to asking how these preferences influence moral deliberation. If associations such as "white = glorious" are learned, then they can be unlearned. Perhaps this is what Mills has in mind when he encourages people to think against the grain and to "learn to trust [our] own cognitive powers, to develop [our] own concepts, insights, modes of explanation, overarching theories, and to oppose the epistemic hegemony of conceptual frameworks designed in part to thwart and suppress the exploration of such matters" (1997, 119).[6]

If white ignorance is the product of an "inverted epistemology," then a revisionist history buttressed by a race-sensitive program in cognitive science should replace race-ignorant with race-cognizant knowing. The historical project speaks for itself: read history through a racial lens, and get the bigger picture. My real interest is with Mills's cognitive science project. I think undoing white ignorance requires something more complex than cognitive therapy, but this is difficult to see given Mills's characterization of ignorance as an inverted epistemology. His language suggests that solutions lie in *reinverting* the epistemology, as one would turn a sweater right side out. The limits of this metaphor raise two concerns. First, I want to understand white efforts to undo ignorance as part of a broader coalition of resistance to the Racial Contract that also includes strategic uses of ignorance by people of color. Next, I think that a more radical and long-lasting epistemic resistance comes from learning to think in new logics, rather than from turning faulty logics right side out. The overall long-term solution to white cognitive dysfunction will need to be some combination of white epistemic retooling *and* the ability to see, understand, and join forces with people of color as they resist the Racial Contract. To convince readers of the limits of Mills's inversion metaphor, I need to shift away from questions about how white agency and ignorance are shaped by the Racial Contract and instead begin in a framework generated by people of color's resistance. For that I turn to María Lugones.

María Lugones on
The Logic of Purity and The Logic of Curdling

Mills focuses on white ignorance and how complex systems of domination disfigure white moral agency. He inherits his tools of analysis from the social contract tradition. María Lugones's *Pilgrimages/Peregrinajes: Theorizing Coalition against Multiple Oppressions* (2003) starts with nonwhite voices and lets the logic flow from them rather than trying to jam them into existing white-created frameworks. Rejecting established political frameworks as a means of sense making, she begins in "a dark place where [she sees] white/Angla women as 'on the other side,' on 'the light side,'" and where she sees herself as "dark but [does] not focus on or dwell inside the darkness, but rather focuses on the other side." She argues that if we stop thinking about oppressed people as victims consumed and exhausted by systems of oppression (e.g., the Racial Contract) and instead considers how oppressed subjects resist systems aimed at disciplining, violating, and erasing them, then different ways of making sense emerge (2003, 12). Her project is at once backward and forward looking. She offers an extensive critique of the logic that shapes modern subjectivity, so her observations apply nicely to the subjects of the Racial Contract. But she also theorizes with an eye toward developing a more dynamic, creative, curdled alternative to modern subjectivity—starting from a "dark place" makes this possible. It is this aspect of her work that I think offers a promising way to expand on Mills's insights on ignorance.

People who struggle against multiple oppressions often describe themselves as having multiple personalities: they feel torn between many identities.[7] For instance, many indigenous women find themselves in tribal solidarity with men of their nations while working against colonialism, but they are frustrated with men's failure to address gender issues. Oppression makes it difficult to see all facets of our identity at once. To highlight this Lugones develops an account of subjectivity that centers on multiplicity. For her, systems of oppression create coexisting logics: a logic of purity (a logic of oppressive systems such as the Racial Contract) and a curdled logic (a logic of resistance and transformation). She illustrates how each logic shapes social identity by tying the two uses of the Spanish verb *separar* (to separate) to a culinary metaphor. She begins in the kitchen. Two kinds of separation can occur during mayonnaise production. The first requires that one cleanly and completely split and separate the egg white from the yolk by moving the yolk back and forth between two halves of the shell so that the white drops gently into a bowl. This is an exercise in purity: no yolk in the white, and no white in the yolk.

The split-separation logic of purity defines two kinds of subjects: unified subjects and fragmented subjects. Both are fictions designed to erase, control, and distort the true multiplicity of all social beings. A good example of the unified subject is the abstract individual of classic liberal theory. Unified subjects are marked by universal traits such as "rational-autonomous-ends-chooser" and not by their privileged racial and gender status. Here, reason *essentially* defines human nature, while sex and race count as *accidental* properties. The fundamental assumption is that unity (essence) underlies multiplicity, and here multiplicity is reduced to an unmarked status that privileges the subject. The essence and accident distinction serves this purpose: subjects appear unified when accidental properties are split-separated out and an unmarked universal human trait (reason) remains. Maintaining the fiction of unity additionally requires that unified subjects—lest they be reminded of their multiplicity—be separated from a second kind of subject: the *fragmented* subject. Fragmentation is a consequence of group oppression that also follows the logic of purity, but unlike unified subjects, a person is split-separated into a fragmented subject when she is reduced to a racially marked identity. Fragmented identities are composed of "*pieces, and parts that do not fit well together; parts taken for wholes, composite, composed of parts of other beings, composed of imagined parts, composed of parts produced by a splitting imagination, composed of parts produced by subordinates and enacting their dominators' fantasies*" (Lugones 2003, 127, emphasis in original). For example, in the Anglo imagination the "American" is split-separated from the "Mexican" and "Mexican/Americans" become simply Mexicans.[8] "The Anglo imagines each rural Mexican/American as having a dual personality: the authentic Mexican cultural self and the American self. In this notion there is no hybrid self. . . . As an American, one is beyond culture; as [a] Mexican one is culture personified. The culturally split self is a character for the theatrics of racism" (135–36). This passion for orderliness that drives the logic of purity is conceptually linked to a desire for control. The U.S. Bureau of Indian Affairs' use of blood quantum to verify tribal status is an exercise in split-separation. Anti-abortion statutes that isolate the fetus from the pregnant woman's body are exercises in split-separation. It is the logic of apartheid, red-lining, citizenship, and anti-miscegenation laws.

Lugones contrasts this first meaning of *separar* with a second sense—"to curdle-separate." Curdle separation counts as culinary failure when making mayonnaise. Mayonnaise is an oil-in-water emulsion. Emulsions are formed when two or more nonmixable liquids (e.g., lemon juice, egg, and oil) are blended so thoroughly that the mixture *appears* homogenized. All emulsions are unstable. Manufacturers must add emulsifiers to puddings and salad dressings to prevent curdling (Winter 1989, 128). Curdle separation is never clean. When mayonnaise curdles, it does not separate into distinct parts; instead, "you are left with yolky oil and oily yolk" (Lugones 2003, 12). Lugones rejects the split-separation logic that generates unified and fragmented subjects in favor of a pluralist logic that recognizes all persons as complex multiple subjects. The logic of impurity—of *mestizaje*—offers a broader understanding of how interlocking oppressions shape subjectivity. A curdled logic produces *multiplicitous* identities such as Creole, Mestizo/a, Métis/se, and Chicano/a.[9] Multiplicitous selves defy control and categorization by "asserting the impure, curdled multiple state and rejecting fragmentation into pure parts" (2003, 123). Curdled logics generate subjects who resist the hard-edged schemas of purity aimed at categorizing, dominating, and controlling the openness of possibilities. Mestizaje is a metaphor for both impurity and resistance. To highlight agency under oppression, Lugones refers to these subjects as oppressed<->resisting subjects. Curdle separation is an active not a reactive process—a creative practice of resistance (Lugones 2003, 145).

As she investigates the split-separation logic of purity, Lugones asks us to keep the logic of curdling and mestizaje superimposed onto it. "The reader needs to see ambiguity, see that the split-separated are also and simultaneously curdle-separated" (2003, 126). These logics flicker back and forth.[10] Think bad radio reception. For example, when I tune my car radio to 90.1 FM, I pull in both the Urbana classical station and the country-western station in Farmer City. Sometimes the classical signal is clearer, and sometimes the country-western station dominates. Other times the receiver pulls in an almost inseparable mix of Hank Williams's vocals and Chopin's piano nocturnes. An analogy can be made with the logics of purity and curdling: both are present (although the purity signal is usually stronger). While listening to the logic of purity, we must also learn to hear the curdled broadcasts that sometimes disrupt and distort purity.

I now return to Mills's account of ignorance with both of these logics in mind. The logic of purity is clearly broadcast in Mills's characterizations of ignorance, but this connection needs to be clarified. In addition, I want to train myself to listen for curdled signals. It is my hunch that a curdled reading of ignorance will offer us a more relational understanding of ignorance by revealing the ways in which people of color have strategically engaged with white folks' ignorance in ways that are advantageous.

The Racial Contract,
Purity, and Two Expressions of Ignorance

Lugones's account of the purity, impurity, and resistance is immensely helpful in understanding how the Racial Contract shapes the ignorance of those who must abide by its epistemic standards. If, as she suggests, "the desire for control and love of purity are conceptual cousins," and if the Racial Contact is about control, then I suspect that the logic of purity is what shapes white ignorance, the erasure of nonwhite history, resistance, and other means of maintaining white supremacy (Lugones 2003, 129). The Racial Contract is a political strategy for controlling multiplicity. It is intolerant of spatial ambiguity: it split-separates polities into white civilized space and wild savage lands occupied by nonwhites. It rejects ontological ambiguity: white signatories of the Racial Contract come to understand themselves as unified unmarked subjects while learning to see nonwhite subjects as less than human, or fragmented. If purity is at the structural heart of the Racial Contract, then all expressions of ignorance will bear its imprint. I think the Racial Contract generates at least two expressions of ignorance. A form of privilege-evasive ignorance, which Mills later calls "white ignorance" (2004), and an expression I call "the ignorance of internalized oppression."[11] It is worth briefly spelling out how purity crafts each expression.

A central feature of white ignorance is the ability to ignore people without white privilege. White ignorance is a form of not knowing (seeing wrongly), resulting from the habit of erasing, dismissing, distorting, and forgetting about the lives, cultures, and histories of peoples whites have colonized. Consider the all-too-common, color-blind responses to racism, such as: "We all bleed the same color," or "We're all human." The logic goes something like this: People who are prejudiced see color and make unfair judgments based on color. To be absolutely certain that we are not making unfair judgements based on color, we should ignore accidental properties, such as color, and just see people. Color blindness is essentially a form of ignoring that equates seeing, naming, and engaging difference with prejudice and bigotry, and not seeing, naming, noticing, and engaging difference with fairness. Purity is at work here. To be color blind you must learn to split and separate race from humanity. Color blindness relies on the cognitive habit of training the multiple (racial diversity) into a fictitious unity (we are all human). The color-blind responses to racism initially seem to be just, until we consider how the illusion of equality is purchased at the cost of multiplicity. Color blindness is just the sort of cognitive dysfunction Mills has in mind. When members of dominant groups actively ignore multiplicity, they practice hearing and seeing wrongly. So, color-blind responses to racism are an

agreement to *mis*interpret the world.[12] They are a perfect instance of
how whites can act in racist ways while at the same time believing they are
behaving rightly!

As Mills observes, an epistemology of ignorance "requires labor at
both ends" (1997, 87–88). If the logic of purity underwrites the Racial
Contract, then all members of the polity, and not just the privileged
ones, are required to live and move within this framework. A second expression of ignorance occurs when oppressed groups become ignorant
of their own multiplicity. What Mills refers to as an "epistemology of victims" acknowledges that people of color may simultaneously understand
the harmful impacts of the Contract while at the same time internalize its
basic message. Here, learning to see wrongly means learning to see your
past as a "wasteland of nonachievement," to loathe the racialized aspects
of your appearance, to distance yourself from your culture, to play up the
white aspects of yourself, and to silence those dark parts of the self that
cause pain (Mills 1997, 109). Cherríe Moraga's early writings make this
distressingly clear:

> I went to a concert where Ntosake Shange was reading. . . . What
> Ntosake caught in me is the realization that in my development as a
> poet I have, in many ways, denied the voice of my brown mother—the
> brown in me. I have acclimated to the sound of a white language which,
> as my father represents it, does not speak to the emotions in my
> poems—emotions which stem from the love of my mother. . . . I was
> shocked by my own ignorance." (2002, 29)

Purity is at work here too. Having split-separated herself into brown-
and-white fragments, Moraga realizes the impact of ignoring the brown
parts of herself. Mills briefly mentions how people of color might resist
this form of ignorance. The solutions run parallel to the revisionist history and cognitive science projects he offers in response to white ignorance. The necessary public political work for people of color begins
with an internal psychological battle to "overcome the internalization of
subpersonhood prescribed by the Racial Contract and recognize one's
own humanity. . . . One has to learn the basic self-respect that can casu-
ally be assumed by Kantian persons, those privileged by the Racial Contract, but which is denied to subpersons (1997, 118–19).[13] Recognizing
one's own humanity requires rejecting European beauty standards, challenging the colonizer's versions of history, and cultivating cognitive resistance to the "racially mystificatory" aspects of white theory. People of
color need to trust their own thinking, to develop their own concepts,
insights, explanations, and theories, and to oppose the epistemic hegemony of the conceptual frameworks designed to suppress views that
challenge dominant understandings.

These expressions of ignorance bear the imprint of the logic of purity, but it does not follow that resistance must also bear this imprint. Purity may be at the heart of the Racial Contract, but we need not rely on this logic for resistance. Mills's allegiance to contract talk as "the lingua franca of our times" (1997, 3) ensures that resistance will take place on the very epistemic turf that gives rise to it. If these expressions of ignorance are the product of an inverted epistemology, then resistance will be understood in terms of reinversion strategies. Reinversion strategies are the only solutions purity has to offer. However, I do not think reinverting inverted epistemologies will have radical long-lasting effects. *Under purity, inverted epistemologies can only be reinverted and not shattered.* The epistemic retooling that Mills describes requires something more structurally complex for it to be effective in the long run.[14] Mills's suggestions for retooling our moral vision are initially helpful, but my fear is that his prescription will only correct our vision until the Racial Contract is rewritten. Learning to see wrongly is a by-product of purity, so, purity-driven solutions, to use Audre Lordes's wonderful metaphor, may count as instances of using the master's tools (purity) to dismantle the master's house. I think the logic of purity can be used in resistant ways, but to see this we need to look at ignorance through a curdled lens.

Strategic Ignorance

Let us dwell in purity for a moment longer. Mills's strategies for undoing the ignorance of internalized oppression focus on one type of resistance—the refusal to accept one's status as subperson—but there are others. Internalizing the logic of purity need not be fatal. If we examine Mills's "epistemology of victims" through a curdled lens we see that it also includes an epistemology of resistance. Lugones theorizes oppressed subjects not only as victims but also as oppressed<->resisting subjects. The logic of curdling reveals additional resistant paths through the Racial Contract. Navigating the dominator's world requires that oppressed<-> resisting subjects employ ways of knowing that reduce the risks of oppression. To extend Audre Lorde's metaphor, the master's tools may not be able to dismantle the master's house, but they might just come in handy when walking through his neighborhood, attending his schools, or working on his assembly line. There are ways of using the dominator's tools that do not replicate dominance. One variety of curdling is to negotiate the Racial Contract in ways that use the logic of purity to your advantage. Perhaps ignorance is a tool that can be used strategically.

James Baldwin once said that segregation worked brilliantly, because it "allowed white people, with scarcely any pangs of conscience whatever, to *create*, in every generation, only the Negro they wished to see" (1961,

69, emphasis in original). Patriarchy also seems to have a knack for cele-
brating only those archetypes of femininity that serve the purposes of
male domination. Happily, members of oppressed groups have long
taken advantage of dominant groups' tendencies to see wrongly and to
misrepresent their lives. Think about how people of color have historically been portrayed as unintelligent, childlike, hypersexual, or primitive. Strategic ignorance is a way of expediently working with a dominant
group's tendency to see wrongly. It is a form of knowing that uses dominant misconceptions as a basis for active creative responses to oppression. It seeks out resistant paths through the logic of purity that turn
white ignorance back on the oppressor jiujitsu style. Some examples follow the practices I have in mind.

One way of using ignorance strategically is to play dumb as a means
of gaining information. In his autobiography, Frederick Douglas explains how he tricked white boys into teaching him to write. He recalls,
"[W]hen I met with any boy who I knew could write, I would tell him I
could write as well as he. The next word would be, "I don't believe you.
Let me see you try it." I would then make the letters, which I had been
so fortunate as to learn, and ask him to beat that. In this way I got a good
many lessons in writing, which it is quite possible I should never have got-
ten in any other way" (2003, 70). Douglas's approach relies on white
ignorance: it presupposes that the white boy he tricks will have an inaccurate understanding of black character. It only works if white folks cannot imagine folks of color being literate or clever.

Strategically acting in ways that conform to white expectations is also
a clandestine way of getting revenge for poor pay, bad working conditions, or avoiding harm. Robin Kelly's research on black working-class
resistance suggests that Southern black laborers had a working understanding of what he calls the "cult of true Sambohood," which defined
black folks' conscious theft as immorality, their calculated slowdowns as
laziness, and their tool breaking as incompetence or carelessness. Kelly
explains how the "mask of 'grins and lies' enhanced black working people's invisibility and enabled them to wage a kind of underground
'guerilla' battle with their employers, the police, and other representatives of the status quo," and that "the mask worked precisely because most
Southern whites accepted their own racial mythology" (1994, 7). Black
domestics "accidentally" broke china while dusting, or pretended they
could not read when confronted with their employers' questions about
civil rights literature. The unnamed narrator in Ralph Ellison's *Invisible Man* wonders if another black man "was dissimulating, like some of
the teachers at the college, who, to avoid trouble when driving through
the small surrounding towns, wore chauffeur caps and pretended that
their cars belonged to white men" (1980, 211). Strategic ignorance

worked precisely because most whites believed that domestics were dishonest, workers were clumsy, or that black teachers could not afford their own cars.

The logic of curdling is visible in strategic ignorance. It is a perfect example of how oppressed<-> resisting subjects, as agents, can animate their ambiguity as a tool for resistance. Strategic ignorance allows oppressed <->resisting subjects to take hold of the double meaning of their actions. In the logic of curdling, the social world is complex and selves are multiple—not fragmented. This means that there is more than one reading of a subject's actions: Douglas is "dumbly clever"; the maid's actions are "clumsy on purpose"; the driver is a "chauffeur car-owner." Purity's hand in white ignorance ensures that the first part of each description (e.g., dumb, clumsy, chauffeur) is the only one that makes sense. In the logic of curdling both readings are visible and sometimes indistinguishable because they flicker back and forth quickly. Oppressed<-> resistant subjects willfully animate this ambiguity to their own advantage. This is the essence of strategic ignorance. As my examples illustrate, strategic ignorance is a political strategy that goes beyond merely inverting existing perceptions. Under the logic of purity, Douglas would just challenge the stereotype of the dumb black man by demonstrating that he really could read and write. His actions will hopefully challenge the white boy's existing perceptions while boosting his own sense of self. This is the strategy that purity offers. Under the logic of curdling, we might understand Douglas as skillfully animating the ambiguous space between literate and illiterate in order to get a lesson in writing. These curdling techniques can either be haphazard techniques for survival, or they can be consciously cultivated into an art of resistance and transformation (Lugones 2003, 145). Unlike white ignorance, strategic ignorance cannot take the form of active ignoring, erasure, and unconscious detachment. Here, ignorance is not bliss. Servants and braceros must be attentive to their employers' moods. Women in violent relationships cannot ignore the shift in body language and tone of voice that signal violence.[15]

Admittedly, most expressions of strategic ignorance keep people of color in the role of "the Negro whites wish to see." The temporary protection that these strategies offer comes at an enormous psychological cost. Acts of strategic ignorance almost always involve some degree of dissemblance, or masking.[16] Dissembling reveals the true multiplicity of subjects. As Ella Surrey remarks: We have always been the best actors in the world. . . . We've always had to live two lives—one for them and one for ourselves" (Gwaltney 1993, 240). Dissembling is a way to keep dominators ignorant of the important aspects of one's life. It allows oppressed <->resisting subjects to present themselves as they are not in order to protect other aspects of themselves that are important.[17]

Thinking beyond Cognitive Science and
Historical Revisionist Solutions

We live in a world where both dominant and resistant logics are present; the split-separated are also simultaneously curdle-separated, so why are we in the habit of turning to the former for clarification? I start with purity because I want to understand how it produces an ignorance-generating ontology. I want to undo my own ignorance. At the same time I recognize how the logic of purity is epistemically cozy for people with race privilege, and I have come to regard epistemic comfort with suspicion. Using the familiar tools of social contract theory to unpack the white ignorance generated by the Racial Contract not only erases strategic ignorance and resistant epistemologies, but it also confines white responses to epistemically comfortable solutions. Whites wanting to undo our ignorance can work hard to reverse the biases revealed to them by the Implicit Association Test. We can thumb through volumes of history to reveal the stories that have been kept from us. We can engage in both of these activities from the safety of our own worlds. These solutions offer a temporary remedy to white cognitive dysfunction, but they do so in ways that rely on isolated, noninteractive, self-reflective, and solipsistic processes. Absent from these solutions is any talk about the relations between races, political alliance building, and the daily interactions between peoples. I want to see the project of undoing white ignorance as part of a broader coalition of resistance that includes strategic uses of ignorance by people of color. Purity flattens an animated and a complex world by erasing relations, and ignorance is the product of that erasure. Love of purity drives misperception by distancing and separating ourselves from those we imagine to be most unlike us. Distance creates gaps in understanding that the imagination then rushes in to fill. Ignorance flourishes when we confine our movements, thoughts, and actions to those worlds, social circles, and logics where we are most comfortable. It grows when we fail to relate to, hang out with, and build community with folks that we are taught to hate, regard with suspicion, or dismiss as different. White ignorance does not exist separately from our failure to engage with people of color.

Ignorance also results from white folks' failure to see ourselves as multiple. I think about my own struggles with white privilege and the ignorance it generates. Who I am is the product of my interactions with others. My continuing journey from privilege-evasive to privilege-cognizant thinking on matters of race did not come from thinking my way out of these problems; it came from hanging out with people of color, interacting, laughing, and making mistakes, while being attentive to my interactions and what they reveal. If privileged groups' desire for wholeness is what gives rise to the split-separation thinking that teaches white folks to see the world wrongly, then combating white ignorance will require that white folks abandon the myth of unified wholeness and learn to see our *own* multiplicity. To understand this we need to return to the kitchen. Recall that an oil-in-water emulsion such as mayonnaise is formed when two or more nonmixable liquids are blended so thoroughly together that the mixture *appears* homogenized. Homogenization is a fiction. If we look at mayonnaise under a microscope, we see a more curdled spread. It is only when we look at it macroscopically that it masquerades as a homogenous condiment. The logic of purity allows white folks to see our privileged identities as whole and complete rather than as microscopically curdled bits superficially held together by emulsifiers. The fiction of wholeness acts as an emulsifier: it presents white identities as stable. Undoing white ignorance requires that white folks work toward cultivating an identity without emulsifiers. We must think of ourselves as curdled beings. In contrast to purity, curdling "realizes their against-the-grain creativity, articulates their within-structure-inarticulate powers. As we come to understand curdling as resisting domination, we also need to recognize its potential to germinate a nonoppressive pattern, a mestiza consciousness, *una conciencia mestiza*" (Lugones 2003, 133). I see no reason white folks cannot cultivate this sort of consciousness. The concept of curdling helps shift our imagination to a new realm of sense. I am not suggesting that we substitute one logic for another: the desire to do so is itself a function of purity. In the name of curdling, purity can have its place if it is used strategically rather than to replicate dominance. In making curdled logics visible, Lugones points to the many frameworks of meaning that can be used to make sense of the world. Possibilities flourish when we dwell in ambiguity. Engaging complexity is one way of overcoming ignorance and establishing relations. If the logic of curdling reveals forms of resistance unseen in the logic of purity, and if it reveals complexity and relations between us, then perhaps it will be a helpful starting point for addressing questions of ignorance.

Notes

1. Mills favors the classic social contract tradition (e.g., Hobbes, Locke, and Kant) over contemporary approaches (e.g., Rawls), because he is interested in origin stories rather than the exclusively prescriptive dimensions of social contracts.

2. Helpful examples of the disjunction between what Mills calls "actual reality" and the "consensual hallucination" are found in Marlon Riggs's brilliant film *Ethnic Notions*, which looks at representations of African Americans, and Carol Spindel's *Dancing at Halftime: Sports and the Controversy over American Indian Mascots*, which contrasts real images of Native peoples with University of Illinois mascot Chief Illiniwek.

3. We cannot acknowledge the true human cost of nation building because it would change how whites have historically thought of themselves as good, civilized, and just: it would change what it means to be white. Whites' ignorance about the centrality of oppression in nation building keeps them believing that they are good people living in a model, one-size-fits-all democracy that is readily exported as a solution to global conflicts. It keeps their identities whole.

4. For examples, see James Allen, ed., *Without Sanctuary: Lynching Photography in America* (Santa Fe, NM: Twin Palms Publishers, 1999).

5. Mills references Alan Goldman's essay, "Ethics and Cognitive Science," which addresses questions such as: What mental images accompany words such as "good," "fair," and "right" when they are used by moral agents making value judgments?

6. The IAT was developed as a tool for exploring the unconscious roots of thinking and feeling, but the test is also a good indicator of unconscious preferences and beliefs. This test can taken online at https://www.implicit.harvard.edu/implicit.

7. My understanding of Lugones's work on subjectivity, purity, and impurity has been greatly enhanced by conversations with Sarah Hoagland and Christa Lebens.

8. In her discussion of dual beings, Lugones uses the form "Mexican/American" and not the more standard hyphenated "Mexican-American" to "signify that if the split were successful, there would be no possibility of dwelling or living on the hyphen" (2003, 134).

9. Métis, or métisse, is the name given to people of mixed indigenous and French-Canadian ancestry. Also, it is important to note that multiplicitous identities do not exclusively describe or refer to people of color. All identity is curdled. Bicultural people are just more familiar with experiencing themselves as multiple because as a matter of necessity they have had to learn how to successfully navigate both their home worlds and the worlds of the oppressor. This shift between worlds is a shift in identity, and it reveals the multiplicity of the self: there is no underlying self that persists through this world travel. Many members of dominant groups fail to see their multiplicity because they move only in worlds where they feel at ease: in places where their identity appears unified and they feel secure. If white folks, for example, spent more time in Latina or Native worlds, or if straight folks spent more time with gay folks, then their multiplicity would be revealed.

10. I am grateful to Penny Deutscher for describing the relationships between purity and impurity as flickering.

11. I am basically following Frankenberg's distinction between privilege-evasive and privilege-cognizant white responses to racism. This distinction is not hard and fast. A great deal has been written on whites resisting their own ignorance about race, but this resistance still takes place in the logic of purity. In this respect, whites may be privilege-cognizant but metaphysically comfortable.

12. Color blindness is a post-civil rights version of the Racial Contract. Whereas earlier drafts held the racial order in place with appeals to white mythologies about invented Africas and Orients and distorted images of blackness, color blindness points in a new direction. Images of the other in the early

white imagination say "we are unlike them," whereas the recent color-blind version says, "we are all the same underneath." Both moves rely on a logic of purity. Neither says we are multiplicituous beings.

13. On the one hand, I cannot help but think that this is assimilationist advice. It sounds as if he advises people of color to parade themselves as pure Kantian agents. On the other hand, Mills proposed solution coincides with the work of black feminists (such as Audre Lorde) who remind us that "the true focus of revolutionary change is never merely the oppressive situations which we seek to escape, but that piece of the oppressor which is planted deep within us" (Lorde 1984, 123).

14. Mills's cognitive solution is not completely ineffective. The harm of oppression is so visceral that it requires immediate attention. Perhaps my privileged stance affords me the luxury of contemplating long-term solutions that privilege fancy theoretical moves over concrete solutions. I focus on theory and not on people. The white girl philosopher in me really wants to solve this problem with clever theoretical moves. However, I do think that more radical responses to ignorance are worth exploring.

15. Isolated acts of strategic ignorance will not change the Racial Contract or the material conditions that make these acts necessary. White employers, battering husbands, or the schoolboys of Douglas's narrative will read these actions as further evidence of subpersonhood and justification for paternalistic policies. This is the double bind of oppression and it is subject to the same sorts of considerations that Sarah Hoagland explores in her wonderful discussion of sabotage. See Hoagland (1997, 41–54).

16. It is interesting to note that the word "dissemblance" comes from the Latin "dis," meaning reversal, and the Old French "sembler," meaning to be like, appear, or seem. It is literally a reversal of appearance. The *Oxford English Dictionary* offers an obsolete usage of the word that means "to pretend not to recognize or notice, to ignore."

17. Darlene Clark Hine's account of how black women used dissembling as a strategy for preserving self-worth is helpful. "The dynamics of dissemblance involved creating the appearance of disclosure, or openness about themselves and their feelings, while actually remaining an enigma. Only with secrecy, thus achieving a self-imposed invisibility, could ordinary black women accrue the psychic space and harness the resources needed to hold their own in the often one-sided and mismatched resistance struggle" (1989, 915).

References

Baldwin, James. 1961. *Nobody Knows My Name: More Notes of a Native Son*. New York: Vintage International.

Douglas, Frederick. 2003. *Narrative of the Life of Frederick Douglas: An American Slave, Written By Himself with Related Documents*, 2d ed., ed. David W. Blight, 1–188. Boston: Bedford/St. Martin's Press.

Ellison, Ralph. 1980 [1947]. *Invisible Man*. New York: Vintage Books.

Frankenberg, Ruth. 1993. *The Social Construction of Whiteness: White Women, Race Matters*. Minneapolis: University of Minnesota Press.

Frye, Marilyn. 1983. "On Being White: Toward a Feminist Understanding of Race and Race Supremacy." In *The Politics of Reality: Essays in Feminist Theory*, 110–28. Freedom, CA: The Crossing Press.

Gwaltney, John Langston. 1993. *Drylongso: A Self-Portrait of Black America*. New York: New Press.

Hine, Darlene Clark. 1989. "Rape and the Inner Lives of Black Women in the Middle West." *Signs* (14)4: 912–20.

Hoagland, Sarah Lucia. 1997. *Lesbian Ethics: Toward New Value*. Palo Alto, CA: Institute for Lesbian Studies.

Kelly, Robin D. G. 1994. *Race Rebels: Culture, Politics, and the Black Working Class*. New York: The Free Press.

Lorde, Audre. 1984. *Sister Outsider*. Trumansberg, NY: The Crossing Press.

Lugones, María. 2003. *Pilgrimages/Peregrinajes: Theorizing Coalition against Multiple Oppressions*. Lanham, MD: Rowman and Littlefield.

Mills, Charles W. 1997. *The Racial Contract*. Ithaca, NY: Cornell University Press.

———. 2004. "White Ignorance" Ethics and Epistemologies of Ignorance Conference. Penn State University, March 26, 2004.

Moraga, Cherríe. 2002 [1981]. "La Güera." In *This Bridge Called My Back: Writings by Radical Women of Color*, ed. Cherrie Moraga and Gloria E. Anzaldúa, 24–34. Berkeley, CA: Third Woman Press.

Tuana, Nancy. 2004. "Coming to Understand: Orgasm and the Epistemology of Ignorance." *Hypatia* (19)1: 194–232.

Winter, Ruth. 1989. *A Consumer's Dictionary of Food Additives*. 3rd ed. New York: Crown, 128.

CHAPTER 5

Denying Relationality

Epistemology and Ethics and Ignorance

Sarah Lucia Hoagland

Ignorance

Aristotle identifies two general categories through which we can be morally excused for our behavior: constraint and ignorance. I cannot be held accountable for failing to keep an appointment with someone if I am in an accident and cannot get to the appointment, or if I do not know the appointment exists (Austin 1970).

However, that someone is ignorant of something does not automatically absolve them of accountability, particularly when they should have known better. Ignorance of the rules of the road, for example, is no excuse when one is driving. Recently a report appeared about the growing frustration on the part of computer technologists toward people who keep letting their computers become infected by opening virus-laden e-mail, admonishing users' willful ignorance. Wrote one technologist: "It takes affirmative action on the part of the clueless user to become infected" (Harmon 2004, sec. A, 1).

On the other hand, Critical Race Theorists argue, when it comes to racism mainstream U.S. society promotes ignorance as part of public policy. For example while the "war on drugs" has resulted in aggressive criminalization and destruction of Black communities, official policy is that the war on drugs is not racially motivated; indeed overt racial rhetoric is largely absent. But, argues Judith Scully, this begs the question: "an individual who carries a suitcase full of explosives into an airport will be deemed guilty of possession of the explosives regardless of whether or not he claims he had no idea what was in the suitcase. A finding of 'guilt' is particularly likely when the individual has an opportunity to find out what is in the suitcase but fails to do so" (2002, 56, 70).

That members of the government may be ignorant of the fact that they are carrying an explosive policy into the country does not absolve them of responsibility, particularly when this can be easily ascertained. Nevertheless the government maintains a "don't ask, don't tell" approach, thereby officially ignoring the design and effects of U.S. drug policies on the Black community. Supporting an epistemology of ignorance with an ethics of ignorance, "the U.S. Supreme Court has declared that racial disparities in law enforcement are constitutional as long as they are not undertaken with discriminatory intent (Scully 2002, note 113, p. 80, referencing *McClesky v. Kemp* [1987] and *U.S. v. Armstrong* [1996]). Charles Lawrence cites *Washington v. Davis* (1976), requiring plaintiffs challenging the constitutionally of a facially neutral law to prove discriminatory purpose (Lawrence 1995). That is, a legal ethics of ignorance that defines public acts of racism by means of private intentions justifies epistemological practices of ignorance. This is U.S. public racial policy. (On the other hand, in March 2005, the U.S. Supreme Court ruled that workers who sue their employers for age discrimination need not prove that the discrimination was intentional [*New York Times*, March 31, 2005]).

One strategy in challenging an epistemology of ignorance brings to light something that is missed by competent practitioners of dominant culture, offering information and analyzing how the dominant or hegemonic frame excludes this information, reframes it so as to render it invisible; this is a strategy of articulating how ignorance can be an active production. Nancy Tuana's work on women's orgasms is an excellent example (2004). Another strategy explores the motivations of competent practitioners of dominant culture who claim ignorance. In this case, interesting psychological theses are offered about self-deception, noting particularly the arsenal of weapons practitioners invoke to excuse themselves. Indeed, Charles Mills has issued a call for a cognitive science that would take up an investigation of difficulties white people manifest in overcoming ignorance in relation to racism, including evasion, self-deception and a cult of forgetfulness (1997, 18–19, 92–97).

My initial interest in exploring ignorance lies in the denial of relationality that is often part of an ethics and an epistemology of ignorance, the denial of substantive relationship between those competent practitioners of dominant culture who are ignorant and those about whom they are ignorant.[1] In this respect, practices of ignorance involve power relations. In this chapter, I argue that epistemological and ethical practices of ignorance are strategic and involve a denial of relationality.

Moreover, as praxis, they are enacted not only from positions of power and privilege but also from locations of resistance. There is a practice among many who are marginalized by dominant logic of *promoting* ignorance among competent practitioners of dominant culture and in the process, destabilizing oppressive relationality. For example at times women keep men ignorant about certain things, and at times blacks keep whites ignorant about certain things. That is, there are strategic practices of ignoring within a logic of oppression and also strategic practices of ignoring within a logic of resistance, though very different things are going on in the two locations.

Relationality

When I speak of relationality, I am not taking up the Rousseauian coming together of two autonomous units in self-interest, nor the mechanistic Foucaultian product of disciplinary structures, nor MacIntyrian state-sanctioned roles. Moreover, I am not talking about a collective whereby, in resisting hierarchal organization, we see ourselves as an amorphous whole, a methodology that was practiced by some feminist collectives.

I am interested in ways our subjectivities are formed through our engagements with each other, both individually and culturally. Fernando Ortiz argues that as two cultures come into contact they affect each other and change, what he calls transculturation (1995, 102–103). Fernando Coronil argues that cultures need to be seen in contrapuntal (musical counterpoint) relation to each other rather than taken to be autonomous units (1996, 73).

Rather than assume engaged cultures to be autonomous units, and their subjects separate, one can understand them as developing through their engagements. For example, Spanish subjects did not pre-exist as colonizers. They became colonizers by interacting, by engaging the Mexica (Aztecs) in the praxis of colonization as they developed tools and policies in administering Spanish rule in reaction and response to resistances and tools developed by the Mexica[2] (see Mignolo 1995). Similarly, Anglo-European scholarly men did not pre-exist as scientists. They became scientists in part through their engagement with pagan and Jewish women healers as they hunted, examined, tortured, and exterminated many of them during the Roman Catholic Inquisition.

European settlers did not pre-exist as white slave owners nor Yorubans as slaves. As Charles Mills suggests, white people do not pre-exist but are brought into existence as whites by the racial contract (1977, 63). Cheryl Harris argues that "the assigned political, economic, and social inferiority of blacks necessarily shaped white identity" (1995, 283). Paget Henry argues that the othering of Africans in Western rationality is a practice of

transformation into the irrational, to be made to disappear phenomeno-
logically, to disappear as a subject (2000, 179).

Claiming subjectivity and resisting the particular relationality of this
violence, Franz Fanon advocates a counterviolence: "For it is the settler
who has bought the native into existence and who perpetuates his existence. The settler owes the fact of his very existence, that is to say, his
property, to the colonial system. . . . Decolonization is the veritable creation of new men. . . . The 'thing' which has been colonized becomes a
man (*sic*) during the same process by which it frees itself" (1978, 36–37).
Significantly, in testifying to the colonialist in EveryEuropean, Franz
Fanon's goal was not that the native resignify himself if that is understood to be the native adopting the colonialist's or settler's framework
and speaking back, resignifying "native." His goal was to destroy both the
native and the settler, for without the native, the settler does not exist.

The battle currently being played out over gay marriage is not about
gays so much as about straight people, about the relationality between
men and women, and the institutional construction of men and women.
The issue of gay marriage is the ontological ground on which the right
wing is positioned to erase, finally, second-wave radical feminism from the
dominant logic as it erased first-wave radical feminism during the fight for
suffrage. In both cases the move occurs through the defense and rein-
forcement of marriage. Marriage and its productions—adultery, loose
women, prostitution, the double standard, whores, virgins, wife beating,
illegitimate children, incest, bastards, marital rape, domestic abuse,
women's economic disabilities—are a critical means by which the state in-
stitutionally intervenes to define what it means to be a woman or a man
and the proper relationship between them (Hoagland 2007).

Whiteness does not exist independently from engagements with people of color. Let me put it this way: There are NO white people in the
United States (including Eastern European immigrants just stepping off
the plane or boat) separate from people of color, NO white people who
are not related to people of color. And I'm not just talking about the fact
that white people benefit from the work of people of color as if it were a
matter of staying in a motel room that we have happened to enter such
that if we are ethically conscious, we will notice and appreciate that someone made the room comfortable for us.

Whiteness doesn't exist independently from engagements with people
of color, even, or especially, if those engagements are white practices of erasure. Discussing actions taken by students and faculty under the presidency
of Oliver Wendell Holmes in 1850, Ronald Takaki argues: "The exclusion
of blacks and white women from Harvard Medical School helped students
as well as faculty identify themselves as white and male" (1993, 202). As
Cheryl Harris argues, "Whiteness was premised on white supremacy rather

than mere difference. 'White' was defined and constructed in ways that increased its value by reinforcing its exclusivity. . . . The concept of whiteness is built on exclusion and racial subjection" (1995, 283).

But these relationalities are rendered invisible through an epistemology that presupposes autonomy and denies relationality between knower and known. Dorothy Smith argues that social relation between knower and known was first constructed and then made invisible through the suspension of the particular subjectivities of both knower and known: the subject studied ceases to be an authority, and the interaction of the researcher—also a subject—is characterized as neutral (1987, 72–73). The academic and professional methodology of detachment safeguards white and male supremacy and monoculturalism. Thus as we approach knowing those different from ourselves, we are positioned to think non-relationally.

Many whites seem enormously unself-conscious about whiteness as a cultural and political phenomenon much as the middle class seems enormously unself-conscious about middle classness as a cultural and political phenomenon. (I say "many" whites because white supremacists, for example, are not unself-conscious about whiteness either as a cultural or a political phenomenon.) More significantly, being ignorant about the relationality between whites and those designated non-white, being ignorant about whiteness, is one way many whites are currently socialized into whiteness. Yet promoting self-consciousness about whiteness does not necessarily lead to relational thinking; it can rather be a solipsistic inward-turning, a non-relational self-examination whereby the focus remains on white folks.[3]

At times the discourse approaches whiteness as being invisible. But, again, what is invisible, transparent, to many whites is our relationality with, our interdependency with, peoples of color. What is a shock among whites, in classes for example or workshops, is that we are indebted to, made possible by, responsible to peoples of color. *I am not making a moral point here; I am making an ontological point.* I am not talking about acknowledging a debt; I am talking about whites' existence. Not something we can pay off, but something to re-cognize and embrace.

That (most) whites walk through our day ignorant of our interdependency with peoples of color is not about the invisibility of whiteness but rather about the erasure of peoples of color as subjects.[4] So I am particularly interested in Charles Mills's introduction of the idea of an epistemology of ignorance embedded in the Racial Contract, an epistemology "which produces the ironic outcome that whites will generally be unable to understand the world they themselves have made" (1997, 18–19).

Relationality involves our forming and being formed, both individually and culturally, in relation through our engagements and practices.

Who we are is in part a function of our relationships—in logic, an internal relation. We are interactive and interdependent. Autonomous thinking promotes both epistemology and ethics of ignorance. My desire has been deeply motivated by the work of, as well as ongoing engagement and dialogue with, María Lugones:

> I am interested here in those many cases in which White/Anglo women do one or more of the following to women of color: they ignore us, ostracize us, render us invisible, stereotype us, leave us completely alone, interpret us as crazy. All of this *while we are in their midst.* The more independent I am, the more independent I am left to be. Their world and their integrity do not require me at all. . . . I am incomplete and unreal without other women. I am profoundly dependent on others without having to be their subordinate, their slave, their servant. (Lugones 2003, 83, emphasis in original)

Logic of Oppression and Logic of Resistance

María Lugones argues that oppression theory portrays oppression in full force, often inescapable (otherwise one is blaming the victim). However given the logic of oppression theory (she cites Karl Marx and Marilyn Frye), it is not clear how a woman can be at all active in her own liberatory process (Lugones 2003, ch. 2). A driving focus of María Lugones's work is the subjectivity of those living under conditions of oppression:

> If we think of people who are oppressed as not consumed or exhausted by oppression, but also as resisting, or sabotaging a system aimed at molding, reducing, violating, erasing them, then we also see at least two realities: one of them has the logic of resistance and transformation; the other has the logic of oppression. But indeed these two logics multiply and they encounter each other over and over in many guises. (Lugones 2003, 12)

I want to look at strategies promoting epistemologies and ethics of ignorance both on the part of those who are operating within a logic of oppression and those who are operating within a logic of resistance.

I. From the Logic of Oppression

Strategic conceptual moves within dominant logic—means and strategies by which the logic of colonial, misogynistic, race supremist, imperial sense is maintained as normalcy both epistemologically and ethically—are extremely interesting to engage critically, particularly in their seamless denials of relationality.

Ignorance and Epistemology from the Logic of Oppression

I begin with a relationship determinedly ignored by Modern Anglo-European philosophers. Latin American philosophers of liberation argue that we cannot understand the Enlightenment without acknowledging its relation to the Conquest. Marveling at how the history of Western philosophy moves from Aquinas to Descartes, skipping entirely the 1500s and Spain's dominance when Europe was yet to be constructed, they argue that the constitution of Modern subjectivity began with the Conquest in 1492 and culminated in Descartes's expression of the cogito in 1636 (Dussel 1995, 17). "I think" is informed, not just preceded, by "I conquer." Moreover, concepts developed in the process of the Spanish colonization of Amerindians, concepts developed to solve Spain's political and bureaucratic problems, ground the Enlightenment, and have become part of our common sense thinking—concepts such as progress, linear development (particularly history and evolution) (Mignolo 1995), and racial codification (Quijano 2000).[5]

European Modernism is framed by colonialism and animates an epistemology of ignorance by positioning Anglo-American-Western European culture as a culmination, related to others not internally, but only sequentially and through natural progression. As Anibal Quijano argues: "The Eurocentric version [of knowledge] is based on two principal founding myths: first, the idea of the history of human civilization as a trajectory that departed from a state of nature and culminated in Europe; second, a view of the differences between Europe and non-Europe as natural (racial) differences and not consequences of a history of power" (2000, 542).

The resulting epistemological methodology, Cartesian methodology, while conceived in resistance to centralized religious authoritarianism, is also a practice of ignorance—a methodological inward-turning, promoting cognitive dismissal of all that lies outside its bounds of sense, and resulting in a highly sophisticated Eurocentrism. Within this tradition, an epistemology of ignorance is an everyday strategic practice of maintaining power relations by denying epistemic credibility to objects/subjects of knowledge who are marginalized, written subaltern, erased, criminalized (for example prisoners, homeless women and men, women whom men pay for sex, workers denied documentation, "illegal" immigrants brought in to support big business, women whom men abuse), and thereby denying relationality (Hoagland, 2003).

For example, an Ashkenazi Israeli-American academic woman, making her home in the United States for the last twenty-five years, was on a U.S. grant in Benin, Africa. She sent greetings back to her colleagues in the United States from "Dark Africa." Two of her colleagues challenged

her phrasing and one, from Ghana, offered to provide her with references as to the origin of the concept and why Africans object to it. Ignoring her colleague's offer, the grant recipient instead turned to French
whites in Benin who assured her that the phrase meant nothing more
than a way to distinguish North Africa from the rest of the continent.[6] By
virtue of whom she acknowledged and addressed and whom she ignored,
she was able to ignore the possibility that she is related to the people she
is talking about (and over there to teach), she could ignore the legacy of
Joseph Conrad's *Heart of Darkness* or Freud's "dark continent" as informing her comfort with the greeting, ignore that she has a place formed in
part by this legacy, and ignore that she is choosing to reaffirm it.

In denying relationality, an epistemology of ignorance denies agency,
subjectivity, to the oppressed even within liberal and progressive argument. At a recent conference a white feminist, considering the ways nice
white folks ignore racism, took on the challenge of addressing the stereotype of blacks as lazy. She offered a fine political analysis of social policies
that fail. She went on to argue that even if the stereotype is true for some,
this doesn't mean their kids will be too. She challenged the Moynihan Report (see Bond and Peery 1970) about the Black family, arguing that
there were violent gang members coming from communities with strong
father figures, notably Italian and Jewish. And so on. Working from a
logic of oppression, her arguments acknowledged black victims of white
racism with an explicit moral condemnation. However, the only agents in
her narrative were whites who oppress, and she did not take up the
specter of resistance.

This is one respect in which whiteness theorizing reaffirms white supremacy. It leaves the agency of peoples of color altogether out of the
picture. In this practice, good whites simply act for black victims. White
ignorance and stereotypes about racism are being challenged, but in a
manner that does not hint at the interdependency between the speaker
and those like her who are concerned with social justice on the one
hand, and the resistant practices of victims of racism on the other. Her
analysis does not address the subjectivity of those being defended.

In resistant logic, slaves and masters are interdependent. In resistant
logic, ascriptions of "laziness" invite very different readings. I argued in
Lesbian Ethics, for example, that slaves breaking tools and fluffy-headed
housewives burning dinners were engaging in sabotage. And these different readings of, say, "laziness" include different portrayals not only of
blacks but also of whites, for example, as dupes of our own arrogance.

These different readings involve an epistemic shift. And resistance to
this shift is part of the logic of oppression, part of the methodological
construction of whiteness embedded in an epistemology of ignorance.
Again, that (most) whites walk through the day ignorant of our interde-

pendency with peoples of color is not about the invisibility of whiteness but rather about the denial of relationality through the erasure of peoples of color as subjects.

Ignorance and Ethics from the Logic of Oppression

Some time ago I was in a position to give a very dear friend, an African American lesbian, a rather large sum of money (for us). It was a real treat, and I knew the joy of being able to do this for her. I was excited that I could do it, I knew what it would mean to her, and my actions came from a deep caring. But I kept thinking about my good feelings, and I began to realize that my pleasure and my sense of moral goodness could only emerge if she is in a position to need and so be grateful for my gift. If she and I were on the same level financially and in her position, that is, in a position where receiving such a sum would be an incredible gift, then she would not accept such a sum from me.

That means my sense of self and the pleasure I receive from giving her that money presupposes her poverty in relation to me, always already presupposes the economic inequity. Yes, those engaged in giving are aware of a certain relationship with those they seek to help, aware that their help is important because of the poverty of the Other.[7] But the self they understand to be in relation to those in need is autonomous.[8] I am arguing, rather, that the two are interdependent: *It is not the other person's need that requires our sense of benevolent charity, as ethical treatises suggest, it is rather our sense of benevolent charity that requires the other person's need* (Hoagland n.d., "From Liberation").

While a relationality is invoked, namely responsibility for, it is simultaneously an affirmation of autonomy: the one who needs our help may be dependent, but the one offering is not. In white Christian service agencies for the old, for example, there is a "division into the able and the needy, into the gerontological community and those they view as isolated and lonely" (Macdonald 1991, 136). An old woman is seen as old, and not as a moral agent. She is seen through the category of old as enacted by professionals, as someone to be handled[9] (Hoagland n.d., "From Liberation").

We who are trained in responsibility in imperialist U.S. are trained to take charge (Pratt, Frye, Lugones, Hoagland). We are positioned to act for the other, to represent the other, but never to recognize ourselves as dependent on her. Particularly for white, middle-class women, those moral instincts are part of our socialization into whiteness. Thus we focus on our character and intentions rather than on our relations, and our sense of existence, our subjectivity, thereby appears to be in no way a product of the engagement.

Consider Frank Capra's 1946 film *It's a Wonderful Life*. Actor Jimmy Stewart plays George Bailey, a man about to give up on life until his guardian angel shows him how his town, family, and friends are all the richer for having known him. As Desmond Jagmohan remarked, the Stewart/Bailey character never once considers how his town, family, and friends have formed him, made him possible (Desmond Jagmohan, personal conversation).

As a result, acknowledging relationality can appear to be a choice. At a Midwest Society for Women in Philosophy (SWIP) conference, one white woman gave a nice presentation in which she described women in her community. In discussion, it was noted that no women of color were mentioned or present in her work. The presenter replied that there were no women of color in her community. Challenging this, African American philosopher Jackie Anderson remarked: "When you're white, you don't have to think about your presence when I'm absent. I'm not an addition. I'm always there. But you don't interrogate my absence. You take the absence as a real absence and that it is your choice to include me" (Midwest SWIP, Spring 2004, Minneapolis, Minnesota).[10]

The ethics of ignorance takes a more proactive form when privileged folks are brought face-to-face with their ontological relationality by those structurally subordinate to them, particularly when we are brought face-to-face with the colonial/slavery/genocidal/imperial legacy of our own locus of enunciation. Indeed, within dominant Western logic, the minute the stage is set to expose knowers as ideologically embedded, disciplinarians (scholars and officials) change the subject to ethics. In a counter-quincentenary performance piece, Coco Fusco and Guillermo Gómez-Peña presented themselves as undiscovered Amerindians living in a cage at different exhibition sites. Their work was interactive, focusing on people's reactions. As Coco Fusco and Guillermo Gómez-Peña assumed stereotypical roles of the domesticated savage, "many audience members felt entitled to assume the role of the colonizer, only to find themselves uncomfortable with the implications of the game." As Coco Fusco notes, "The performance exposed the sense of control over Otherness that Columbus symbolizes" (1995, 47, 50).

While the performance was satirical, white Western audiences interpreted the work literally. And when discovering their mistake, rather than taking the opportunity to think about the self exposed, like René Descartes many chose to frame the act as deception. Officials chose an evasive and self-deceptive move, expressing outrage over the fact that they and many members of the viewing public had been fooled. They complained, for example, that the performance was staged not in art galleries but in a place of "truth," namely museums. But this was precisely Coco Fusco's and Guillermo Gómez-Peña's point—to locate their performance exactly where colonial/Western relations were continuing to be performed through museum representation, representation erasing the relationality, erasing the interdependency between those viewing and those exhibited (Fusco 1995).

There are worlds of sense-making purposefully excluded by dominant logic through an epistemology and ethics of ignorance. The problem is not only a lack of awareness when we find ourselves lodged in ignorance, a lack of self-consciousness, for example, an ignorance that is dispensed with by learning the facts and trying to widen our horizons or unlearn certain things. The work involves epistemic and ethical shifts, involves challenging conceptual coercion by denying the denial of relationality, involves embracing engagement and the risks of change that brings, involves entering non-dominant worlds of sense.

II. From the Logic of Resistance

Dominant logic doesn't only work to obscure interdependent relation, it is a practice of conceptual coercion; in significant ways it forecloses the possibility of a destabilizing critical response, recognizing only those responses that reinforce its own status. For example, Tera Hunter notes that white planter society portrayed freed slaves who refused to work under the same conditions they experienced during slavery as lazy, not as self-respecting (1997).

For me, one example of conceptual coercion is Sigmund Freud's work. There is no place for me to speak there; I am only spoken about, even when I'm speaking. I don't care what creative stuff he offered, it was drawn on the bodies of Austrian women abused by their fathers. After first believing the women, as we have learned through his letters, which he had ordered destroyed, Sigmund Freud subsequently chose to create his theory that children and women fantasize rape, making a decision to discredit their testimony, because he could not accept the implications for the social order of patriarchal rule (Rush 1980). Through his practice of knowing, an epistemology of ignorance, Sigmund Freud helped establish the silencing of women . . . at least in relation to men in power; as Nancy Tuana notes, had these women reported being raped by servants, the discrediting would not have occurred (personal conversation). Any objection from women is reincorporated into his construction of women. Sigmund Freud mapped out terrain that, by and within its own framings, is inescapable. This is my rage.

It is to avoid such epistemic coercion that in my work I advocate conceptual separatism. My interest has always been in ways mainstream common sense erases meaning that would destabilize it. The understanding I am after flourishes in María Lugones's work on multiple (not fragmented) realities (Lugones 2003; Hoagland 2004).

There are different logics at work. An epistemology of ignorance from a logic of resistance can involve a refusal to take up the dominant logic and a denial of the relationships it designates, a resistance to animating the self constructed there. One may be interpellated within the dominant logic,[11] but one is not *only* constituted within it. The possibility of sense-making or of resistance is not located solely within the dominant logic. To say one is subordinated, indeed to say one is silenced, is not to say one is passive and unable to respond. *One can be both subordinated and resistant. One can be both silenced and speaking* (Hoagland n.d., "Hate Speech").

Ethics and Ignorance from a Logic of Resistance

Because epistemology and ethics of ignorance as practiced in dominant logic do not only deny interdependent relation but foreclose possibilities of challenge, there are significant differences in practices within marginalized locations, within a logic of resistance. They involve active subjectivity and agency, strategies and practices of moving resistantly within the ignorances of power.

For example, Dwight McBride explores the complex relationship between slave witnesses and those who would receive their testimony. Whites' understanding of slavery functions as public understanding of slavery. Abolitionist literature played to white subjectivity thereby framing and limiting the discourse within which slave witnesses had to fit to be intelligible in publicly protesting slavery. Dwight McBride explores strategies used by Frederick Douglass, Phillis Wheatley, Olaudah Equiano and Mary Prince as they entered hegemonic discourse, as they strategized and became intelligible to and for, white abolitionists.[12] Within abolitionist logic, they are seen only as victims to be interrogated, simply reporting their experiences. They are not understood to be handling their progressive white audience (2001).

Discussing Black womanist ethics, Katie Cannon argues that the ethical premises of autonomy and freedom embedded in the white concept of responsibility were irrelevant for Black women during slavery and segregation. As a result, she argues, "Black women and men, as early as the 1600s, refused to obey the moral precepts held up to them by white Christian slaveholders. They resented the white man's message of docility, which acted to render them defenseless in the face of white violence. Living under a system of cheating, lying and stealing, enslaved Blacks learned to consider these vices as virtues in their dealings with whites" (1988, 76).

Maintaining whites in ignorance about resistant practices is a strategy embedded in an ethics of survival. When there is engagement on the part of those marginalized, enslaved, oppressed, at times resistance will involve a con. Indeed, it is only in imperial cultures that trickery, and the play of engagement, are a threat to power. María Lugones notes that the trickster is central to many non-dominant cultures. And critical skills emerge within the logic of resistance—one can play on others' ignorances. For example, María Lugones can play the Latin American as gringos construct her—stereotypically intense—or she can play the real thing. An Angla who knows nothing of Latina culture will be unable to tell the difference (Lugones 2003, ch. 4). The trickster, the clown, is crucial for dismantling the seriousness of tyranny and the power of privilege, leaving one a fool who persists in a state of ignoring.[13]

To avoid remaining fools, competent practitioners of the dominant logic can work to become critical practitioners. However, those working to enter an ethics of resistance can nevertheless become dangerous, particularly having been ignorant. In Sherley Anne Williams's story of the slave, Dessa Rose, a white woman named Ruth, in coming to know and then befriend Dessa Rose, became dangerous to her as they all plotted and executed an escape. As Ruth came to consider slaves human, she wanted to tell "everyone" (that is, whites) the "truth." Dessa Rose remarks: "Miz Lady . . . thought that if white folks knew slaves as she knew us, wouldn't be no slavery. . . . But it was funny, cause that was the thing I had come to fear most from her by the end of that journey, that she would speak out against the way we seen some of the peoples was treated and draw tention to us. And what she was talking now would sho enough make peoples note us" (1986, 231, 239).

Ruth became dangerous because her understanding and empathy involved what Elizabeth Spelman calls, boomerang perception (1988)— Ruth looked at Dessa Rose and came right back to herself. Ruth's ignorance, even when coming to acknowledge Dessa Rose as human, was the failure to recognize how she herself was constructed in relation to Dessa Rose. As a result, she was not yet particularly competent to enter another world, changing her own relationality, not competent at "playful world travel" (Lugones 2003, ch. 4), and initially not particularly competent to maintain the ignorance of those in power and to keep the secrets of the con. Having been socialized in an ethics of ignorance, she lacked the skills, the virtue, of an ethics of resistance, skills that include promoting the ignorance of those who are in charge.

Epistemology and Ignorance from a Logic of Resistance

From within resistance, one may choose to challenge hegemonic logic on its own terms, to resist within the public transcript. But there are also strategic resistant practices of ignoring the public transcript, that is, of not responding on its terms. These strategies and practices involve hidden transcripts (Kelley 1994; Scott 1990), strategies that can include maintaining the dominator's ignorance and destabilizing the oppressive relationality.

Strategies of manipulation, for instance. Jean-Paul Sartre gives an example of a woman who goes out with a man for a conversation in the middle of which he grabs her hand. She ignores this gesture. All Jean-Paul Sartre can see in her action is bad faith; in fact for him this is a paradigm of bad faith. A woman engages in conversation, a man grabs her hand, she ignores it. They had agreed to a meal and conversation. He changed the articulated parameters of the encounter in favor of an unspoken game she is to know about and subtly acquiesce to but had no part in agreeing to; and she parries his move with a countermove that interrupts (at least momentarily) his coercion (Hoagland, 1999).

From a location of oppression whereby one is designated ignorable while simultaneously encoded as subordinate, one is resisting being (only) the self constituted there, denying dominant relationality. The skills involved, the virtues, include what W. E. B. Du Bois calls double consciousness. There is, for example Uncle Remus's story of B'rer Rabbit, who used his wits by playing on B'rer Fox's ignorance in order to get out of his clutches (Lester 1987; also see Bell 1992). Or slaves who wrote passes for themselves and others to move about off their plantations while whites presumed illiteracy. The skills involve maintaining a critical practice and moving in a resistant logic, rejecting or destabilizing a particular relationality, even while playing into it, by maintaining the ignorance of those who dominate. Denying relationality in this respect, especially while maintaining the ignorance of dominators, denies some of the foreclosures of domination.

Conclusion

Again, it is not as if two groups—slaves, for example, and masters—stand autonomously, independently of each other. Masters are who they are as a result of their engagement with those they name slaves. (And masters can be fooled because they practice an epistemology of ignorance within the logic of oppression.) And slaves are who they are as a result of their engagement with those they resist in power. That engagement is part of our legacy, and that engagement has been described in the public transcript, oppressive logic, as slavish. But from a resistant logic I find a different world and significant sets of skills.

Taking up a flexibility learned of necessity by women of color in dealing with white/Anglo organization of life in the U.S., María Lugones notes complex skillful and creative practices such as the ability to shift from mainstream constructions of life as an outsider to other spaces not

anchored to white racist logic. This flexibility can be exercised resistantly;
it holds liberatory possibilities. To challenge the dominant mapping of
our lives, those concerned with an epistemology and ethics of ignorance
can cross barriers and take up resistant worlds of sense, resist dominant
relationality, understanding another by what María Lugones calls "playful
world travel" (Lugones 2003, 77–78). But if one insists on the public and
counterpublic transcript as the only sense, one promotes both an epistemology and ethics of ignorance within the logic of oppression. For dominant logic must erase resistant logics, render them invisible, render them
nonsense, to maintain its own legitimacy (Hoagland 2002).

A white working-class academic refused to do something asked of her
on the job. Two white working-class lesbians argued about it. One lesbian
saw this as simply doing what others expected working-class people to do.
The other lesbian suggested a different reading: "Why should I try to
please someone who can't be pleased!" In the first lesbian's epistemology,
the only site of understanding is the dominant site wherein working-class
people are expected to perform inadequately in the academy, and to challenge that, working-class people must go out of their way, working twice as
hard. The second lesbian, acknowledging how the dominant logic cir-
cumscribes situations and frames them to privilege certain relationships,
could see the woman through another logic. The first lesbian didn't get it;
she only imagines within dominant discourse, and, more importantly, she
insists on others meeting her there.

We are all positioned to remain loyal in particular ways to relationality framed by ignorances fostered in the logic of oppression; even
when we maintain a double consciousness with regard to our own resistances, we may miss that of those working within different resistant
logics (Lugones 2004, ch. 7). For example, Franz Fanon's ability to
write black women and white women as objects within the play of dominance and resistance between "settlers" and "natives" (1978) is part of
my rage, a rage matched by María Lugones's rage at Mary Daly's ability
to write only Anglo-European women as resisters and threats to patriarchal order while writing African, Indian, and Chinese women as only
victims (personal conversation; see, e.g., Katherine 2000; Sharma and
Bilimoria 2000).

Our practices could be different; we do not have to go for the denial
of relationality and the resulting ignorances of what Elizabeth Spelman
calls pop-bead logic and of fragmentation, but rather take up our interdependency. And we do not have to follow the dominant relationality.
(How many faculty members, for example, when there is trouble in the
classroom, turn to students for help, and how many turn, instead, indeed
can only imagine turning, to the administration or the campus police?

That is, how many of us go up the disciplinary pyramid of power relations when seeking support rather than going sideways or down?[14])

Ultimately, ethics and epistemologies of ignorance come back to relationality, interdependence. Through world travel, border crossing, we can find the conditions for coalition and for expanded subjectivities (Lugones 2000). When there is engagement on terms not countenanced by the dominant logic, then relationality changes and so does who we are becoming. Identities are interactive; our possibilities emerge from within the collectivities we engage. Within these collectivities are the possibilities of the interdependencies of non-dominant differences.

From whom do you seek intelligibility? By whom do you wish to be known? To whom do you give credence by virtue of your response? As spoken word artist e. nina jay writes:

> moviemakers are so clever—they is so clever
> I think about slasher movies
> women in showers and summer camps and motels
> and in beds with boys they hardly know
> I think about how the camera makes me
> feel like I am chasing her too
> I think about how angry I get at her for
> not running fast enough or for falling or
> how they write her character so stupid
> you want to hate her want her to smarten up
> want her to get taught a lesson and I realize
> that I want her to get killed too—
> why should she have done something so stupid—
> didn't she see how dark it was?
> didn't she see that shadow?
> didn't she hear that music?

Afterword

When I presented an earlier version of this chapter—more flowing and minus section heads—María Lugones raised a question in the discussion period I was unable to take in. She began by wondering which logics I am foregrounding and which are in the background and, thinking of Mary Daly's work, I got lost in the metaphor. As the discussion progressed, my mind went blank and I did not absorb most of what was said. I asked her later to tell me more about her concerns and she noted this: I had written an earlier paper on whiteness theorizing which she had read, and my criticism was something of what I mention in this chapter—that whiteness theorizing tends to be solipsistic rather than relational regarding people of color, it fails to address people of color as agents, and it centers whiteness which ipso facto reinscribes white dominance (Hoagland n.d., "We're Not"). She was seeing my work in this chapter as a move away from centering whiteness by moving to resistance, not remaining in dominant logic, the logic of oppression. However, she was concerned that I had not yet moved to complex communication (of which she spoke in her keynote for this conference) (Lugones 2006). It is not that easy, given the epistemology and ethics of ignorance, to simply move into others' worlds of resistance, nor to meet others there.

This chapter suggests that the refusal to travel to marginalized worlds is a practice of ignoring central to an epistemology and ethics of ignorance; it hints at epistemic and ethical shifts necessary to cease reinscribing dominant relationalities through dominant ignoring. But my brief suggestions about becoming critical practitioners of dominant culture, playful world travel, border crossing, and traveling to non-dominant worlds of sense do not take on the extraordinary complexities involved in thinking concretely with others, in the communicative difficulties when going for coalition against oppression not through sameness but through difference.

In working for social justice and to destabilize the dominant ethics and epistemology of ignorance, how is a Latina working-class lesbian graduate student and worker at the Michigan Womyn's Music Festival to engage a white upper-class lesbian animal communicator, and where? How does a middle-aged African American lesbian civil rights activist engage a young African American spoken word artist, and where? How does a middle-class Indian lesbian working with INCITE! engage a white U.S. working-class lesbian working with young girls in the sex trade, and where? How does a gay Jewish upper-class political educator engage a gay Latino political educator organizing in New York City, and where? How does an antiracist Jewish lesbian engage Palestinian peace activists, and where? How does a white lesbian separatist engage a Latina popular educator? And where? And how do academics, *qua* academics, meet any of these people? And where?

Interlude

I read this afterword to Joshua Price, one of the people informing in the previous paragraph and who was one of the presenters at this conference. He objected that he was not just this gay Jewish guy; knowing almost everyone I mention, he argued that designating like this flattens them. Yes, I agreed.

I sit here now, with María Lugones, reading this afterword and describing Josh's concerns, and we recognize, in talking, that categorizing in this way doesn't capture the complexity of communication, that it needs to be complicated. As we talked, we shifted from categories to geographies, spatialities, relations, and as a result, rather than imagine struggling to communicate from distinct categories which can inspire the urge to think in terms of fragmentation and add-on theorizing and to find common ground, we shifted to accessing distinct worlds of meanings in concrete geographies.

We can think of descriptions of folks that get us into very different relationships, meanings, practices, exclusions—relationships which take women into very different worlds of sense. Consider an African American lesbian conversant in the community politics of African American lesbians on the South Side of Chicago which differs markedly from the North Side African American lesbian community in whose politics she is also conversant, not to mention community politics of white lesbian feminists and separatists on the North Side. Consider how she finds folks to talk with. In struggling for social justice in coalition, how might one access her different communities and worlds of meaning in order to engage her?

That is, I need to trouble more than one world of meaning to engage her. It is not as if I am going to an African American lesbian's world of meaning in "playful world travel" and that's going to do it. How do I meet her in the geographies where she makes sense, the spatialities where she's understood? These are the communicative problems requiring competent critical epistemic and ethical skills; and it becomes clear that there isn't an easy door to walk through in order to meet others.

End of Interlude

This is a problem of efforts both of assimilation and of separatism (understood as pure separation [Lugones 2003, ch. 6]). It is as much a problem for those who think there is only one frame of meaning (or only one that matters, that merits acknowledgment) as it is for those who work for a completely separate world of meaning. Both directions ultimately will read other resistors through the dominant logic/categories, and in the process reinscribe dominant relationalities (Lugones 2003, ch. 7).

Charles Mills notes that whites are ignorant of the world we have created (1997). I have been arguing that construction and maintenance of dominant ignorance involve strategic praxis, both from a logic of oppression and a logic of resistance. But another way of putting it is that whites and others in dominant relationalities lack epistemic privilege (conversation with María Lugones). This is not to say that from marginalized positions anyone holds knowledge which no one else has access to; nor is this about standpoint. It is to say that those lacking epistemic privilege *lack* critical abilities. It is to say that as we are materially privileged in particular ways, our epistemic abilities are suspect. It is to say that our abilities of understanding and analysis have been undermined or compromised in key ways as a *result* of our material privileging.

For example, in working collectively with the Escuela Popular Norteña, a popular education school focused in Latino communities, I have come to realize that part of how many white feminists' abilities have been compromised is through our reaction to violence—turning to the state and organized police, legal, and medical forces (see, e.g., Silliman and Bhattacharjee 2002; Shah 1997). We went from grassroots collective action to promoting state intervention. This is an epistemology and ethics of ignorance accomplished through a denial of relationality (Hoagland 2007). For men of color on the other hand, I suspect the compromising of abilities is something quite different.

So I am wanting to think of ways to bring a dissonance, a disbelief that nothing but the dominant logic makes sense, a destabilizing of certainty and hence hierarchal relationality. I'm interested in thinking about ways of opening up, listening, learning from others. This cannot be grasped in theory, separate from praxis and engagement. And it involves not just shifts in attention but also both epistemic and ethical shifts. The questions are not: From whom do you seek intelligibility? By whom do you wish to be known? To whom do you give credence by virtue of your response? The question is: As those concerned with social justice, will we struggle to develop the skills to meet each other as well as others in unfamiliar geographies, spatialities, and *without* boomerang perception, *without* translation?

Notes

I have received invaluable insights and help from Anne Leighton, Jackie Anderson, Alison Bailey, and María Lugones. An earlier version of this chapter was a keynote presentation at the Ethics and Epistemology of Ignorance Conference, Rock Ethics Institute, Penn State University, March 27, 2004. I thank Nancy Tuana and Shannon Sullivan for all of their work in making this conference happen and for encouraging and supporting the work it inspired. I also thank Nancy Tuana in particular for her continuing interest in and support of my work.

1. I am following María Lugones's distinction between competent practitioners of a culture—practitioners who have mastered the dominant culture and fit right in, and critical practitioners of the dominant culture—practitioners who do not take dominant logic at face value (Lugones 2003, ch. 1).

2. For example, unable to hold their own when debating Mexica (Aztec, pronounced "mecheeka") tlamantini (Mexica philosophers or wise ones) over the rationality of their Christian god, Spanish jesuits simply shot them (Dussel 1995, 112). In resistance, Mexica, like Guaman Poma de Ayala (a Mexica noble

used by Spanish colonizers to create maps and write histories of the Mexica), codified much Mexica cosmology in a way that the Spanish could not then recognize but which was thereby preserved and is available to us today (Mignolo 1995).

3. Indeed, most whiteness theory is a conversation among whites to the exclusion of people of color, a veritable continuation of the nineteenth-century practice of training white selves to be good masters—the white anti-racist's burden (conversation with Anne Leighton).

4. For example, in significant respects, whiteness is not invisible to a suburban white woman in her thirties finding herself driving through a black neighborhood in her city.

5. For example, encountering sophisticated and complex civilizations such as the Mexica, the Spanish began replacing the Other in space by the Other in time (Fabian calls this the denial of coevalness [1983, cited in Mignolo 1995]). As a result, cultures existing simultaneously with Spanish culture were rendered less developed (both conceptually and through economic de-development) (Mignolo 1995, xi), and non-Europeans could be considered pre-European and placed on a linear historical continuum from primitive to civilized (Quijano 2000, 556). In this way, creations developed by other cultures—mathematics (Mayan) and agriculture (Incan) for example—could be appropriated and subsequently considered European developments.

6. These same colleagues suggested that U.S. citizens are obsessed with racism. I, too, have come across French whites who evade questions of racism by calling it an American obsession, apparently to avoid the self exposed in their own relation to colonialism and slavery—the French Foreign Legion and Haiti come to mind.

7. Just as I have argued that men who base their identity on being protectors of women require that women be in peril (Hoagland 1988), so I am arguing that those who base their moral identity on being generous require that others be impoverished.

8. This is the problem with the logic of charity and hierarchal relationship—the self that is the One who extends itself downward understands itself as autonomous, independent of the Other, while understanding the Other as needing the One and so dependent. Thus dependency is shunned in dominant logic at all costs, and autonomy admired. And interdependency ceases to be an epistemic reality.

9. Some years ago I was asked to develop a course on ethics and aging. One requirement I included involved students talking over class material with an old person, and I suggested that be someone over 70. The director of the program argued that I should not use age as an indicator because it was arbitrary (which, of course, was my point) and wanted instead to use the concept of frailty. Thus students were to focus on what (middle-age) professionals determine to be the state of being old, namely frail. Moreover, I was also directed to avoid questions of the social construction of old age and ageism and to address only ethical dilemmas that gerontological workers face as a result of their having to handle the old, to ignore ethical dilemmas the old face as a result of their having to be handled by the middle aged in an ageist society. That is, the only ethical agent I

was to address was the caregiver. An epistemology of ignorance is promoted by an ethics of ignorance, an ethics denying relationality.

10. In a class on multiculturalism, I asked students to describe concretely how their situation was multicultural. One white student said she could not do this because there were no people of color in her community. A black student asked her: "When you go to a party, are there ever any racial jokes?" "Yes," she said. "Then there *are* people of color in your community," was the reply. Not only are people of color present, a particular relationality informs the identity of her (white) community.

11. I am here following Judith Butler following Althusser, "Being *called a name* is also one of the conditions by which a subject *is constituted* by language" (Butler 1997, 2).

12. And he notes how Ralph Waldo Emerson came to understand white male subjectivity as a result of its location in the system of slavery—the reckless sense of "authority and autonomy . . . that flow[s] from . . . absolute control over the lives of others" (McBride 2001, 74, citing Emerson).

13. To avoid becoming fools, practitioners of white supremacy as normalcy work to protect themselves from a con while simultaneously asking for one, work to always already know the Other, to avoid responsibility, respons-ability, the ability to respond. The perfect john. And as johns are incompetent lovers, an ethic and epistemology of ignorance from the logic of oppression prepares us to be incompetent, particularly in our inability to engage, to listen to Others, to enter the story (Hoagland 2003).

14. "In an apparatus like an army or a factory, power takes a pyramidal form, but the summit doesn't form the source or principle from which all power derives. The summit and the lower elements stand in a relationship of mutual support and conditioning" (Foucault 1979, 159).

References

Alcoff, Linda, and Libby Potter, eds. 1993. *Feminist Epistemologies*. New York: Routledge.

Aristotle. 1962. *Nicomachean Ethics*. Translated by Martin Ostwald. New York: Bobbs-Merrill.

Austin, J. L. 1970. "A Plea For Excuses." In *Philosophical Papers*, ed. J. O. Urmson and G. J. Warnock, 175–204. London: Oxford University Press.

Beauvoir, Simone de. 1952. *The Second Sex*. New York: Vintage.

Bell, Derrick. 1992. *Faces at the Bottom of the Well*. New York: Basic Books.

Bond, Jean Carey, and Pat Peery. 1970. "Is the Black Male Castrated?" In *Black Woman*, ed. Toni Cade, 113–18. New York: Signet.

Bordo, Susan. 1987. *The Flight to Objectivity: Essays on Cartesian Culture*. Albany: State University of New York Press.

Bulkin, Elly, Minnie Bruce Pratt, and Barbara Smith. 1984. *Yours in Struggle: Three Feminist Perspectives on Anti-Semitism and Racism*. Ithaca, NY: Firebrand Press.

Butler, Judith. 1997. *Excitable Speech: A Politics of the Performative*. New York: Routledge.

Cannon, Katie. 1988. *Black Womanist Ethics*. Atlanta, GA: Scholars Press.

Code, Lorraine. 1993. "Taking Subjectivity into Account." In Alcoff and Potter (1993).

Coronil, Fernando. 1996. "Beyond Occidentalism: Toward Nonimperial Geohistorical Categories." *Cultural Anthropology* 11:1: 52–87.

Crenshaw, Kimberlé Williams, Neil Gotanda, Gary Peller, and Kendall Thomas, eds. 1995. *Critical Race Theory: The Key Writings That Formed the Movement*. New York: The New Press.

Du Bois, W. E. B. 1986 [1903]. *The Souls of Black Folk*. In *DuBois*, ed. Nathan Huggins, 357–547. New York: The Library of America.

Dussel, Enrique. 1995. *The Invention of the Americas: Eclipse of "The Other" and the Myth of Modernity*. Translated by Michael D. Barber. New York: Continuum.

Fabian, Johannes. 1983. *Time and the Other: How Anthropology Makes Its Object*. New York: Columbia University Press.

Fanon, Franz. 1978 [1963]. *Wretched of the Earth*. New York: Grove Press.

Foucault, Michel. 1979. *Discipline and Punish*. New York: Vintage.

———. 1980. *Power/Knowledge: Selected Interviews and Other Writings, 1972–1977*. New York: Pantheon Books.

Frye, Marilyn. 1983. "In and Out of Harm's Way: Arrogance and Love." In *The Politics of Reality: Essays in Feminist Theory*, 52–83. Trumansburg, NY: The Crossing Press.

———. 1992. "A Response to *Lesbian Ethics*: Why Ethics?" In *Willful Virgin: Essays in Feminism*, 138–46. Freedom, CA: The Crossing Press.

Fusco, Coco. 1995. "The Other History of Intercultural Performance." In *English Is Broken Here: Notes on the Cultural Fusion in the Americas*, 37–64. New York: The New Press.

Glissant, Édouard. 1989 [1981]. *Poetics of Relation*. Translated by Betsy Wing. Ann Arbor: University of Michigan Press.

Harmon, Amy. 2004. "Geeks Put the Unsavvy on Alert: Learn or Log Off." *New York Times*, February 5.

Harris, Cheryl. 1995. "Whiteness as Property." In Crenshaw (1995).

Henry, Paget. 2000. *Caliban's Reason: Introducing Afro-Caribbean Philosophy*. New York: Routledge.

Hoagland, Sarah Lucia. 1988. *Lesbian Ethics: Toward New Value*. Chicago: Institute of Lesbian Studies, PO Box 25568. Chicago, IL 60625.

———. 1999. "Existential Freedom and Political Change." In *Re-reading the Canon: Feminist Interpretations of Jean-Paul Sartre*, ed. Julien Murphy, 147–74. University Park: Penn State Press.

———. 2002. "Making Mistakes, Rendering Nonsense, and Moving toward Uncertainty." In *Re-reading the Canon: Feminist Interpretations of Wittgenstein*, ed. Naomi Scheman, 119–37. University Park: Penn State Press.

———. 2003. "Practices of Knowing: Transcendence and Denial of Epistemic Credibility, or Engagement and Transformation." *International Studies in Philosophy* 35:2.

———. 2004. "Walking Together Illegitimately." *Off Our Backs: The Feminist Newsjournal* 34:7–8 (July–August): 38–47.

———. n.d. "Hate Speech, Performatives, and Resistance." Unpublished manuscript.

———. 2007. "Heterosexualism and White Supremacy." *Hypatia: A Journal of Feminist Philosophy* 22:1: 166–85.

———. n.d. "From Liberation to Care . . . Have I Missed Something?: Care, Ageism, and Feminist Ethics." Unpublished manuscript.

———. n.d. "We're Not the Only Ones Here." Paper presented at the Thirteenth Annual Conference, Philosophy, Interpretation, Culture, Binghamton University, April 12, 2003, as well as Midwest SWIP and Central APA.

Hoagland, Sarah Lucia, and Marilyn Frye, eds. 2000. *Re-reading the Canon: Feminist Interpretations of Mary Daly.* University Park: Penn State Press.

Hunter, Tera W. 1997. *To Joy My Freedom.* Cambridge, MA: Harvard University Press.

INCITE. 2000. http://www.incite-national.org.

Katherine, Amber. 2000. "(Re)reading Mary Daly as a Sister Insider." In Hoagland and Frye (2000), 266–97.

Kelley, Robin. 1994. *Race Rebels: Culture, Politics, and the Black Working Class.* New York: The Free Press.

Kusch, Rodolfo. forthcoming. *Indigenous and Popular Thought in América.* Translated by María Lugones and Joshua Price. Durham, NC: Duke University Press. Originally published as *El pensamiento indigena y popular en américa.*

Lawrence, Charles R. III. 1993. "If He Hollers Let Him Go: Regulating Racist Speech on Campus." In Matsuda et al. (1995).

———. 1995. "The Id, the Ego, and Equal Protection: Reckoning with Unconscious Racism." In Crenshaw et al. (1995).

Lester, Julius. 1987. *The Tales of Uncle Remus: The Adventures of Brer Rabbit.* New York: Penguin Books.

Lugones, María. 2000. "Multiculturalism and Publicity." *Hypatia* 15:3: 175–81.

———. 2003. *Pilgrimages/Peregrinajes: Theorizing Coalition against Multiple Oppressions.* New York: Rowman & Littlefield.

———. 2006. "On Complex Communication." *Hypatia: A Journal of Feminist Philosophy* 21:3: 75–85.

Lustbader, Wendy. 1991. *Counting on Kindness: The Dilemmas of Dependency.* New York: The Free Press, Macmillan.

Macdonald, Barbara, with Cynthia Rich. 1991 [1983]. *Look Me in the Eye: Old Women, Ageing and Ageism.* Expanded ed. Minneapolis, MN: Spinster's Ink.

MacIntyre, Alasdair. 1981. *After Virtue: A Study in Moral Theory.* Notre Dame, IN: University of Notre Dame Press.

Matsuda, Mari J., Charles R. Lawrence III, Richard Delgado, and Kimberlé Crenshaw, eds. 1993. *Words That Wound: Critical Race Theory, Assaultive Speech, and the First Amendment.* Boulder, CO: Westview Press

McBride, Dwight. 2001. *Impossible Witnesses: Truth, Abolitionism, and Slave Testimony.* New York: New York University Press.

Merchant, Carolyn. 1990. *The Death of Nature.* San Francisco: Harper & Row.

Mignolo, Walter. 1995. *The Darker Side of the Renaissance.* Ann Arbor: University of Michigan Press.

Mills, Charles W. 1997. *The Racial Contract.* Ithaca, NY: Cornell University Press.

Ortiz, Fernando. 1995 [1947]. *Cuban Counterpoint: Tobacco and Sugar.* Durham, NC: Duke University Press.

Pratt, Minnie Bruce. 1984. "Identity: Skin Blood Heart." In Bulkin et al. (1984).

Price, Joshua. Unpublished manuscript. "Actuarial vs. Participatory Epistemic Paradigms."

Quijano, Anibal. 2000. "Coloniality of Power, Eurocentrism, and Latin America." *Neplanta: Views from South* 1:3: 533–80.

Rousseau, Jacques. 1968. *The Social Contract.* New York: Penguin Books.

Rush, Florence. 1980. *Best Kept Secret: Sexual Abuse of Children.* Englewood Cliffs, NJ: Prentice Hall.

Sartre, Jean Paul. 1956. *Being and Nothingness.* Translated by Hazel E. Barnes. New York: Philosophical Library.

Scott, James C. 1990. *Domination and the Arts of Resistance: Hidden Transcripts.* New Haven, CT: Yale University Press.

Scully, Judith A. M. 2002. "Killing the Black Community: A Commentary on the United States War on Drugs." In Silliman and Bhattacharjee (2002).

Shah, Sonia, ed. 1997. *Dragon Ladies: Asian American Feminists Breathe Fire.* Boston: South End Press.

Sharma, Renuka, and Purushottama Bilimoria. 2000. "Where Silence Burns: *Sati* ("Suttee") in India, Mary Daly's Gynocritique, and Resistant Spirituality." In Hoagland and Frye (2000), 322–48.

Silliman, Jael, and Anannya Bhattacharjee, eds. 2002. *Policing the National Body: Race, Gender, and Criminalization.* Cambridge, MA: South End Press.

Smith, Dorothy E. 1987. *The Everyday World as Problematic: A Feminist Sociology.* Boston: Northeastern University Press.

Spelman, Elizabeth. 1988. *Inessential Woman.* Boston: Beacon Press.

Takaki, Ronald T. 1993. "Aesculapius Was a White Man: Race and the Cult of True Womanhood." In *The Racial Economy of Science*, ed. Sandra Harding, 201–209. Bloomington: Indiana University Press.

Tuana, Nancy. 2004. "Coming to Understand: Orgasm and the Epistemology of Ignorance." *Hypatia: A Journal of Feminist Philosophy* 19:1: 194–232

Williams, Sherley Anne. 1986. *Dessa Rose.* New York: Berkeley Books.

CHAPTER 6

Managing Ignorance

Elizabeth V. Spelman

James Baldwin's searing indictment of white America in *The Fire Next Time* begins with this vivid declaration:

> [T]his is the crime of which I accuse my country and my countrymen, and for which neither I nor time nor history will ever forgive them, that they have destroyed and are destroying hundreds of thousands of lives and do not know it and do not want to know it. (Baldwin 1993, 5)[1]

Baldwin offers several explanations for such ignorance. First, and most generally, he remarks that "For the horrors of the American Negro's life there has been almost no language" (1993, 69); the absence of such language threatens the availability of understanding even to those who have experienced the horrors. But even in the case of nameable and articulable horrors, he insists, "White America remains unable to believe that Black America's grievances are real; they are unable to believe this because they cannot face what this fact says about themselves and their country" (Baldwin 1985, 536). Moreover, they have immunized themselves from the kind of criticism that might correct their misunderstandings. After all, "the white world is threatened whenever a black man refuses to accept the white man's definitions" (Baldwin 1993, 69). Moreover, "there is simply no possibility of a real change in the Negro's situation without the most radical and far-reaching changes in the American political and social structure. And it is clear that white Americans are not simply unwilling to effect these changes; they are, in the main, so slothful have they become, unable even to envision them" (Baldwin 1993, 85).

Baldwin is claiming, in short, that whites do not have but also do not want to have knowledge of the injuries they inflicted through slavery and the other expressions of racism so manifest in the everyday lives of black

119

Americans; that whites lack awareness of and interest in what it is about
them and their institutions that has wreaked such havoc in the lives of
blacks; and that they have not developed the imaginative skills that would
allow them to envision a world in which such horrible powers would have
been tamed. About such failures of knowledge and awareness and imagination, Baldwin remarks: "But it is not permissible that the authors of
devastation should also be innocent. It is the innocence which constitutes the crime" (Baldwin 1993, 5–6).

Ignorance, as Baldwin hopes to drive home to his readers, is at least
sometimes an appalling achievement; managing to create and preserve it
can take grotesquely prodigious effort. And where there are costs and
benefits associated with what one knows or doesn't know, with what one
wants to know or doesn't want to know, ignorance is likely to need management. Baldwin's provocative claims invite us to explore some of the
strategies deployed and the stakes involved in managing ignorance.

I

What is the nature of the ignorance that Baldwin has so vividly described? Baldwin has said that there is something whites are unwilling to
believe, namely, that black America's grievances are real. We can put
Baldwin's argument crudely but perhaps helpfully in the following way,
letting g be "Black America's grievances are real," and letting W be the
rhetorically conceived white American that Baldwin has in mind[2]:

> (1) W does not believe that g is true and does not want to believe that
> g is true.

W's not wanting to believe that g is true suggests that W has some worries
that g might be true; indeed, on Baldwin's view, W has fears that were g
true, this would have unbearable implications for his understanding of
himself and his country. So though W does not believe g is true, W is not
quite sure g is false, which in turn suggests that:

> (2) W does not believe that g is false but wants to believe that g is false.

We might regard (1) and (2) together as an elasticized version of Baldwin's claim that whites are unwilling to believe that black America's grievances are real. Such unwillingness to believe that g is true means neither
simply that W does not believe g is true nor that W believes g is false (nor,
then, that W has in some sense willed to believe that g is false). If he really
did believe g was false, he wouldn't have to be so vigilant about immuniz-
ing himself, about trying to ensure that he won't have to countenance evidence that might point to g's being true.

W's ignorance involves not a simple lack of knowledge of g nor the embrace of a false belief about g (the false belief that g is false). W ignores g, avoids as much as he can thinking about g. He wants g to be false, but if he treats g as something that could be false, then he would also have to regard it as something that could be true. Better to ignore g altogether, given the fearful consequences of its being true. Better not to have thought at all than to have thought and lost. W is quite happy about not believing g is true but unhappy about not believing g is false. Ignoring g, not thinking about it, allows W to stand by g's being false, to be committed to g's being false, without believing g is false.

W has a complicated propositional attitude, as it is sometimes put, toward both (a) g is true and (b) g is false. Such attitudes often are quite complex, especially when the stakes involved in having or not having them are high. To take an example briefly from another context, Carolyn Betensky has offered a particularly perspicacious exploration of such complexity in her analysis of the place of ignorance in Frances Trollope's 1840 novel *The Life and Adventures of Michael Armstrong, the Factory Boy*. Trollope's book focuses on a manufacturing class family that takes a young factory worker under its wing. Part of what Trollope does, according to Betensky, is raise questions about who, among the characters in the novel (and among the likely readers of the novel), has or doesn't have, should or shouldn't have, and wants or doesn't want to have knowledge about the conditions of factory workers.

> *Michael Armstrong* divides its manufacturing-class characters into camps: there are those who know what is happening to the workers and hide this information from others, those who do not know and do not care to know, those who know but do not want to know, and those who do not know but want to know and who stand up against those who would keep them from knowing. (Betensky 2002, 67)

In her reading of the novel, Betensky aims to show how different degrees of sympathy and varying amounts of moral credit attach to the novel's characters according not only to what they know but how they feel about what they know, and what, if anything, they intend to do about it. For example, in the case of a central set of characters—the wife of a callous manufacturer and her children—Betensky remarks that their "lack of a will to know [about the condition of workers in the manufacturer's factory] drains off the moral capital they are initially invested with in their depiction as comely innocents" (Betensky 2002, 67).

Returning to the case at hand, think of the range of attitudes or postures one might have toward either or both of the claims, that g ("Black America's grievances are real") is true, and that g is false. One might be thoroughly ignorant of, not even aware of, such a claim or claims, or aware of a claim but indifferent to it, so indifferent as not to have a belief or desire about it. One could believe it is true or believe it is false. One could not quite believe it yet want to believe it, or not quite believe it and hope one does not come to believe it; or, for that matter, believe it but not want to believe it or disbelieve it but not want to disbelieve it.

W (Baldwin's rhetorical conceived white American) does not believe and does not want to believe that g is true, and W does not believe but wants to believe that g is false. W's wanting to believe that g is true—wanting to believe that it is just false that blacks' grievances are well founded—does not eventuate in W's believing that g is false. That means that whatever else Baldwin is saying about W, he is not saying that W is self-deceived. For whatever else self-deception involves (and there is considerable disagreement about some of its features),[3] it certainly involves having a false belief (otherwise there is no deception). But W is in the interesting position of neither believing that g is true nor believing that g is false, and so of having neither a true nor a false belief about g's being true or false. What Baldwin accuses her of is not self-deception but ignorance. Unwilling to think about g's being true or false, W ignores g. That is different from being ignorant of g. If W were ignorant of g, it would be odd to describe her as not wanting to believe that g is true or wanting to believe that g is false. W's wanting g to be false is not a matter of taking up g's being true or false as a matter of belief, as a matter of something for which evidence is a relevant consideration. W does not think about whether g is true or false. And yet she is hardly indifferent to its being true or false. Her ignoring g allows her to stand by g's being false, to be committed to g's being false, without believing that g is false.

Indeed, as Baldwin sees it, white America's ignorance of—or rather ignoring of—these matters is rooted in such deep fear and bewilderment that whites on the whole have rendered themselves incapable of freeing themselves from it. And yet, Baldwin insists, "We [blacks] cannot be free until they [whites] are free" (Baldwin 1993, 10)—that is, black liberation cannot be achieved until whites come out from under the yoke of such ignorance. Indeed, Baldwin adds, not only the lives of blacks but also of the nation blacks share with whites[4] depend on removing "the masks [whites] fear [they] cannot live without and know [they] cannot live within" (Baldwin 1993, 95). The fear connected to removing the mask of ignorance has to do with the implications of W taking seriously the idea that blacks might have grounds for grievance; and yet at some level, Baldwin implies, W knows about the costs of living with such ignorance but cannot be counted on to know how to lead herself out of it.

What or who will lead W out of ignorance? As we saw earlier, Baldwin alludes to the necessity for "the most radical and far-reaching changes in the American political and social structure" (Baldwin 1993, 85). But he also proposes that it falls to blacks to "make America what America must become" (Baldwin 1993, 10). And they will do this, Baldwin says, motivated neither by hatred nor forgiveness but by a pity-laced love that "shall force our brothers to see themselves as they are" (ibid.).

Baldwin doesn't provide much detail about this black-led white exodus from ignorance, but there is no doubt about the central point he wishes to make in this connection: that there is, there has to be, a way out of the destructive ignorance of which he accuses white America. Indeed, if there is anything hopeful in his analysis, it is that exit is possible (though of course many whites, and many blacks, may disagree, not necessarily for the same reasons, with either or both his prognosis and his proposed remedy). One plausible route to undoing such ignorance would seem to be to understand the labor it takes to create and sustain it. To one such set of labors we shall shortly turn our attention. But before we do, it is important to point out that the very nature of the ignorance Baldwin attributes to white America and the cultural context in which he made such attributions suggest that he had a particular slice of white America in mind.

Recall Baldwin's charge of criminal ignorance against white America: ". . . the crime of which I accuse my country and my countrymen" . . . is "that they have destroyed and are destroying hundreds of thousands of lives and do not know it and do not want to know it" (Baldwin 1993, 5). In my interpretation of this charge, I have said that W, the rhetorically conceived white American of whom Baldwin speaks, does not believe that g is true—does not believe that black America's grievances are real; but neither does he believe that g is false. Now there surely are white Americans (Baldwin had to face them with unrelenting regularity) who believe that g is false, for example, members of explicitly declared white supremacist groups who not only believe that black grievances are unfounded but do so in the very face of, with knowledge of, the destruction of black lives which W, Baldwin has said, does not know and does not want to know. The doxastic profile of S, the rhetorically conceived white supremacist, shares only some of the features of W's doxastic profile:

Like W (the rhetorically conceived white American),

(3) S does not believe that g ("Black America's grievances are real") is true and does not want to believe that g is true.

But unlike W,

(4) S does believe that g is false.

In W's case, her not wanting to believe that g is true has to do with her not being able to face the consequences of its truth for her understanding of herself and her country. Revelations of the truth of g, of the history of white destruction of black lives, Baldwin seems to be suggesting, would be shameful to W.[5] S *might* be ashamed if he were to believe that g is true, but S has no doubt that g is false. One important reason for the strength of his belief is that he does not read the history of white destructiveness of black America as grounds for black grievance. Explicitly embracing the view that whites are superior to blacks, S has a much higher threshold for shame than W when it comes to white/black relations. Thus S does not have to ignore the question of whether g is true or false. Unlike W, S is not prepared to take the history of white destruction of black life as evidence for the truth of g. S is not among those who, in Baldwin's words, "have destroyed and are destroying hundreds of thousands of lives *and* [emphasis added] do not know it and do not want to know it" (Baldwin 1993, 5). In S's case, only some of the conjuncts hold: S is among those who partake in the destruction, but S not only knows it but wants to know it; indeed he celebrates it.

Earlier I described the white American about which Baldwin speaks as "rhetorically conceived." Baldwin has a rumbling prophetic voice, and sometimes uses bold broad brushstrokes to bring attention to the perilous state in which he finds the nation. I don't think Baldwin would deny that there are at least some white Americans who neither ignore the question of whether black grievances are real nor doubt they are real, but W is not among them.

In this connection it is notable that the specific charge lodged here by Baldwin does not involve the attribution of racism but of ignorance. This is not to say that the two are not connected, nor that he does not treat them as being connected. In fact, the kind of ignorance of which Baldwin accuses W helps define a kind of cowardly form of racism that puts W somewhere between whites who take racism to be a moral stain upon and a social and political disaster for the nation, and whites who believe that America belongs to whites and are prepared to do whatever it takes to make it that way. It seems clear that Baldwin takes W to be morally much closer to the latter group (constituted by the likes of S, discussed earlier) than to the former (of course these three groupings hardly exhaust the possibilities). The kind of ignorance about which Baldwin is concerned is closely related to his view that "a civilization is not destroyed by wicked people; it is not necessary that people be wicked but only that they be spineless" (Baldwin 1993, 55). Writing in the mid-1960s—albeit always with an eye to U.S. history—Baldwin presumably could see, in committed white civil rights workers, on the one hand, and in indefatigable white resistance to civil rights, on the other, examples of whites who had the courage of their convictions. As worried as Baldwin was by the latter group (or for that matter by certain limitations in the former), the whites who seemed the object of his caustic scorn were those who avoided having convictions, who managed ignorance. I am not suggesting that Baldwin did not think that explicitly declared white supremacists were ignorant in some sense or other but that he was in the main not writing about them or to them. What most seems to concern Baldwin is the spineless ignorance of those whites who do not really want to know about the lethal history and presence of white racism. It is not even so much that they know and don't care, but that they don't care to really know.

Part of the rhetorical force of Baldwin's accusation of ignorance is the variety of ways, in *The Fire Next Time* and other texts, in which he undermines the presumption of whites' superiority to blacks. They include Baldwin's assumption of the authority and power of himself as a black man to forgive or not forgive whites, and the exercise of that authority and power in the refusal to forgive ("the crime . . . for which neither I nor time nor history will ever forgive them" [Baldwin 1993, 5]), and his withering portrait of whites as basically confused, bewildered, pathologically fearful beings, in need of a pitying love from those who have acquired the knowledge necessary to lead them out of their dangerously pathetic state, that is, from the very blacks who have suffered so grievously because of them. In a similar way Baldwin turns the racial tables in exercising the epistemic and moral authority to describe whites as suffering from fear-induced ignorance. But it would have been simplistic to focus his charges on those people his readers, especially his white readers,[6] would recognize as explicitly declared white supremacist groups or iconic bigots. That might do something to turn the racial tables, but it would let W off the hook, allow W to think that Baldwin is talking about people W already thinks are ignorant, whose fierce bigotry W may safely regard as paradigmatic of such ignorance—it would allow W to think that Baldwin is not talking about *her*. It is as if Baldwin anticipates an inclination in his likely white readers to write off the ignorance of which he speaks as something characteristic of *other* whites—people in whom Ws as a group may have a special investment seeing as their less educated and morally impoverished fellow citizens of the poor and working classes. Baldwin aims to dash any hopes such whites might have of adding to their moral capital (to use the phrase so well deployed by Betensky) by not being white supremacists or bullying bigots.

There is an old saw that "what you don't know can't hurt you," often with the suggestion (even if not the logical implication, strictly speaking) that what you *do* know *can* hurt you, that knowledge can be harmful. In her reading of Trollope's *Michael Armstrong*, Betensky explores a kind of aesthetic and social harm thought threatening to upper-class women were they to come to know about the condition of factory workers. There

are some things ladies just shouldn't know: being a lady is not simply
compatible with but requires certain kinds of ignorance. On the other
hand, given the same class structure under scrutiny in Trollope's novel,
the alleged ignorance of the poor and working classes is among the traits
that mark them as inferior to the better-educated classes (though part of
that education is learning what one can or ought to be ignorant about).
In short, depending on the context, ignorance can count in one's favor
or as a mark against one. People are rewarded or punished for what they
know or do not know, want to know or do not want to know, and because
of that they may well have an interest in the management of their own
and others' ignorance. Management of such ignorance is both an individual and a social labor. The timid wives of cruel manufacturers in Trollope's *Michael Armstrong* are rewarded by members of their class for not
wanting to know but criticized by Trollope for their lack of such desire.

What are the rewards or punishments for the kind of commitment W
(the rhetorically conceived white American) has to not knowing—for W
individually and for Ws as a group? Audre Lorde famously asked, "What
are you paid for your silence?" What does W hope to be paid for her ignorance? What does she hope to gain from it? Baldwin has suggested
that W will not then have to take under consideration what presumably
she would regard as ugly claims about herself and her country (and her
regarding these as ugly is one of the things that distinguishes W from S,
the rhetorically conceived white supremacist). Baldwin took a few tenta-
tive steps toward describing the labor it would take to undo such ignorance. U.S. history provides us with vivid and instructive examples of why
and how W manages to create and sustain it.

II

The decades after the Civil War in the United States provide a host of examples made almost to order in support of Baldwin's claim about white
America's ability to manage ignorance by inoculating itself against inquiry into and knowledge of the horrors of white racism. The particular
examples I have in mind have to do with some of the efforts to repair the
damage inflicted by that war and the effective erasure of history that such
repair managed to achieve (whatever else repair entails, it typically
involves some degree of erasure).

The damage from the war took many forms. For one thing, of
course, there was enormous injury to persons and property: to soldiers
and civilians North and South; to roads and buildings, particularly in the
South, where cities such as Richmond and Atlanta lay in ruins. The war
also delivered a blow to the social and economic order of the South. And
it represented the fact that slavery had come to be a divisive issue among

nonslaves—that (in the words of historian Eric Foner) it had "divided the nation's churches, sundered political ties between the sections [North and South], and finally shattered the bonds of the Union" (Foner 1990, 1). This meant that among the repair jobs facing Americans was finding some way to mend the ever-deepening rift between factions that can be described variously (though the distinctions are not extensionally equivalent) as Confederate and Union; pro- and anti-slavery; Southern and Northern; Democratic and Republican; white and black. Reconstruction, in Foner's words, was the "central problem confronting the nation" (Foner 1990, 33); some kind of reconciliation seemed to be called for, given that, as historian David Blight has put it, "the whole social fabric needed healing and rebuilding" (Blight 2001, 129).

It is by now widely agreed among historians that such efforts at reconstruction and reconciliation in the end failed to put much of a dent in the white domination of every dimension of American life. Such domination, having been constructed, needs regular maintenance and repair; and though white domination surely was not destroyed by the war, it seemed to suffer some more than glancing blows. So the agents of white domination needed to do more than the ordinary amount of maintenance and repair work on it.[7] Blight's recent book illuminates a moment in the repair schedule of white domination in which the labor of ignorance plays a major role.

What Blight describes as a postwar "culture of reconciliation" was manifest in particularly clear form in reunions of Union and Confederate soldiers and in the pages of widely read journals and magazines. At a major reunion in Gettysburg in 1913, fifty years after the end of the war, President Woodrow Wilson, insisting that it would be an "impertinence to discourse upon how the battle went, how it ended," that it would not be appropriate to comment on "what [the war] signified," went on to embrace and feed the reconciliationist spirit:

> [The last fifty years] have meant peace and union and vigor, and the maturity and might of a nation. How wholesome and healing the peace has been! We have found one another again as brothers and comrades, in arms, enemies no longer, generous friends rather, our battles long past, the quarrel forgotten—except that we shall not forget the splendid valor, the manly devotion of the men then arrayed against one another, now grasping hands and smiling into each other's eyes. How complete the union has become and how dear to all of us, how unquestioned, how benign and majestic, as state after state has been added to this, our great family of free men! (Blight 2001, 11)

The *Louisville Courier-Journal* gushed, "God bless us everyone, alike the Blue and the Gray, the Gray and the Blue! The world ne'er witnessed such a sight as this. Beholding, can we say happy is the nation that hath no history?" (Blight 2001, 9). By this point reconciliationists had put decades of concerted effort into "banish[ing] slavery and race from the discussion" of the war (Blight 2001, 107). For example, during the period 1884–1887, *Century* magazine published article after article meant to help readers make sense of the war; but as Blight points out, "A reader looked in vain for any discussion of the causes or consequences of the war"; about the issues of slavery and race the editors and their writers were "resoundingly silent" (Blight 2001, 175), out of conviction that bringing up such impolitic matters would undermine the careful, fragile work of reconciliation.

That such reconciliation was purchased at the price of real racial reconciliation and genuine, lasting emancipation was not lost on African Americans such as Frederick Douglass. He had a very robust sense of emancipation, insisting that it should lead to blacks' full membership in "the great national family of America," and that the work of the nation "does not end with the abolition of slavery, but only begins" (Foner 1990, 12, 34). The Civil War was destined, he had urged, "to unify and reorganize the institutions of the country," to achieve "National regeneration" (Blight 2001, 18). But he was also insistent that such reorganization and regeneration could not take place if black life and liberty were not secured. As he saw it, the point of the war and Reconstruction was to allow the nation to be "entirely delivered from all contradictions" (Blight 2001, 43), and yet the calls for sectional reconciliation were predicated on forgetting that such contradictions had existed and continued to exist. As Blight has put it: "While black life and human rights were so insecure, Douglass resented what he called 'this cry of peace! peace! where there is no peace'" (Blight 2001, 123). Douglass was appalled by what he derided as a "great love feast of reconciliation" (Blight 2001, 127). He had a strong sense that for the vast majority of Northern and Southern whites in the 1870s—even those who had been staunch allies in the abolitionist and Radical Reconstruction movements—peace among them was much more important than thinking about blacks' lives and liberties, healing among whites more crucial than justice for blacks. As Douglass remarked in 1875: "If war among the whites brought peace and liberty to the blacks, what will peace among the whites bring?" (Blight 2001, 132).[8]

These are just a few of the highlights of the richly detailed case Blight makes about how a powerful politics of national reconciliation—that is, reconciliation between white Northerners and white Southerners, white Union soldiers and white Confederate soldiers—ended up requiring that "America's bloody racial history was to be banished from consciousness" (Blight 2001, 205).

Though a call for reconciliation cannot be made without reference to some kind of rift or renting—otherwise what is the need for the call?—and though, therefore, reconciliation cannot be consciously achieved without alluding to and thus threatening to keep fresh the very damage it hopes to mend, there was considerable success in securing reconciliation among whites while erasing or keeping invisible[9] the gaping racially related wound reconciliation was supposed to heal. It was, Blight urges, as if the warring parties could only come together again as a healed nation if they didn't mention that what they fought over was among other things the condition of the slave. This is, after all, part of the pernicious logic of white solidarity: such solidarity would not have been possible if whites had differed over the proper treatment of blacks. Reconciliation between groups of whites formerly at war could not be achieved if the question of black and white equality were kept in the fore; it required, instead, notions of the rough equality of the North's and South's past wrongdoing, of the North's and South's suffering, of the valor of soldiers in the North and South, and of the North's and South's economic prospects—descriptions of the war requiring that all moral and political judgments differentiating between the former factions be suspended.

This meant in effect that the repair of the nation—or rather of relations among the white portion of the nation's population—required dashing or dampening the prospects of a real transformation of the conditions of life for ex-slaves. Let's forget that spat we had—or in any event only remember it in such a way that we also just forget about the people over whose freedom we fought. "The national reunion required a cessation of talk about causation and consequence [of the war], and therefore about race. The lifeblood of reunion was the mutuality of soldiers' sacrifice [i.e., white soldiers' sacrifice] in a land where the rhetoric and reality of emancipation and racial equality occupied only the margins of history" (Blight 2001, 191–92). Healing for whites required ignoring the claims of justice for blacks (Blight 2001, 3).[10]

Let us return now for a moment to Baldwin: "White America remains unable to believe that Black America's grievances are real; they are unable to believe this because they cannot face what this fact says about themselves and their country" (Baldwin 1985, 536). Blight's complex narrative makes clear to us the work it can take to achieve such an inability, to create and to sustain ignorance of this sort. In order for reconciliation among formerly warring whites to be possible, Blight has told us, "America's bloody racial history" had to be "banished from consciousness." Following along lines I suggested earlier, let's try describing the kind of ignorance created and sustained by such banishment in the following way, letting c be "The Civil War involved fierce debates over slavery and race," and letting R be the white reconciliationists:

(5) R does not believe that c is true and does not want to believe that c is true.

Again, R's not wanting to believe that c is true suggests that R has some worries that c might be true (indeed, if Blight is correct, one of the big worries R had about c being true is that its being true, or rather its being believed to be true, could not help but undermine white solidarity after the war). This in turn suggests that

(6) R does not believe that c is false but very much wants to believe that c is false.

R's ignorance, as suggested earlier, following a lead implicit in Baldwin, is to be understood as an unwillingness in R to believe that c is true—yet an unwillingness that means neither simply that R does not believe that c is true, nor that R believes that c is false. R's not thinking about c allows him to stand by c's being false, to be committed to c's being false, without believing it is false.

Blight's careful work enables us to see how such commitment is developed and sustained. First of all, we can see why it makes sense to be cautious about saying that R believes c to be false: if R did in fact believe that, then why would the very thought of c have to be banished from consciousness? We also can see why the commitment was felt to be so important—on it seemed to hinge the possibility of reconciliation among whites after the war. Blight's account shows how such commitment is created, expressed, and sustained. President Wilson's speech expressed but also helped build a commitment to c's being false, as did the writers for *Century* and the reconciliatory white soldiers. It is a commitment that is driven not by the force of arguments about the truth or falsity of c but indeed arises out of the need to keep such arguments out of mind's way. It is a commitment the value of which is warranted by similar commitments from others and the fruits of being loyal cocommunicants in the House of White Solidarity. What is shared is not a *belief* subject to warrant or nonwarrant but a *commitment* subject to approval or disapproval, encouragement or discouragement, support or abandonment. Such commitment both sustains and is one of the dividends promised by the management of ignorance.

Notes

Many thanks to Frances Foster and Martha Minow for careful critical readings of earlier drafts, to Monique Roelofs for catching the baby on its way out with the bathwater, and to Shannon Sullivan and Nancy Tuana for the opportunity to start whittling away at my ignorance of ignorance.

1. Portions of the first two paragraphs here on Baldwin are reproduced from chapter 4 of Spelman (2002).

2. For the information of readers unfamiliar with standard philosophical format, here and later I use uppercase letters to refer to persons (e.g., W, S) and lower-case letters to refer to propositions (e.g., g, c). W's profile is explored in more detail later.

3. For a recent discussion see Mele (2001).

4. In *The Fire Next Time* Baldwin is concerned with relationships between blacks and whites, and among blacks. He does not address relationships between blacks, or whites, and other groups within the United States.

5. Baldwin says nothing to suggest that he would describe W as unconsciously believing g, or otherwise "really" believing g but being unaware of doing so.

6. The first section of what came to be *The Fire Next Time* was published in the *New Yorker*, the second in *The Progressive*.

7. It is against the background of the unceasing maintenance and repair of white supremacy that the current movement for reparations to black America for slavery and its continuing legacy must be seen.

8. Such questions were very much on the mind of W. E. B. Du Bois some decades later—another part of the story not addressed here.

9. There is a difference between invisible mending—fixing something to look as if it has never been torn—and trying to keep a wound invisible and thereby unavailable for mending.

10. Blight describes Ku Klux Klan hearings held in 1871, during which "ordinary freedmen, public officials, poor white farmers, Klansmen, and former Confederate generals came before federal officials and described, or evaded, what the war had wrought"; the kind of reconciliation proposed between North and South was predicated on avoiding the "mountain of ugly truths" produced by such hearings (Blight 2001, 117).

References

Baldwin, James. 1985. *The Price of the Ticket.* New York: St. Martin's Press.

———. 1993. *The Fire Next Time.* New York: Random House.

Betensky, Carolyn. 2002. "Knowing Too Much and Never Enough: Knowledge and Moral Capital in Frances Trollope's *The Life and Adventures of Michael Armstrong, the Factory Boy.*" *Novel: A Forum on Fiction* 36:1: 61–78.

Blight, David. 2001. *Race and Reunion: The Civil War in American Memory.* Cambridge, MA: Harvard University Press.

Foner, Eric. 1990. *A Short History of Reconstruction 1863–1877.* New York: Harper & Row.

Mele, Alfred. 2001. *Self-Deception Unmasked.* Princeton, NJ: Princeton University Press.

Spelman, Elizabeth V. 2002. *Repair: The Impulse to Restore in a Fragile World.* Boston: Beacon.

Part II

Situating Ignorance

CHAPTER 7

Race Problems, Unknown Publics,
Paralysis, and Faith

Paul C. Taylor

I

This chapter has given me no end of trouble. It is perhaps fitting for a discussion about ignorance that the source of this trouble remained opaque to me for quite some time. It is perhaps as fitting that it eventually revealed itself as a kind of ignorance—ignorance of the unexcavated deposits that certain deep and, I had thought, uprooted commitments had left in me.

Despite this difficulty, I was eventually able to do most of the work that I had planned. I was able to highlight the epistemic dimensions of a pragmatic or radical constructionist account of race and indicate the role that such an account might play in banishing a kind of social ignorance in and around the United States. Those thoughts will take up the next three sections of this chapter, which we might think of (but will have no further occasion to refer to) as a postpositivist realist theory of racial identity (Moya and Hames-Garcia 2000).

The remainder of the chapter will explore the thoughts that came to me as I tried, and failed, to carry further the opening argument about racial identity. Certain steps in the argument led me into impasses that I had not anticipated. I will try to find these moments of blockage and hesitation instructive, principally by tracking them to their affective and existential sources and by tracing out their impact on the production and maintenance of social ignorance. I do not expect to say anything radically new in these sections; I hope only to offer a series of interconnected reminders and warnings about the various challenges that complicate the task of social inquiry.

II

Contemporary U.S. society systematically promotes social ignorance. That is, it encourages its citizens and other participants—on whose behalf I will henceforth speak of "we" and "us"—not to know things that are profoundly important for the ethics, politics, and administration of social life. (I repeat: It *encourages* us not to know. Many of us nevertheless find out, in displays of determination that I will have no further occasion to credit, for reasons of expository convenience, in my references to "our" ignorance.) All sorts of institutions and agents invite or pressure us to accept doubtful propositions as true, to ignore the actual effects and conditions of our conjoint conduct, to neglect the institutions by means of which we might conduct meaningful social inquiry, and to act on the basis of tendentious pictures of the social world.

As a student of Dewey and Du Bois, which is to say, as a pragmatist and a race theorist, I am particularly interested in certain cases of social ignorance. These are the ones, very broadly speaking, in which race thinking encourages us in our will not to know, thereby blinding us to the suffering that results or may result from certain policy choices. Here, in no particular order, are some examples:

We act as if race serves as an adequate proxy for criminal dangerousness. Under certain circumstances we call this racial profiling. But we can reasonably indulge in this practice only if we ignore at least three important considerations: that public safety officials can access more reliable indicators of criminality with relatively little cost; that charging and sentencing biases routinely distort criminal records and other "markers" of criminality; and that class and race inappropriately structure many individual encounters with the justice and corrections systems, thereby shaping one of the favored signs of a criminal predisposition—the criminal record (Kennedy 1998).[1]

We assume that undocumented immigrants swarm across our borders uninvited, drain our public resources, and contribute nothing to society. But we can sustain these beliefs only if we ignore the evidence that immigrant workers, including undocumented workers, pay more in taxes than they receive in social benefits (Porter 2005; Fix and Passel 2001) and if we look away from the symbolic and duplicitous politics that makes a spectacle of policing borders while tacitly allowing employers to hire inexpensive undocumented labor (Andreas 2001).

We think of Arab and Muslim cultures as inexplicably and uniquely proficient at spawning terrorists, perhaps because of some primordial tendency to "militancy," "radicalism," or premodern conservatism. But this view makes sense only if we ignore a handful of important historical and cultural facts. First, neither Muslims nor Arabs have a monopoly on terrorism, as the history of white supremacy, the Central Intelligence Agency (CIA), and the birth of Israel will show. Second, since the fall of the Ottoman Empire, and most evidently in the context of Cold War politics, Western countries have had a non-negligible role in creating the modern "Middle East" (Friedman 1990; Ali 2003; Fromkin 2001). We have supported and sometimes installed conservative and otherwise repressive regimes, and we have supported and trained radical Islamist fighters, both of which are significant factors in the emergence and consolidation of terrorism as a political technique (Bass 2003; Ali 2003). And third, due in part to the unfortunate history to which I have just alluded, the significant Muslim traditions that insist on tolerance, free thinking, and human rights have been overwhelmed on the ground and overshadowed in popular perception (Sen 2000).

In each of these cases, we effectively agree not to know some quite important things about our social world and the people in it. Sometimes this means accepting manifest falsehoods, and sometimes it means declining to engage in inquiry that seems likely to reveal some claim as a falsehood. Either way, unfortunate social realities, realities that we might refer to as "ignorance-related injustices," remain in place.

When stakeholders in a democracy decline to consider factors that might materially affect their policy choices, then we need some explanation. We might appeal to the predictable apathy of a population blessed with the basic material comforts; or to the possibility that what seems to be a democracy is really a polyarchy, governed by elites who benefit from and encourage a disengaged citizenry; or to the citizenry's awareness of and rational response to the structural obstacles to truly effective political participation; or to a cultural tendency to historical myopia. But in my three initial cases, some part of the explanation should surely appeal to our now-familiar ideas about how racial stereotypes do their work. Deepseated racial assumptions make it easier for us to assume that certain people are dangerous or lazy or fanatical: racial myths make it easier for us to ignore the complex realities that our fellows inhabit and represent.

III

We have just seen how race thinking can function as an ignorance-generating mechanism. Racialized assumptions about the worth and capacities of human individuals run parallel to and reinforce racialized habits of regard and disregard. The result is that we circumscribe our networks of care, concern, and goodwill in ways that allow us to mistreat others and ignore their suffering.[2]

Interestingly, though, race thinking can also help *banish* social ignorance: it can help us block the formation, consolidation, and maintenance

of ignorance-related injustices. Of course, only some forms of race thinking can do this work. The older forms—call them, collectively, classical
racialism—led people to believe that nature has sorted humanity into distinct and hierarchically ranked types, each with its own complement of
physical, moral, and mental traits. Many people spilled a great deal of ink
and, especially in the nineteenth century, measured a great many skulls
and other body parts in the attempt to give this belief the imprimatur of
scientific validation. As Stephen Jay Gould (1996) and others have shown,
these attempts did little more than reveal classical racialism's great efficiency and productivity at generating ignorance. But certain forms of *critical* racialism have emerged since the decline of the classical paradigms,
and they can be more defensible and useful. I mean in particular to rec-
ommend a view that I call radical constructionism (Taylor 2004).

A radical constructionist holds that races are populations of people
who are similarly situated vis-à-vis certain mechanisms of social stratification, mechanisms that asymmetrically distribute social goods in ways that
track our commonsense racial distinctions. More succinctly and only a little imprecisely, each race comprises people who stand in similar relations
to the stratifying mechanisms of white supremacy. On this account, races
work in social theory the way centers of gravity work in physics: both are
posits that allow compact and perspicuous renderings of the workings of
certain forces, forces that we can describe at lower levels of abstraction
only with considerable difficulty. On this account, a person's racial identity is a counterfactually specifiable information-bearing trait. To know
that Betty is black is to know that she would have had to ride the Jim
Crow car in 1940s' Georgia; to know that Tom is Asian is to know that he
would have been prevented from achieving naturalized citizenship or
even, typically, from entering the country between 1880 or so and the
1960s. And to know these things is to know that the people of whom different counterfactual claims are true tend to have different life chances
even now. For example, and other things being equal, some people are
likely to have a greater store of net financial assets than others, and some
are likely to get better loan terms than others. Some are more likely than
others to commit or suffer criminal victimization, and some are more
likely than others to be charged if arrested, convicted if tried, and given
a stiff sentence if convicted.

The method of radical constructionism, then, involves identifying
the patterned differences between individual social locations by linking
bodies and bloodlines to a conjunction of probabilistic and statistical social markers. This approach infuses the familiar form of race thinking
with slightly less familiar content. "Race" is, as many people have pointed
out, a fluid and historically variable concept. But its central function
across all of these historical variations has been to assign generic mean-

ing to human bodies and bloodlines. Before the 1950s or so, people overwhelmingly assigned these meanings in ethical and factual error: it just is not the case that hair texture and skin color covary with moral worth or intelligence. But now, after advances such as the birth of genetics and the maturation of sociology, we can assign these meanings in responsible ways that pick out important social patterns. It just *is* the case that we distribute social goods in ways that create discernible patterns, and that these patterned distributions mark the boundaries of definite, if fluid, populations. And—once more, to be clear—we can call these populations "races" because doing so does the theoretical work that modern racial discourse has always required of its basic concept: it assigns deeper generic meanings to human appearance and ancestry.

To say all of this is nearly to say that races are what John Dewey referred to as "publics" (1954 [1927]). They are populations of people who collectively suffer the consequences of conjoint social actions. Dewey pointed out that the rise of industrial capitalism left publics too often inchoate: people are too often unaware of the ways in which they share common cause with others. So 2,000 people may develop cancer from a toxin introduced to their living environment by a single factory but never know of each other until an enterprising trial lawyer unites them for a class action suit. Similarly, Korean, Chinese, and Japanese immigrants to the United States may experience similar kinds of anti-Asian racism but decline to think of themselves as sharing anything—for quite good reasons, mind you—until an enterprising pan-Asian activist brings them all together to respond to the murder of Vincent Chin.

This Deweyan account reveals the unavoidably epistemic—which of course is not to say *entirely* epistemic—burden of democratic politics in the industrial and postindustrial era. The challenge is to make publics self-aware and active, to end our ignorance of our common suffering. Remaining true to democracy as a form of life requires that we refine the techniques for identifying, uniting, and mobilizing those people who are affected by the far-reaching consequences of the increasingly globalized conjoint actions that constitute contemporary life.

In a similar way, connecting Dewey's publics to a version of critical racialism reveals the unavoidably—and again, not entirely, or even mostly—epistemic burden of racial politics. Some of the conjoint actions that give contemporary life its distinctive shapes asymmetrically burden the people we would pretheoretically think of as members of certain races. So making publics aware of themselves means making these races aware of themselves—not as cultural groups or as national units but as sets of individuals who are similarly situated vis-à-vis the mechanisms of social stratification. It means making individuals aware of the conditions that people with bodies and bloodlines like theirs are likely to face in the social world, conditions of which they ought to be aware as they chart their paths through life.

The comparison with Dewey's account of inchoate publics helps clarify the distinct contribution that radical constructionism might make to critical racialism. And discussing this contribution helps make clear the relevance of this argument for a discussion of social ignorance. The position that I have briefly described might seem quite familiar: it closely resembles the idea that race talk is a useful tool for identifying the victims of racism. There is a long tradition of this practical racialism, stretching from the nineteenth-century African American convention movement (Glaude 2000) to the debate over Ward Connerly's "racial privacy" movement (Taylor 2004). When Connerly proposes to bar state governments from keeping track of racial statistics, his opponents rightly argue that those statistics allow us to determine the compliance rate for antidiscrimination laws, and that depriving ourselves of these statistics will block us from obtaining important knowledge about how society is functioning. Here we can already see the utility of race thinking for social inquiry and the relevance of these issues for a discussion of social ignorance.

While radical constructionism adopts the motivating insight of this practical racialism, it goes even farther, in two ways. First, radical constructionism is a perspective on racial metaphysics, that is, it is a way of insisting that races are real, even though there are no biological races. So the claim is not just that race talk is useful, it is that race talk is useful *because the world is populated by things that we have good reasons to think of as races*. The people I have called practical racialists tend to remain agnostic on this ontological point, to the detriment, I think, of their linguistic proposals. (It is hard to urge people to use racial discourse while also conceding that doing so means trafficking in illusions or fantasies.) Luckily, it is possible to be more ambitious, and more consistent, than this. To put the point a bit hastily, in pragmatic language that I do not have space to defend, good inquiry tells us what kinds of entities to accept into our ontologies. This is, in a way, the point of scientific investigation. Banishing our ignorance about the social world—*Who are the people in our prisons? Oh, look, they are overwhelmingly black and brown people*—reveals what Daniel Dennett in another context refers to as real patterns, in just the way that talk of centers of gravity does. And if centers of gravity are real then races are too. (Yes, this is a decent-sized "if," but discussing that issue would exceed the scope of this chapter. Suffice it to say that I think centers of gravity exist, and that it is odd to have to say so.)

The first advance that radical constructionism makes over practical racialism, then, is its insistence on racial discourse as a truth-generating, ignorance-banishing, theoretical vocabulary with metaphysical implications. The second advance has to do with the nature and provenance of the patterns that race talk identifies. The claim is not just that explicit, conscious, and pernicious racial discrimination makes race talk useful. It is that there are institutional and systemic forces that systematically reproduce inequalities across generations; that this continues to happen even after the abolition of *de jure* racism; and that this phenomenon has arguably more impact on life chances than conscious racism. Think of the long-term effects of distributing social goods along racial lines, from cheap Western land—or, for that matter, the ability just to own property—in the nineteenth century to favorable home mortgage terms in the twentieth. Both of these policies favored whites, and both give their recipients a decades' long head start in the creation and accumulation of wealth. The inequalities that result distinguish the life chances of nonwhite peoples from their white counterparts at every income level, in ways that are impervious to the recent achievement of formal equality. We too often ignore facts such as these in our haste to celebrate, for example, the growing black middle class, and this insistence on unknowing leads us to ignore the broader social forces that distort the distribution of social goods. Radical constructionism helps us avoid this by focusing, as we saw earlier, on the social patterns that these patterned inequities create, and on the probabilistically defined social locations that result from them.

IV

We might see more clearly how this appeal to radical constructionism might work by considering an additional case. I am thinking of the latest coup in Haiti, completed in the spring of 2004, and of Colin Powell's casual dismissal of the claim that U.S. forces kidnapped President Aristide and spirited him out of the country. This is a paradigm case of the social production of ignorance, not because it is so obvious that the United States behaved as Aristide said it did, but because it is not obvious that it *did not* behave that way, and because no one in power seems—*seemed*, I guess, since it has receded so far into the background of its public agenda—to have the slightest interest in conducting the investigations needed in order to find out.

Few people in the United States saw any need to investigate Aristide's claim; it struck most Americans as, in Powell's words, an "absurd" accusation. But this response is available to so many, and available for Powell to foment, only because we willfully embrace a thoroughgoing ignorance about the history of U.S. interventions in Latin America and the Caribbean. Anyone who knows anything about the history of, say, the Monroe Doctrine and the Roosevelt Corollary, or, for that matter, of the CIA, has to find Powell's dismissal absurd.

This sort of obscurantism infects our deliberations about Haiti quite easily, thanks principally to long-standing racialized myths about dark people being backward and unfit for self-governance. It is true that Haiti's leaders have often governed poorly, but that alone has not afflicted the country with poverty and political unrest. The United States and other Western countries have contributed mightily, beginning with France's insistence on being compensated for lost colonial property, including owned humans, that was expropriated during the freedom struggle. The European imperial powers, wary of a free black republic in the new world, isolated the island nation from the beginning, adding to its unethical start-up debt an artificially circumscribed vista for economic growth. And U.S. imperial and Cold War policy led to several rounds of colonial and neocolonial intervention in the twentieth century, with direct occupation between 1915 and 1934, and Cold War client regimes after that. These interventions structured Haiti's government and economy in ways that were more congenial to the needs of outsiders than to the needs of citizens, a trend that continued under the hegemony of western-dominated international financial institutions, such as the International Monetary Fund (IMF) and the World Bank.

Classical race thinking encourages us in our ignorance of this history. It enables us to rely, tacitly or expressly, on the assumption that black folks cannot be expected to govern themselves properly. And this allows us to explain failed, flawed, or troubled black states without appealing to any factors outside of their native incapacities—which is to say, the incapacities of the natives.

On the other side, though, critical race thinking, especially of the radical constructionist variety, enjoins us to return to the forgotten histories and contexts of new world African politics. Black people, radical constructionism reminds us, are among the peoples that Western culture routinely depicts as unfit for self-governance. Degrading myths of black laziness and irrationality intertwine with honorific myths of white civilization and civilizing missions, and these myths collectively motivate utterly unsatisfying accounts of real social problems and phenomena. Consider this line from the "Haiti" entry at the Infoplease reference Web site:

> After a succession of dictatorships a bankrupt Haiti accepted a U.S. customs receivership from 1905 to 1941. Occupation by U.S. Marines from 1915 to 1934 brought stability. Haiti's high population growth made it the most densely populated nation in the hemisphere. (Pearson Education 2002)

A literary critic could have a field day with this, but I will say just a few things. First, to say that Haiti "accepted" a customs receivership completely fails to capture the geopolitical context of U.S. gunboat "diplomacy." Second, the nineteen-year occupation may have brought stability but it also brought forced labor, a constitution rewritten for the benefit of U.S. business, and the loss of Haitian sovereignty. Third, what in the world does population growth have to do with anything else in the passage? Why mention it—other than to complete the familiar picture of Negroes as not just being incapable of self-government but also hyper-fertile? (It may be worth mentioning that Infoplease is run by the largest educational publisher in the world, which owns the Prentice Hall imprint as well as *Financial Times* and Penguin Putnam publishers.)

One need not be a radical constructionist to interpret this passage critically, but the radical constructionist emphasis on inquiry and patterns does make it easier to cultivate the habit of critical interpretation. Black, brown, and yellow peoples around the world have been overwhelmingly subject to practices such as gunboat diplomacy, and the diplomats have traditionally described their interventions with rhetoric about stability and failed governance. These patterns stand out if one is in the habit of looking for patterns. Sometimes narratives, events, or images emerge that seem to fit the pattern—like a coup that topples a leftist leader whose sanity U.S. leaders have publicly challenged, and whose progressive economic policies they gave less publicly undermined. On these occasions, radical constructionism encourages us to be skeptical, to inquire further, and to realize that doing otherwise might mean conceding to a familiar mechanism for generating ignorance.

Of course, I am not claiming that racial myths are the only factors that sustain our ignorance on matters of grave social import. We certainly have to consider the eclipse of journalism by infotainment, the U.S. government's traditional obscurantism about its foreign policy, the unfortunate partiality of our standard measures of policy success (such as the Dow Jones average and GDP), and the Bush administration's unusual determination to block social inquiry into the consequences of its actions. My point is just that race thinking can join these other factors in blocking the road to inquiry, and that critical race thinking can reopen this road.

There is more to say about the role that radical constructionism might play in banishing social ignorance, but at this point we should pay more attention to the various conditions under which social ignorance takes root and grows. While I have spoken entirely of institutional and discursive conditions, other kinds of conditions, existential and volitional, can be just as important and much more immediately affecting. My attempt to recruit Haiti into the argument has made this clear to me.

V

Sometimes I find myself provoked into odd counterfactual assertions. After hearing a politician's homophobic rant, I say, *If I were gay, I would be angry all the time.* Or after watching Puerto Rican athletes compete in international competition, as if the island "commonwealth" were not a dependent U.S. possession, or colony, in all but name: *If I were Puerto Rican. . . . It must be intolerable,* I think, *to live under these conditions.*

Of course, there are plenty of potentially intolerable situations. The people in them learn to tolerate them, to get on with their lives while maintaining, if they are emotionally skilled enough, a healthy but not debilitating sense of outrage. Some of them fight against the intolerable, which means learning to live with it while insisting that no one should *have* to live with it, *and* while trying to see to it that no one does. This is a delicate balancing act, one that we might begin to capture with Cornel West's language of revolutionary patience (1988) or with his insistence on the tragicomic sense of life (West and Gates 1997).

My counterfactuals indicate my distance from the intolerable situations in question. They do more than this, of course, or so I hope. They express my sympathy with the affected parties, as well as my awareness of a cause to which I might contribute. But they also reveal that I am not forced to confront the intolerable in just these forms.

Marrying a Haitian woman and beginning to raise a Haitian American child completely collapsed my distance from the intolerable Haitian situation. For the first time, I had to attempt this tragic balancing act in connection with the travails of these particular people. I had to cultivate a sense of righteous outrage, somehow shorn of any self-consuming bitterness, rage, or despair. And I had to do this while facing up to the depressing persistence of the disturbing social patterns. Once again, as in Guatemala, Chile, and elsewhere, people with at least financial ties to the United States were crucial participants in a coup that removed a popularly elected (but still deeply flawed) leftist leader.[3]

I knew that these kinds of things happened, and I knew, more or less, how they happened, and why right-thinking people should object to them. But I had been forced into a new way of experiencing what I knew. Once more, to put it in pragmatic terms that I will not defend: I had been forced to *have* an experience that I had only previously accepted truths about. I had found something like revolutionary patience in dealing with other intolerable situations, including the ones that condition African American strivings in the United States. But this newly expanded area of immediate ethical concern upset the balance that I had achieved between the prerequisites for despair and outrage and the imperative of continued functioning and productive engagement.

Suddenly, or not so suddenly, philosophizing about the production of ignorance seemed a profoundly idle task. I could not make myself put pen to paper or face the empty computer screen. I could not think of anything to say that could do justice to, or lessen, the enormity of the struggle to which I meant to be contributing.

VI

I am tempted to trace this speechlessness, this inability to act in the mode appropriate to a philosopher and academic, to a crisis of faith. Shaken faith, as a kind of object loss, can lead to disappointment, despair, and debilitation. And I find that there are deep faiths in play here.

Engaging in public moral deliberation is an act of faith. One stakes oneself on the audience's receptiveness and goodwill, on the ability of words, of information, to illuminate and persuade. Du Bois ascribes a version of this faith to himself in one of his autobiographies. He says, "I regarded it as axiomatic that the world wanted to learn the truth and if the truth was sought with even approximate accuracy and painstaking devotion, the world would gladly support the effort." He believed further that "when the truth was properly presented, the monstrous wrong of race hate must melt and melt quickly before it" (Du Bois 2002, 603, 760).

I took up philosophy because of my adherence to a faith like this. Some part of me, early on, generalized Du Bois's axiom to all situations involving politics and social ethics. I believed that the key to correcting society's moral errors lay in making public the nature of the errors and the alternatives to them. I thought, in what now strikes me as an odd leap, that philosophizing was a way to do that.

This optimism about moral discourse lost its appeal for Du Bois when he learned that a lynched black man's knuckles were on public display at a nearby store. Nothing as dramatic as that knocked the scales from my eyes. I just realized over time that injustice issues not just from what the optimistic Du Bois thought of as "ignorance and deliberate ill-will" but also from deeper sources in the structures of discourse, in the habits and practices of embodied existence, and in political economy. This was a turn to what Susan Bordo refers to as systemic critique, which attempts to uncover, identify, and connect the causal factors that conspire, on many different levels, to create and maintain problematic social realities (Bordo 1995, 31–32).

The turn to systemic critique bears on the problem of social ignorance in at least two ways. First, it contributes to our inventory of ignorance-generating mechanisms. Du Bois's early optimism can, as he put it, obscure the role of unreason in human affairs—the role of structural factors and passions in the production and reproduction of injustice.

Second, and more important just now, the turn to systemic critique highlights the ineliminable role of social inquiry in moral agency. For the optimist, the first step toward social change is to give reasons, to persuade. For the critic, such as Marx or Foucault or even Dewey, reasoning and persuasion occur on a terrain already shaped by power relations, prejudices, myths, ideologies, passions, and neuroses—all of which require excavation and analysis. For the optimist, moral argument assumes something of an ideal speech situation, distinguished by enough common ground and goodwill for people to recognize and respond to the pursuit of moral truth. For the critic, moral argument must begin by revealing the ways in which communication and collective deliberation have been systematically brought up short of the ideal.

VII

Trying to philosophize about Haiti has forced me to uproot the last vestiges of my early faith in moral optimism. Perhaps better, philosophizing about Haiti has reminded me that optimism is not an enemy for the critic to vanquish once and for all. It is, rather, a perennial temptation, one for the critic to fight off, repeatedly.

Insisting on the permanence of struggle, even against one's own demons and bad habits, pulls against another optimistic faith that I brought to philosophy. Political philosophy, of the right sort, presupposes that there is some point in struggling against injustice: one must believe that the cosmos is not, in some sense, essentially unjust. Some part of me once adopted a version of this faith by imagining a kind of end point, a moment of shining victory beyond which justice would forever reign. More sober parts of me resisted this but still imagined a trajectory of continual improvement, of upward progress toward a just ideal. It goes without saying that these are differently utopian sensibilities, and I wish it could go without saying that I have since excavated and sought to chasten them. But I wonder if they had subtly reasserted their hold over me sometime before my encounter with Haiti. I wonder if some part of my despair over the continuing crisis grew out of the tension between my utopian impulses and the dreary, repetitive reality of U.S. foreign policy.

I am admitting here to a kind of political optimism or millenarianism. I believed on some level that the point of struggle was to finish off injustice, to achieve or steadily approach a final reconciliation of human needs, desires, and conditions, at least in some particular domain. As with the optimist about moral deliberation, forcing the political optimist to see the world soberly practically guarantees a period of profound unsettlement. *If evil cannot be vanquished once and for all*, it seems reasonable to say, *then what is the point? If we are not even making steady progress, if the same things keep happening*—sometimes with the same people behind them, as in the current administration's recycling of the likes of Otto Reich and John Negroponte—*then why bother fighting?*

The answers to this mode of despair are pretty straightforward and clearly related to the problem of social ignorance. We might say first of all that the correct response to a depressingly persistent and persistently depressing situation is to ask whether we have engaged with it as intelligently as we might have. Here the paralysis of despair can be self-deluding, an indulgent alternative to discovering—which is to say, banishing ignorance about—our own shortcomings and possibilities for improvement.

We should note secondly that the millenarian approach can obscure the small but significant victories that come from continued struggle. Howard Zinn (2003) reminds us of a time when picketing the White House to protest the Vietnam War might have seemed futile, since it did not end the war. He then goes on to point out that the hubbub apparently helped Nixon decide against using atomic weapons. Similarly, the Innocence Project may not have succeeded in abolishing the death penalty, but it has saved many lives. Food pantries have not ended the problems of poverty and hunger, but they have helped many families survive particularly lean times. If we look only for the ultimate victory, then we may blind ourselves to the nearer goals that we can reach. In addition, we should not forget that victories once won have to be preserved. Even truly democratic forms of life, if any were ever to exist, would require continued care.

VIII

Philosophizing about Haiti helped me detect and uproot yet another form of optimism. In addition to the discursive and utopian faiths mentioned so far, I found myself committed to a kind of communitarian faith, to a kind of optimism about the grounds for and reasonable extent of social trust.

Society works only if it possesses sufficient social capital (Putnam 2001). This is a property that societies possess to the extent that they have social networks marked by cooperation and reciprocity. These networks emerge and function properly only if we trust others: only if we can believe, often enough, that other people intend to safeguard our interests—even if they do so only out of their own self-interest (Hardin 2004). Sometimes we can justify this trust with good enough reasons: the teacher returns our children to us at the end of the day unharmed and edified; the grocer or restaurateur furnishes us with food that does not harm us; the pharmacist fills our medicine bottles with the prescribed chemicals, not with poisons. But participating in a large enough social entity, such

as a large social movement or a continent-spanning republic, fairly requires that our trust ascend to the level of faith. Especially in an age of
prostrate media, pliant regulators, and prosperous lobbyists, we act in
Pauline fashion on the evidence of things unseen, on the assurance of
things hoped for, when we assume that our federal representatives actually represent average citizens, or that multinational corporations actually
care about the health or happiness of any ordinary individual.

This social faith assures us that trust in our basic institutions is warranted and rewarded. And like the other faiths we have considered, it
can blind us to important realities. It can encourage us to ignore the
utter indifference with which corporations typically regard the well-being
of real people, as well as the corrosive effects of this and other social conditions on our democratic prospects. It can blind us to the malfeasance
of our fellows and our leaders, and to the manifest fact that the occu-
pants of offices on which we would like to bestow our trust—like cabinet
secretaries in presidential administrations—do not by virtue of their
position automatically become trustworthy.

This blindness can be particularly damaging in the United States,
where federal officials become vehicles for the expression of the timeless
idea of America. America is supposed to be a seamlessly benevolent force
in the world, a place where soldiers do not abuse prisoners or bury the
bodies that represent collateral damage in mass graves; a place that supports freedom and democracy over repression and dictatorship. Many people are deeply committed to the values of freedom and democracy and to
the idea that the United States might help instantiate these values around
the world. But many more take it on faith that the United States just does
instantiate these values, with the result that they lose the ability to notice
the instances in which the American reality ceases to live up to the ideal.

When confronted with the charge that prisoners had been abused
while in U.S. custody, Defense Secretary Rumsfeld and others responded
that such behavior was un-American and, hence, highly unlikely. (Notice
that this is still more circumspect, and epistemically responsible, than
Powell's claim of absurdity.) Once again, the history of U.S. intervention
in Latin America undermines this inference, what with the myriad ties
between repressive military governments, brutal U.S.-backed insurgen-
cies, and the recently renamed School of the Americas at Fort Benning,
Georgia (Ireland 2004; Gill 2004). But our tautological commitment to
American moral righteousness, our need to believe that the officials we
trust are in fact trustworthy, and our inattention to history all conspire to
prevent us from being sufficiently critical and curious.

I was surprised at Colin Powell's hasty dismissal of Aristide's kidnapping
charge, and I was surprised at my surprise. I did not think, and do not think,
that I trusted Powell in any deep way. But I could still feel the disappoint-

ment of having someone I ought to be able to trust prove unreliable. (Here I finally begin to feel the force of Kant's claim that "[t]he non-resisting subject must be able to assume that his ruler has no *wish* to do him injustice" (1991 [1793], 84). I feel the force, I should say, of the "must.")

IX

Ever since I stopped talking about radical constructionism, I have been speaking in almost religious terms. My inability to philosophize about Haiti, to dispassionately apply to Haiti the critical race theory that I began by recommending, followed, I have decided, from crises of faith. I diagnosed myself as still affected by certain forms of optimism: optimism about moral deliberation, about the trajectory of political or liberatory activity, and about the warrant for social trust. The recent coup in Haiti, and the U.S. response to it, made my optimistic commitments explicit by undermining them. And in so doing, it reminded me of the volitional and existential obstacles that faith and shaken faith can lay across the path of inquiry.

Faith can produce ignorance by replacing the will to pursue truth with the conviction of inviolate truth attained. Shaken faith can produce ignorance by replacing the will to know with debilitation, disappointment, and despair. One might feel, some part of me once felt, that the world must be a place where reason can by itself move people to right conduct, or where justice can win a final victory, or where our leaders tell us the truth and the United States is a seamlessly benevolent influence on the world. *The world just has to be this way*, we say, those of us who have had the right sort of grounding in the Western tradition, or else the ground of our social being will vanish from beneath us.

But the problem here has less to do with accepting problematic faith claims than with interpreting indispensable faith claims in problematic ways. In order for social life on the liberal democratic or social democratic model to work, we must believe that reason and deliberation can have roles in social change, we must believe that the universe is not essentially unjust, and we must believe that we can trust at least some people, some of the time. The challenge is to hold these faiths in the manner prescribed by Wittgenstein's philosophy of religion. On this approach, faith is not a report of facts but an expression of passionate commitment; it is a way of regulating for all in our lives. Faith claims are, to switch metaphors and thinkers, the stars we steer by rather than the destinations we expect to reach.

With this in mind, I remind myself that faith issues most saliently not in conviction but in action—or, better, and in terms borrowed from Dewey's philosophy of religion (1986 [1934]), that it issues not in convictions about facts but in the conviction that certain ends ought to reign supreme over conduct.[4] I remember that a faith in the utility of moral discourse leads us not to rely solely on words but to use words to recruit allies in struggle and to provide them and ourselves with guiding analyses and existential sustenance. (Is this why we speak of "moral support"?) I remember that faith in the efficacy of struggle leads us not to anticipate final victory but to adopt a tragic sense and to work toward small victories that we know might never come. And I remember that the faith in others that we call trust is not a license for naïveté but an indispensable and defeasible tool for creatures bound to social life.

Notes

1. See also (Cole 2000) and (James 2002).

2. This way of putting the point draws on Glen Loury's (2003) account of reward and development bias and on the contributions by Jorge Garcia and Adrian Piper (in Boxill 2001).

3. The International Republican Institute and the National Endowment for Democracy have provided substantial financial support for elite opposition in Haiti and Venezuela. See Chomsky (1993) and Pina (2003).

4. "[T]here is a difference between belief that is a conviction that some end should be supreme over conduct, and belief that some object or being exists as a truth for the intellect. Conviction in the moral sense signifies being conquered, vanquished, in our active nature by an ideal end; it signifies acknowledgment of its rightful claim over our desires and purposes. Such acknowledgment is practical, not primarily intellectual" (Dewey 1934, 15).

References

Ali, Tariq. 2003. *The Clash of Fundamentalisms: Crusades, Jihads, and Modernity.* New York: Verso.

Andreas, Peter. 2001. *Border Games: Policing the U.S.–Mexico Divide.* Ithaca, NY: Cornell University Press.

Bass, Warren. 2003. *Support Any Friend: Kennedy's Middle East and the Making of the U.S.–Israel Alliance.* New York: Oxford University Press.

Bordo, Susan. 1995. *Unbearable Weight.* Berkeley: University of California Press.

Boxill, Bernard, ed. 2001. *Race and Racism.* New York: Oxford University Press.

Chomsky, Noam. 1993. *Year 501.* Cambridge, MA: South End Press.

Cole, David. 2000. *No Equal Justice: Race and Class in the American Criminal Justice System.* New York: New Press.

Dewey, John. 1954 [1927]. *The Public and Its Problems.* Athens, OH: Swallow Press.

———. 1986 [1934]. *A Common Faith.* Volume 9 of *John Dewey: The Later Works.* Edited by Jo Ann Boydston. Carbondale: Southern Illinois University Press.

Du Bois, W. E. B. 2002. *Writings.* New York: Library of America.

Fix, Michael, and Jeffrey Passel. 2001. "U.S. Immigration at the Beginning of the 21st Century." The Urban Institute home page. <http://www.urban.org/url.cfm?ID=900417>.

Friedman, Thomas. 1990. *From Beirut to Jerusalem.* New York: Anchor-Random House.

Fromkin, David. 2001. *A Peace to End All Peace: The Fall of the Ottoman Empire and the Creation of the Modern Middle East.* New York: Owl Books-Henry Holt.

Gill, Lesley. 2004. *The School of the Americas.* Durham, NC: Duke University Press.

Glaude, Eddie. 2000. *Exodus: Religion, Race, and Nation in Early Nineteenth-Century Black America.* Chicago: University of Chicago Press.

Gould, Stephen Jay. 1996. *The Mismeasure of Man.* New York: Norton.

Hardin, Russell. 2004. *Trust and Trustworthiness.* New York: Russell Sage Foundation.

Ireland, Doug. 2004. "Teaching Torture." Alternet Web site. Accessed July 22, 2004. <http://www.alternet.org/rights/19313/>.

James, Joy. 2002. *States of Confinement: Policing, Detention, and Prisons.* New York: Palgrave-Macmillan.

Kant, Immanuel. 1991 [1793]. "On the Common Saying: 'This May Be True in Theory, but It Does Not Apply in Practice.'" In *Kant: Political Writings,* ed. H. S. Reiss, 61–92. New York: Cambridge University Press, 1991.

Kennedy, Randall. 1998. *Race, Crime, and the Law.* New York: Vintage.

Loury, Glen. 2003. *The Anatomy of Racial Inequality.* Cambridge, MA: Harvard University Press.

Moya, Paula, and Michael Hames-Garcia, eds. 2000. *Reclaiming Identity.* Berkeley: University of California Press.

Pearson Education. 2002. *Haiti.* Information Please Web site. <http://www.infoplease.com/ipa/A0107612.html>. Accessed April 18, 2005.

Pina, Kevin. 2003. "Is the U.S. Funding Haitian 'Contras'?" *The Black Commentator* 36:3 (April). <http://www.blackcommentator.com/36/36_guest_commentator.html>.

Porter, Eduardo. 2005. "Illegal Immigrants Are Bolstering Social Security with Billions." *New York Times,* April 5.

Putnam, Robert. 2001. *Bowling Alone.* New York: Simon and Schuster.

Sen, Amartya. 2000. "East and West: The Reach of Reason." *New York Review of Books* 47:12 (July 20): 33–39.

Taylor, Paul C. 2004. *Race: A Philosophical Introduction.* Cambridge: Polity.

West, Cornel. 1988. *Prophetic Fragments.* Lawrenceville, NJ: Africa World Press.

West, Cornel, and Henry Louis Gates. 1997. *The Future of the Race.* New York: Vintage-Random House.

Zinn, Howard. 2003. *A People's History of the United States, 1492–Present.* New York: HarperTrade.

CHAPTER 8

White Ignorance and Colonial Oppression

Or, Why I Know So Little about Puerto Rico

Shannon Sullivan

I am not much of a basketball fan, but news of the first round defeat of the United States men's basketball team in the 2004 Summer Olympic Games caught my attention. The United States was trounced (92–73) by the Puerto Ricans—a stunning loss for a heavily favored team that was composed of some of the top professional basketball players in the National Basketball Association (NBA). But what struck me was the particular team that defeated the United States. I was not surprised that an underdog could be victorious but rather that, given my vague knowledge that Puerto Rico is somehow part of the United States, a country effectively could be beaten by itself in the Olympics. How could Puerto Rico field its own team, separate from the United States? Perhaps I was wrong that Puerto Rico was still part of the United States; perhaps an independence movement had taken place of which I was unaware. This seemed doubtful, but I could not otherwise explain the existence of a separate Puerto Rican team. And so I found myself stymied by the question, what exactly is the relationship of Puerto Rico to the United States?

The short answer, I now know, is that Puerto Rico is an "insular area" or unincorporated territory of the United States that was granted a limited form of self-government in 1948, the same year that the International Olympic Committee recognized Puerto Rico as sufficiently independent to participate separately in the Olympic Games (Dryer 2004). But there also is a longer, more complicated answer that involves the United States' past and present status as a (neo)colonial power. That answer is related to at least three other questions: why do I and many other white people in the United States tend to know so little about the United States' relationship with Puerto Rico, how does that ignorance operate, and what are some of its consequences?[1] The answers to these questions point to the crucial role that white ignorance plays in the construction and maintenance of white privilege, including the knowledge that it generates about nonwhite people. They also point to the intimate relationship between power, knowledge, and ignorance, and the relationship of all three to processes of racialized colonization.

These questions could be addressed in the context of a number of colonial situations, both without and within the United States. France's relationship with Algeria, for example, could be described as one in which "[t]he [white] European knows and he does not know. On the level of reflection, a Negro is a Negro; but in the unconscious there is the firmly fixed image of the nigger-savage" (Fanon 1967, 199). And a thorough analysis of the different ways that the United States exoticized and colonized islands with predominantly nonwhite populations must include Hawai'i, which was annexed by the United States in 1898 and made a state in 1959 and which today continues to fight for its independence (http://www.hawaii-nation.org/index.html). I focus on Puerto Rico in particular because it is "the oldest colony on earth" owned by "the oldest representative democracy on earth" (Fernandez 1996, 262). As such, the ongoing oppressive relationship between the United States and Puerto Rico strikes me as especially egregious. I also wish to examine the case of Puerto Rico because of the growing Latinization of the United States. This transformation makes particularly important and timely the issue of the United States' relationship with a Latino/a and Spanish-speaking island that both is and is not part of itself.

I am less interested here in ignorance as a simple lack of knowledge than I am in ignorance as an active production of particular kinds of knowledges for various social and political purposes. Of course, there is plenty of the former kind of ignorance when it comes to the United States' relationship with Puerto Rico, and United Staters' lack of knowledge about Puerto Rico has had harmful, racist effects.[2] But the epistemic relationship between the two lands is much more complex than the simple opposition between ignorance and knowledge indicates. This is because rather than oppose knowledge, ignorance often is formed by it, and vice versa. In such cases, ignorance is better thought of as ignorance/knowledge. The notion of ignorance/knowledge does not collapse ignorance and knowledge into one another. It instead denies, or at least places under suspicion, the purported self-mastery and self-transparency of knowledge, as if nothing properly escaped its grasp. It helps one to peek behind knowledge of Puerto Rico to see what unknowledges help compose it and upon which that knowledge depends.

The simple opposition of knowledge and ignorance tends to imply that they are unrelated to power or, better put, that knowledge and ignorance can be understood outside of the multiple relations of force that compose human transactions. Following Foucault (1978), I do not intend "force" as something necessarily or overtly violent. The term *force* instead is meant to capture the way that all relations operate as a dynamic interplay of energy, pressure, and capability and, as such, are relationships of power. This being said, it is important to add that not all relations of force are the same, nor does the powerful interplay of human transaction place all people on a level playing field. The creation of ignorance/knowledge through relations of force often is unbalanced and unequal, as is the case in colonized lands. But as a dynamic, relational process, it involves the active participation of all "sides" and includes the possibility of resistance to and transformation of the forms of ignorance/knowledge produced.

In what follows, I provide a brief historical overview of the United States' acquisition of Puerto Rico and then examine the expanding nation's creation of ignorance/knowledge of its new colony. Focusing on the role that the educational system played in the U.S. colonization of Puerto Rico, I explore how Puerto Ricans, unlike Filipinos, were construed as similar enough to white U.S. citizens to be capable of Americanization. I then turn to Puerto Rican resistance to U.S. domination, explaining how it has been manipulated by the United States to produce colonialist discourses of ignorance/knowledge and yet has not been totally co-opted by that production. Closing with the need to acknowledge relationality between the United States and Puerto Rico, I both caution that such an acknowledgment cannot completely dispel the ignorance that underlies knowledge of the island and suggest that this ignorance sometimes might function as revolutionary rather than oppressive.

The United States' Colonization of Puerto Rico

Puerto Rico became a colony of the United States in 1898, handed over by Spain after its defeat in the Spanish-American War. The Philippines, Guam, and Hawai'i were other spoils of the war for the United States, but it was Cuba that was central to the United States' conflict with Spain. As Spain's rule of Cuba became increasingly harsh in the late nineteenth century, Cuba's struggle for independence broke into violent revolution in 1895. As the U.S. media generated popular support for the Cubans by reporting on Spain's alleged atrocities, the United States was provided its justification for intervention in the revolution when the U.S.S. Maine was sunk in Havana harbor in February 1898. When the U.S. Congress passed and President McKinley signed a resolution two months later declaring Cuba free and independent, war on Spain effectively had been declared (Cushing 1997).

The congressional resolution in favor of Cuban independence can make it appear as if the United States' primary motivation for fighting Spain was to promote freedom and end colonial imperialism. But the story is much more complicated than this. The turmoil in Cuba jeopardized U.S. businesses' substantial investments in Cuba's sugar and tobacco industries, which McKinley was under great pressure to protect (Cushing 1997). Equally important to the United States was its need for foreign markets in which to sell its goods. As then Senator Albert J. Beveridge imperialistically explained, "American factories are making more than the American people can use: American soil is producing more than they can consume. Fate has written our policy for us: the trade of the world must and shall be ours, and we will get it as our mother [England] has told us how" (quoted in Cabán 1999, 22). A U.S. foothold in the Caribbean was essential to economic expansion in Latin America and Asia, especially China. The isthmian canal proposed by the United States in the 1880s (today known as the Panama Canal, opened in 1914) would provide the "landlocked" country a waterway to the Far East. Military protection of the passageway was of paramount importance and depended on U.S. naval control of the Carribean (ibid., 26–27).

By the end of the nineteenth century, the United States was powerful enough to enter the fray with European countries and Japan to compete for imperial control of the remainder of the world. As political economist Paul Reinsch explained in 1900, "[A]ll are straining every nerve to gain as large a share as possible of the unappropriated portions of the earth's surface. . . . By rapid preemption the available area is becoming exceeding limited, so that the eyes of the civilized world are already turned to the South American continent for further fields of exploitation" (quoted in Cabán 1999, 16–17). The primary "available area" referred to by Reinsch was Africa. By 1900, the so-called scramble for Africa, initiated by German Chancellor Otto von Bismarck at the Berlin West African Conference in 1884, was nearly complete, and the conference's goal of dividing up Africa among European powers without igniting war between them had been achieved. While in 1880 Africans ruled 90 percent of Africa, by 1900 only Ethiopia and Liberia were free of European imperialism (Sellen 1999). With Africa "exhausted," the United States feared that South America would be the next target of European imperialism, threatening U.S. control of the Western hemisphere. In particular, President McKinley worried that the increasingly feeble and financially strained Spain would sell its Pacific and Caribbean islands to Germany (Cabán 1999, 29). Fighting for Cuba's independence and taking possession of Puerto Rico would help keep Europe out of the United States' so-called backyard, as well as establish the United States as an equal player in the global power games initiated by Europe.[3]

Cuba's struggle with Spain was transformed into the Spanish-American War as the United States hijacked the Cuban revolution for its own purposes. The United States was never interested in Cuban freedom as such but rather in using Cuba's fight with and independence from Spain to further the United States' expansionist aims. One of the results of this hijacking was the United States' possession of Puerto Rico. Too vital to U.S. interests to be allowed independence, Puerto Rico also was perceived as being too dissimilar to the United States to incorporate into the Union. The solution to the problem of what to do with Puerto Rico after the war was provided by the Foraker Act of 1900, which accomplished a first in U.S. history by legally establishing Puerto Rico as a colony of the United States (Cabán 1999, 8). Puerto Rico was officially and ambiguously designated as belonging to, but not part of, the United States (Santiago-Valles 1994, 64), a relationship that remains largely unchanged today, even though Puerto Rico is now considered by the United Nations a U.S. commonwealth rather than a U.S. colony.

The Creation of "Porto Rico"

At the beginning of the twentieth century, this account of how Puerto Rico came to be a U.S. colony would have been much more familiar to the average United Stater than it is today. Nevertheless, in 1898, most people in the United States knew very little about Puerto Rico, unsure, for example, whether it could be driven to from Florida or was one and the same as the Philippines. But United Staters were eager to learn about their new possessions, and U.S. officials were concerned that those possessions were presented properly and correctly to U.S. citizens. As William Buchanan, former U.S. diplomat to Argentina, explained in 1899, "the greatest importance should attach to a proper representation of what they (the Phil.) and other Islands possess; and to a correct first impression being formed here with regard to the problems we have to solve, and as to what we have gained by the acquisition of these new possessions" (quoted in Duany 2002, 45). A correct portrayal of the Philippines and Puerto Rico was a proper portrayal, that is, one that accurately reflected both the (allegedly) legitimate appropriation of the islands as U.S. property and the problems and benefits that accompanied ownership of them. United Staters' ignorance of their new possessions needed to be fought with a particular kind of knowledge that would "justify . . . the acquisition of new territory" and the United States' new position as owners of overseas colonies (ibid.). The lack of United Staters' knowledge of their new colonies was to be filled with a knowledge built of certain ways of not knowing them. United Staters' ignorance of Puerto Rico would not so much be eliminated as it would be replaced by an ignorance/knowledge of various facets of Puerto Rican life and culture, actively produced to serve the interests of white U.S. citizens.

The creation of ignorance/knowledge of Puerto Rico had already begun with the 1898 Treaty of Paris, which ceded the islands to the United States. In doing so, it officially designated Puerto Rico as "Porto Rico" for ease of pronunciation by non-Spanish speakers (Duany 2002, 60). While this change in Puerto Rico's name might appear a minor linguistic matter that was insignificant compared to the United States' military and impending economic domination of the island, the name change paved the way for such domination by creating a new geo-social space for U.S. control. Recalling that the word "colonize" stems from the same Roman/Latin words as "design," "develop," "cultivate," and "define," one can see how the United States' colonization of Puerto Rico began with its redefinition as a place wholly intended to satisfy U.S. interests (Santiago-Valles 1994, 24). Not quite a blank slate because of its Spanish heritage—that is, its white-not-quite "baggage"—Puerto Rico was designated as raw material to be cultivated and developed as the United States saw fit. Made nonsensical from a Spanish-speaking perspective with the substitution of a nonexistent word, Puerto Rico ("rich port") and U.S. ignorance of it were replaced with the object of colonialist ignorance/knowledge known as Porto Rico.

Just as the annexation of Puerto Rico ultimately occurred because of the United States' concerns about Cuba, the development of Porto Rico took place in close conjunction with the United States' relationship with the Philippines. Puerto Ricans initially welcomed the United States' intrusion into their battle with Spain, viewing the United States as a country in favor of democratic self-rule and opposed to colonization. Puerto Rican leaders looked to the U.S. Constitution as proof that the United States would quickly turn over control of the island to Puerto Rican leaders after Spain was pushed out. As the Puerto Rican newspaper *La Democracia* assured its readers, "from a people who are descendants of [George] Washington, no one should expect a sad surprise . . . we trust, with full confidence, in the great Republic and the men who govern her" (quoted in Fernandez 1996, 4). In contrast, Filipinos resisted U.S. military presence on their island from the beginning and continued to violently struggle for their independence after Spain's defeat. As a result, Filipinos were conceived by white United Staters as savage and warlike, while Puerto Ricans were portrayed as docile and gentle. When census reports produced soon after the Spanish-American War characterized Puerto Rico, and not the Philippines, as predominantly white, the contrast between the two islands was strengthened. Filipinos were construed as primitive and barbaric, while Puerto Ricans were seen as potentially capable of civilization and progress (Duany 2002, 54–55). Puerto Ricans thus were saddled with the Porto Rican characteristic of being receptive to so-called Americanization. On the "Tropical Chain of Being," Puerto/Porto Ricans were located toward the middle to top, much higher than Filipinos, who were stationed near its lowest rung (Santiago-Valles 1994, 73).

Their respective locations on this chain help explain the different ways that Puerto Rico and the Philippines were portrayed in the world fairs of the early twentieth century held in the United States. From roughly 1850 to 1940 throughout Western Europe and the United States, world fairs were popular ways to exhibit the cultures and inhabitants of colonial possessions, all in the name of generating and dispersing archaeological and ethnological knowledge to the public. Both Puerto Rico and the Philippines were displayed in the 1901 Pan-American Exposition in Buffalo, New York, and the 1904 Louisiana Purchase Exposition in St. Louis, Missouri. In Buffalo, reproductions of Filipino houses, scenery, and villages were built in which to display indigenous Filipino "tribes" and customs in their "natural" habitat, while the exhibitions of Puerto Rico focused on its agriculture, architecture, and natural resources. No Puerto Rican people or cultural practices were included in the Puerto Rican display, while live, semi-nude Filipino people engaging in their "Native" activities were among the "objects" for visitors to gawk at in the Filipino exhibition. The Filipino exhibit in Buffalo was so popular that the St. Louis exposition greatly expanded it to include nearly 1,200 Filipinos in four separate villages, while the small Puerto Rican display continued to focus on the island's material resources (Duany 2002, 39–50).

The two expositions demonstrate the different degrees to which Puerto Ricans and Filipinos were exoticized by the United States. Puerto Ricans were not considered "advanced" enough to properly represent their island, which is why the United States had to "undertake to do for these people what they cannot do so for themselves" (Duany 2002, 45). But unlike Filipinos, Puerto Ricans were seen as being receptive to civilizing influences; they were not so different from white United Staters that all hope was lost. While the United States' exoticization of Puerto Ricans was less extreme than that of the Filipinos, it is important to recognize how colonial oppression sometimes operates through enforced sameness rather than imposed difference. This is especially true in the United States' relationship with Latin America. While the ignorance/knowledge produced about the "Asiatic" Filipinos construed them as a savagely indecipherable other to the United States, the ignorance/knowledge generated about Puerto Ricans and other Latin American peoples constructed them as "a reform[able] recognizable Other, as a *subject of difference that is almost the same but not quite*" (Homi Bhabha, quoted in Santiago-Valles 1994, 88, emphasis in original). This "colonial mimicry" enables imperialist control through conflation of identities and erasure of differences. In the Western Hemisphere, in particular, colonial mimicry has been a central building block of the myth of America/*Américas*. According to this myth, the United States ("America") is the entirety of the *Américas* (and, remembering Canada, also the Americas and *Amériques*) and can speak legitimately for the entire Western Hemisphere. The Western Hemisphere is a blank slate on which white European descendants are to write their destiny via the pursuit of freedom and progress, and the United States is at the vanguard of this civilizing movement because it is where this project has excelled (Kenworthy 1995, 18).

Constructing Puerto Rico as less exotic than the Philippines enabled the United States to fold Puerto Ricans into the myth of America/*Américas*. Precisely because Puerto Ricans (allegedly) were relatively familiar and similar to United Staters, they were targeted for colonial intervention in not just different but greater ways than were Filipinos. Let me be clear that to claim that U.S. colonialism has played a greater role in the history and lives of Puerto Ricans than Filipinos is not to slight the powerfully oppressive effects of, for example, being put on display at world fairs as nonhuman, barbaric people. It instead is to suggest that it is no coincidence that Filipinos were granted their independence by the United States in 1947, while Puerto Ricans continue in limbo as an unincorporated territory today. While flagrant racism made the Philippines seem unsuitable for possible annexation to the United States, that same racism also helped Filipinos gain their sovereignty. A relatively "benign" racism treated Puerto Ricans more benevolently by recognizing their humanity—albeit (allegedly) not yet fully developed—but this benevolence contributed to extensive and ongoing colonialist intervention long after most other countries gave up their colonies at the end of World War II.

Education, Colonization, and Ignorance

In the name of "doing good" overseas, the United States colonized Puerto Rico by attempting to foster women's rights, increase literacy and better educate children, develop the island's economy, and improve public health via scientific progress (Briggs 2002). I do not have enough space here to explain how each of these seemingly worthwhile projects resulted in deeply ambivalent and often problematic results. I instead single out education, briefly focusing on the role that it played in the colonization of Puerto Rico. Because Puerto Ricans were construed as being almost the same as United Staters, they were seen as educable. But because they were not perceived as exactly the same, they were seen as being incapable of educating themselves and needful of outside help.

The role of education in the colonization of Puerto Rico is especially pertinent to my purposes, given how the theme of ignorance is explicitly woven through it. Simply put, United Staters' ignorance of Puerto Rico led them to view Puerto Ricans as ignorant and to believe that their (alleged) ignorance interfered with their ability to become true Americans. U.S. Commissioners of Education sent to investigate Puerto Rico soon after the end of the Spanish-American War decried its illiteracy and lack of public education, and they placed the blame for Puerto Rico's educational deficiencies on Spanish colonialism. In what now can be seen as a remarkable moment of irony, Spain was accused of deliberately keeping Puerto Rican people ignorant in order to more easily subject them to Spanish control. Democratic self-governance was said to depend upon a fund of common knowledge that Puerto Ricans lacked (Navarro 2002, 33, 66). In the name of anticolonialism, the United States must bring that fund of knowledge to Puerto/Porto Rico. As one U.S. commissioner exclaimed, "[p]ut an American schoolhouse in every valley and upon every hilltop in Porto Rico, and in these place the well-fitted and accomplished American schoolteachers, and the cloud of ignorance will disappear as the fog flies before the morning sun" (quoted in Navarro 2002, 35).

The so-called democratic fund of knowledge needed by Puerto Rico turned out to be the combined emulation of a Protestant, Euro-American, male, middle-class point of view and depreciation of the island's Puerto Rican and Spanish heritage. The Puerto Rican educational system was modeled explicitly on the Tuskegee and Hampton Normal and Agricultural Institutes, which "trained" freed blacks in the United States, and the Carlisle Indian Industrial School, which "trained" Native Americans. None of the institutes taught much industrial education in terms of prevailing standards of applied science and technology. They tended to focus instead on habituating students in "proper behavior" and "old-fashioned virtues": "cleanliness, decorum, promptness, and truthfulness," as well as "individual salvation, industry and thrift, [and] hard work" (Navarro 2002, 120, 124). Transported to Puerto Rico, the Tuskegee-Hampton-Carlisle model resulted in similar efforts to "correct" Puerto Rican behavior, decorum, and morality as the students were assimilated into the culture and history of "Western civilization." The curriculum of the Normal School in Puerto Rico included manual training, lessons in American history, geography, and civil government, celebrations of U.S. patriotic holidays, and physical exercises and daily bathing. No Puerto Rican history was studied. Perhaps most important to the Normal School was its teaching of the English language. While Spanish grammar was taught and instruction necessarily took place in Spanish (at least at the beginning), mastery of English was viewed as being crucial to Puerto Rican students' education. As the director of one of Puerto Rico's agricultural schools explained, "[T]here is no means of Americanizing the island so sure as to give its boys and girls the use of the English language and a modern industrial training," again broadly understanding industrial training to include practical lessons in "health, manners, and deportment" (Navarro 2002, 88).

The intended and partially achieved result of this educational system was the erasure of Puerto Ricans' knowledge about themselves, their history, and their island through their combined infantilization and feminization.[4] The United States' ignorance of Puerto Rico, in the simple form of a gap in knowledge, was being foisted onto Puerto Ricans. But in addition to this gap in knowledge, a more complex type of ignorance also was at work. In the name of the eradication of colonialist-imposed ignorance, the United States instituted new types of ignorance in the form of a particular kind of knowledge. In the words of one U.S. congressman in 1900, Puerto Ricans should be kept "in leading strings until [the United States] has educated them up to the full stature of American manhood" (Santiago-Valles 1994, 64). Puerto Ricans were to know themselves as Porto Ricans, which meant knowing that they (allegedly) were a relatively uncivilized, childlike, ignorant, and weak (read: feminine) people with no cultural or political history of any value who were fortunate enough to receive help correcting this problem from a benevolent democracy that had only their best interests at heart. Puerto Ricans were implicitly told that by becoming ignorant of who and what they were before 1898, they could remake themselves into true, manly Americans. Free public education was a central motor behind the generation of Porto Rican ignorance/knowledge upon which this remaking depended.

Free public education also was presented to Puerto Ricans by the United States as the key to possible statehood for the island. As the commissioner of education for Puerto Rico explained after a series of meetings with Puerto Rican teachers in 1901, "[W]e have reached the point now in Porto Rico when, in the major portion of the island, it is understood that the open door to the Federal Union is the free public school" (quoted in Navarro 2002, 60). Perhaps the commissioner genuinely believed that fully educated (= Americanized and masculinized) Puerto Ricans would be allowed into the union. Or, as the commissioner's phrase "it is understood that" suggests, perhaps the commissioner's goal in these meetings was to dangle the (false) promise of statehood in front of Puerto Ricans to get them to buy into a colonial model of education. In any case, it is clear from congressional debates held and Supreme Court decisions made soon after the annexation of Puerto Rico that the United States had no intention to incorporate the island as a state. From the perspective of the United States, Puerto Rico was a laboratory for designing and testing effective processes of Americanizing and masculinizing foreign lands that could then be used elsewhere in Central and South America, but never a potential state (Cabán 1999, 8, 16). Puerto Rico was, in other words, both the product and instrument of the America/*Américas* myth that legitimated U.S. hegemony in the Western Hemisphere. Through its production of colonialist ignorance/knowledge about both Puerto Rico and the United States, the educational system installed on the island was a crucial component of the laboratory that enabled the myth of America to flourish.

Resistance and the Production of Ignorance/Knowledge

Perhaps surprisingly, another crucial site for the manufacture of U.S. colonialist ignorance/knowledge of Puerto Rico has been Puerto Rican resistance to U.S. domination. Puerto Rican resistance has been used against Puerto Ricans as a sign of their alleged need for U.S. colonialist paternalism. Their resistance has been transformed into a site of U.S. ignorance/knowledge of Puerto Rico as Porto Rico. But Puerto Rican resistance has not been totally co-opted by this colonialist process. Puerto Ricans have been effective in using ignorance/knowledge of them as Porto Ricans against itself for their own benefit.

Early on in the island's colonization, Puerto Rican leaders determined that dramatic confrontation with the United States would only lead to Puerto Rican "claims [being] lost in emptiness, and our rights in violence." They reached this decision after President Theodore Roosevelt made clear in 1907 that the United States would not hesitate to invade the island militarily if Puerto Ricans violently opposed the United States as Cuba and the Philippines had. Party leaders thus decided to try to fight U.S. domination from "within the regime, to hurt it from close up" (José De Diego, quoted in Fernandez 1996, 45).

They soon had an opportunity to do so. On the first day of the new 1909 legislative session of the Puerto Rican House of Delegates, the dominant Unionist Party proposed that the House should refuse to enact any legislation or pass any bills coming from the Puerto Rican governor or executive council (both of which were appointed by and supported the United States) as a protest against the existing political relationship between Puerto Rico and the United States. (Puerto Rico could enact its own laws and bills but only as long as they did not conflict with those of the United States.) When the president of the executive council protested, the House introduced and passed a number of bills of its own, including one that would shift the power to shape educational policy from the United

States to Puerto Rico. The hope of House members was to engage in a bit of bargaining: the House would approve the president's proposed budget if the president would pass the House's new bills. With neither side backing down, the Puerto Rican government was paralyzed, and its struggle caught the attention of United States President Taft, to House members' delight. Unionist leaders in the House were allowed to present their case for increased self-governance to President Taft and achieved a modest victory when Taft responded by creating a commission to examine the island's problems (Fernandez 1996, 46–47).

The ultimate result of Taft's involvement was an amendment to the Foraker Act to include the automatic appropriation of the previous year's budget if a new budget were not passed in a timely fashion. Taft reported to the U.S. Congress on Puerto Rico's attempts to "subvert" the U.S. government, which was seen as particularly problematic, given that Puerto Rico was "the favored daughter of the United States" who had received the blessings of U.S. guardianship in the form of improved schools, road, medicines, and free trade (Taft, quoted in Fernandez 1996, 48). Positioned via U.S. ignorance/knowledge as an ungrateful female child, Puerto Rico was partially excused for its lack of appreciation. As Taft explained, the United States "must have been conscious that a people that enjoyed so little opportunity for education could not be expected safely for themselves to exercise the full power of self government" (Taft, quoted in Fernandez 1996, 48). Taft acknowledged the United States' partial responsibility for the political mess in Puerto Rico but in such a way that only increased both the (alleged) need for the United States to rule the island and the United States' ignorance of Puerto Rico as anything but a dependent child. The United States should have known better than to give infantile, feminine Puerto Ricans more political power than they could safely handle, Taft effectively declared, just as a parent knows not to give dangerous weapons to their children. Correcting its "mistake," the U.S. Congress approved Taft's request that it act "for [Puerto Ricans'] own good" and take away the political powers of appropriation that Puerto Ricans "had shown themselves too irresponsible to enjoy" (Taft, quoted in Fernandez 1996, 48).

Instead of leading to increased autonomy, the Puerto Rican leaders' decision to fight within the U.S. political and colonial system reduced their ability to officially govern themselves. But I resist reading the Puerto Rican House's 1909 struggle with the United States as a complete failure. It can be understood instead as an early form of *jaiba* politics, which is modeled on the mountain crab (*jaiba*) that moves sideways when crawling forward. An indigenous Puerto Rican tradition, *jaibería* includes everyday "practices of nonconfrontation and evasion, . . . of taking dominant discourse literally in order to subvert it for one's purpose, of doing whatever one sees fit not as a head-on collision . . . but [as opposition] through other means" (Grosfoguel et al. 1997, 30). Rooted in *jaibería*, *jaiba* politics seeks to achieve its goals through ambiguity and subversion. It tends to operate indirectly, ambivalently shifting laterally with any forward advance it makes. Because such "seductive" characteristics are stereotypically associated with women, *jaibería* sometimes is positively depicted by its adherents as producing a feminization of Puerto Rican politics, turning against itself the United States' ignorance/knowledge of Puerto Ricans as docile and unmanly (ibid., 28). A nonheroic position that rejects any quest for purity, *jaiba* politics often is complicit with structures of domination—and herein lies its strength as well as its weakness. While there are no guarantees that *jaiba* politics will be effective and some uses of it can be entirely complicit with the status quo, its stealthy ambiguity enables it to use the tools, rhetoric, and goals of domination, including those of ignorance/knowledge, against themselves. This is especially important when there is no viable position outside structures of domination from which to fight it, or—to say the same thing—when attempting to occupy such a position is merely a showy gesture of self-indulgent "heroism" so that one can be on record as openly opposing an oppressor, even knowing in advance that this form of opposition will be futile.[5]

This was the case in Puerto Rico in 1909. Especially after Roosevelt's explicit military threat, the Puerto Rican House of Delegates had very little viable room to move outside U.S. colonial control of the island. Violent resistance to U.S. occupation most likely would have resulted in a great deal of Puerto Rican bloodshed and very little, if any, increase in Puerto Rican autonomy. Choosing to work from within the system, which meant partially working with rather than solely against U.S. ignorance/knowledge of Puerto Rico, House delegates used *jaiba* politics to oppose U.S. domination with nonviolent, legislative struggle. While the delegates unfortunately moved more sideways (or even backward) than forward in this particular instance, their decision to use the U.S. system against itself by democratic arguments that appealed to constitutional precedent can be affirmed as an important moment in Puerto Rican resistance to U.S. colonialism.

The need for and use of *jaiba* politics in Puerto Rico continues today. This is not to slight the anticolonialist efforts of those such as *Los Macheteros* (the cane cutters), a Puerto Rican revolutionary group that has engaged in violent opposition to the United States for the last twenty-plus years. But largely because the United States branded the group "terrorists"—a devastating rhetorical strategy that the United States continues to deploy throughout the world today—*Los Macheteros* have been relatively unsuccessful at decreasing U.S. exploitation of Puerto Rico. After *Los Macheteros* attacked the U.S. Navy in 1979, for example, killing two sailors and injuring ten others, the group's goals were quickly dismissed by U.S. authorities as illegitimate, because the "terrorist" organization was considered "beyond the pale" (Fernandez 1996, 246–47). Direct, and especially violent, opposition to U.S. domination of Puerto Rico might appear more "manly" and thus satisfy common expectations of what counts as "real" resistance to oppression, but it rarely has resulted in significant changes to the U.S.-Puerto Rican relationship.

Contemporary Puerto Rican nationalists have uncritically accepted U.S. ignorance/knowledge of Puerto Rico by criticizing *jaibería* as a deplorable sign of a colonial mentality and a lack of virility (Grosfoguel 2003, 10; Grosfoguel et al. 1997, 31). *Jaibería* also has been portrayed by imperial elites in the United States as mere Puerto Rican indecision, which (allegedly) is the only reason that the United States' paternalistic relationship with Puerto Rico persists. Puerto Ricans' frustration over their situation has been characterized as "self-induced," a product of their inability to give the U.S. Congress a "clear indication" of what they want. The United States' indecision about what to do with Puerto Rico allegedly is only a by-product of Puerto Rican ambiguity and inconsistency, as manifest in recent Puerto Rican plebiscites in which the vote is fairly evenly split between statehood and commonwealth status.[6] Ever since the U.S. Congress transformed Puerto Rico into an *Estado Libre Asociado* (a Free Associated State, or Commonwealth) in 1952, Puerto Rico supposedly has been at liberty to change its status whenever it likes.[7] That it has not made a change allegedly has nothing to do with the hegemony of U.S. interests and desires and everything to do with deficiencies in Puerto Rican character (Carr 1984, 11, 407–408).

But, in fact, contemporary instances of *jaiba* political action can be seen as representing deliberate decisions and as achieving more than *Los Macheteros* (or the 1909 House delegates) were able to accomplish. *Jaiba* resistance has not completely been co-opted by colonialist productions of ignorance/knowledge. In 1917, for example, citizenship was imposed on Puerto Ricans, without their say, to undermine growing independence movements on the island, not to transition Puerto Rico into statehood and grant Puerto Ricans equality with "real" United Staters (Fernandez 1996, 33).[8] To this day, U.S. citizenship does not mean the same thing for Puerto Ricans and other U.S. citizens. Singling out two important differences, unlike other U.S. citizens, Puerto Ricans do not have representatives or senators in Washington, D.C., and they cannot vote in federal elections (Duany 2002, 123). While U.S. citizenship thus has played and continues to play a significant role in Puerto Rico's subject status, it also has become a tool for mitigating some of the worse effects of (neo)colonialism. Puerto Ricans have learned to use their U.S. citizenship to redistribute wealth from the mainland to the island by, for example, faking illness to obtain Social Security benefits, thereby avoiding the alternatives of debilitating, underpaid factory work and fruitless, demoralizing quests for nonexistent jobs. These *jaiba* strategies of adopting a "postwork" subjectivity and an entitlement attitude undermine, without completely overthrowing, the capitalist stranglehold that the United States has on Puerto Rico, partially offsetting the political, economic, and other inequalities between them (Grosfoguel et al. 1997, 29–30; Grosfoguel 2003, 11).

To call this achievement one of freedom from colonialism admittedly would be inaccurate, but this is primarily because it is off base to characterize Puerto Rico's current situation in terms of a sharp dichotomy between independence and subjugation. In a world in which the United States economically and otherwise exploits free nations throughout Central and South America (and elsewhere), Puerto Rican sovereignty is less a beneficial ideal than it is a fictional narrative, because it falsely promises complete escape from the modern-capitalist world system ruled by the United States (Grosfoguel 2003, 6, 8–9). Fighting for Puerto Rican independence is not a subversive position when the United States no longer needs Puerto Rico as a way to gain hegemony in the Western Hemisphere and tends to view the island as merely a drain on its economy. Worse than fictional, the "ideal" of Puerto Rican independence can be harmful to the majority of Puerto Ricans, promoting the interests of the petty bourgeois at the expense of the poor and working class (Duany 2002, 16; Grosfoguel 2003, 63). The meaningful question before Puerto Ricans today is not whether they will be free of or subjugated by the United States, as if passive complicity with U.S. (neo)colonialism is the only available alternative to a place of struggle allegedly "outside" its domain. Rather, it is one of how Puerto Rico can protect and increase the unemployment, Social Security, civil rights, and other benefits that it has wrested from the United States via its "insider" status and its creative use of the mainland's ignorance/knowledge of the island (Grosfoguel 2003, 67–68, 74). The answer to that question is not necessarily found in any of the political solutions to the problem of Puerto Rico's relationship to the United States. While independence at this time likely would be harmful for Puerto Rico—indeed, today an anti-independence position is viewed by its proponents as a rejection, not an acceptance, of U.S. neocolonialism (Grosfoguel 2003, 2)—neither statehood nor ongoing commonwealth status is a panacea. This is because, by themselves, these "solutions" risk transforming only the political definition of Puerto Rico without addressing the power inequalities that exist between it and the United States (Grosfoguel et al. 1997, 32). These inequalities must be the focus of attention if meaningful change in U.S.-Puerto Rican relationships is to occur.

Conclusion:
Reciprocity as a Response to Ignorance

Why do I know so little about Puerto Rico? Because, seemingly, there is so little that is worth knowing: Puerto Ricans are a childlike, ignorant people, helplessly dependent upon the United States for any and all solutions to the island's problems. This is to say that I know so little about Puerto Rico because I know so much about it: my ignorance of the island is formed out of complex structures of colonialist ignorance/knowledge that champion an asymmetrical and a nonreciprocal relationship between the United States and Puerto Rico. Because it (supposedly) possesses all of the power and knowledge vis-à-vis Puerto Rico, the United States (allegedly) gains nothing valuable or beneficial from the island—only economic headaches—and thus does not depend on Puerto Rico in the way that Puerto Rico depends on the United States. Given this purported lack of symmetry and reciprocity, no wonder that being knowledgeable about Puerto Rico seems pointless or trivial to many white United Staters.

Rather than a reflection of the relationship between Puerto Rico and the United States, the denial of reciprocity and meaningful relationality is a classic strategy of hegemonic cultures for safeguarding their dominant position (Hoagland, ch. 5 this volume). If white United Staters acknowledged their interdependence with Puerto Rico, then it would be difficult for them to continue to treat Puerto Ricans as insignificant and to neglect their "response-ability," in the sense of answerability, to the island. It also would be difficult to continue to ignore the coconstitutive relationship between the United States' colonial history and its racial categories. Racial identities are not built and maintained merely within the confines of a single nation, even one, such as the United States, populated by many different racial groups. They are formed in relation to various patterns and histories of colonialism. Put another way, an understanding of the different racial groups that compose the United States is impoverished if it neglects the global and colonial histories that have helped shape them. The different racializations of the Irish in Great Britain and the United States, for example, resulted in part because of the different colonial relationships that the Irish people had with each nation (Grosfoguel 2003, 155). Colonized by England, the Irish were black in Great Britain and also upon arrival in the heavily English-populated United States. But in part because the United States did not have a colonial relationship with Ireland, the Irish were able to become white in the United States. The Irish in the United States used racist tactics to distinguish themselves racially from African Americans, so the story is more complicated than one of colonial history alone (see Ignatiev 1995), but the point still holds that racial relations internal to the United States cannot be separated from that history.

In no case is this point more relevant than in that of Puerto Rico. To be a white United Stater is to have a racial identity formed not only in complex relation with African Americans, Latinos/as, Asian Americans, and other full citizens of and immigrants to the United States, it also is to have a racial identity formed in relation with the colonized Puerto Rican subject-citizens of the United States. Although I usually do not think of myself in this way—and this is no coincidence—the relationship between my white U.S. citizenship and Puerto Ricans' subject citizenship is crucial to my identity as a white person. My white "Americanness" depends in part on the United States' colonial relationship with Puerto Rico,[9] and it is in my white-privileged interests to remain completely ignorant of that fact. If I do not acknowledge the reciprocal and interdependent relationship between the United States and Puerto Rico, then I can continue to neglect my "response-ability" to the island while simultaneously thinking of myself as a good person. I can, for example, ignore the issue of possible Puerto Rican statehood because of its seeming unimportance without acknowledging how my white privilege depends on keeping at bay the "threat" of further Latinization of the United States that the island's statehood would bring (Grosfoguel 2003, 8; see also Gonzalez 2000, 261).

Because of the complex relationship between ignorance and knowledge, the solution to white ignorance about the colonial oppression of Puerto Rico cannot be merely to seek more knowledge about the island. White United Staters should not deliberately cultivate huge gaps in their knowledge about the United States' colonialist history. But because of the coconstitutive relationship between ignorance and knowledge, all quests for knowledge tend to be accompanied by ignorances and blind spots that are difficult to detect. It would be dangerously naïve to claim that white United Staters should simply educate themselves about Puerto Rico, for doing so does not necessarily break with the United States' century-long colonialist tradition of treating Puerto Ricans as a mere object of study for the colonizer's gaze. That tradition has a great deal of ignorance built into the knowledge that it has produced about Puerto Rico. White people do need to educate themselves about the lives and worlds of people of color, but to effectively tackle racism, they also need to turn their gaze upon themselves and simultaneously examine the active operation of their ignorance (Frye 1983, 118).

Yet this self-reflective move can never be complete, since no person is self-transparent. What to do then about the ignorance that will remain even in the midst of well-intentioned efforts to examine it? I suggest that the ignorance in formations of ignorance/knowledge sometimes can serve as something other than an "aggressive ignorance" that is a tool of "epistemic imperialism" (Lugones 2003, 18). It occasionally can function as a revolutionary failure of knowledge, an epistemic engagement with another in which I allow that something about the other has escaped me (Davis 2002). In the case of Puerto Rico, my acknowledged ignorance of the island thus can help me be suspicious of the times in which I think I fully understand it. I now know, for example, not only why Puerto Rico was allowed to field its own Olympic basketball team independent of the United States but also why I was not able to explain the relationship between the two lands when I first heard about the Puerto Ricans' victory. Yet this does not mean that my colonialist ignorance/knowledge of Puerto Rico has been completely dismantled. Porto Rico is not that easy to dispel. Cognizant of its continued existence, perhaps my ignorance can help remind me of the limitations of knowledge, as well as of the ways that knowledge can support rather than challenge (neo)colonialism. Such a failure of knowledge will not be pure, but the risk of its complicity with colonialist ignorance/knowledge offers a chance of meaningful change in relations between Puerto Rico and the United States.

Notes

Thanks to Nancy Tuana and two anonymous reviewers for helpful comments on an earlier draft of this chapter.

1. As Paul Taylor's chapter in this volume attests, not only white people in the United States are experientially distant from or ignorant of the realities of life in Puerto Rico, and the Carribean and Latin America more broadly. The issue of ignorance based on racial privilege that extends to nonwhite people is an important one deserving in-depth treatment, but it is beyond the scope of my efforts here.

2. I use the somewhat awkward word "United Staters" in place of "Americans" to refer to citizens of the United States so that I might resist the customary erasure of other (South, Latin, Central, and North) American nations in the Western hemisphere.

3. The "yard" metaphor is the geographical equivalent of calling African American men "boy": it inflates the importance of the United States while demeaning other American nations, promoting the America/*Américas* myth discussed later (Kenworthy 1995, 40–41).

4. On the preservation of Spanish as the principal language of Puerto Rico as a form of resistance to U.S. domination, see Cabán (1999, 132).

5. For other accounts of "impure" and "feminine" resistance to oppression that complement *jaiba* politics see, respectively, Lugones (2003), especially pages x and 13–14, and Nandy (1983), especially page 104.

6. The movement for independence lost its popular support in Puerto Rico in the 1950s, gaining only 4 percent of the vote in a 1993 referendum (Fernandez 1996, 261).

7. Note how equating *"Estado Libre Asociado"* and "Commonwealth," as commonly is done, is problematic because it allows the United States to have its cake and eat it too. When it is in the United States' interest to emphasize Puerto Rico's freedom in relation to the mainland, Puerto Rico's status as a "Free Associated State" can be touted. But when that purported freedom conflicts with U.S. interests (e.g., when contemporary Puerto Ricans press for statehood), then the United States can deny Puerto Rican autonomy because of the island's status as a mere commonwealth.

8. In the words of then President Woodrow Wilson as he inaugurated the U.S. citizen-child, "[W]e welcome the new citizen, not as a stranger but as one entering his father's house" (Fernandez 1996, 55).

9. Because of space constraints, I leave out the role of my gender in this relationship, but a longer account would have to complicate my status as a "true" American since I am a woman.

References

Briggs, Laura. 2002. *Reproducing Empire: Race, Sex, Science, and U.S. Imperialism in Puerto Rico.* Berkeley: University of California Press.

Cabán, Pedro A. 1999. *Constructing a Colonial People: Puerto Rico and the United States, 1898–1932.* Boulder, CO: Westview Press.

Carr, Raymond. 1984. *Puerto Rico: A Colonial Experiment.* New York: New York University Press.

Cushing, Lincoln. 1997. "Centennial of the Spanish-American War 1898–1998." Accessed July 23, 2006. <http://www.zpub.com/cpp/saw.html>

Davis, Dawn Rae. 2002. "(Love Is) The Ability of Not Knowing: Feminist Experience of the Impossible in Ethical Singularity." *Hypatia* 17:2: 145–61.

Dryer, Alexander Barnes. 2004. "Why Puerto Rico Has Its Own Team: How the Insular Territory Made It to Athens." Accessed August 17. <http://www.slate.msn.com/id/2105234>

Duany, Jorge. 2002. *The Puerto Rican Nation on the Move: Identities on the Island and in the United States.* Chapel Hill: University of North Carolina Press.

Fanon, Franz. 1967. *Black Skin, White Masks.* Translated by Charles Lam Markmann. New York: Grove Press.

Fernandez, Ronald. 1996. *The Disenchanted Island: Puerto Rico and the United States in the Twentieth Century.* 2d ed. Westport, CT: Praeger.

Foucault, Michel. 1978. *The History of Sexuality: Volume I.* Translated by Robert Hurley. New York: Random House.

Frye, Marilyn. 1983. *The Politics of Reality: Essays in Feminist Theory.* Freedom, CA: Crossing Press.

Gonzalez, Juan. 2000. *Harvest of Empire: A History of Latinos in America.* New York: Penguin Books.

Grosfoguel, Ramón. 2003. *Colonial Subjects: Puerto Ricans in a Global Perspective.* Berkeley: University of California Press.

Grosfoguel, Ramón, Frances Negrón-Muntaner, and Chloe S. Georas. 1997. "Beyond Nationalist and Colonialist Discourses: The *Jaiba* Politics of the Puerto

Rican Ethno-Nation." In *Puerto Rico Jam: Rethinking Colonialism and National-ism*, ed. Ramón Grosfoguel and Frances Negrón-Muntaner, 1–36. Min-neapolis: University of Minnesota Press.

Ignatiev, Noel. 1995. *How the Irish Became White.* New York: Routledge.

Kenworthy, Eldon. 1995. *America/Américas: Myth in the Making of U.S. Policy toward Latin America.* University Park: Pennsylvania State University Press.

Lugones, María. 2003. *Pilgrimages/Peregrinajes: Theorizing Coalition against Multiple Oppressions.* Lanham, MD: Rowman and Littlefield.

Nandy, Ashis. 1983. *The Intimate Enemy: Loss and Recovery of Self under Colonialism.* New York: Oxford University Press.

Navarro, José-Manuel. 2002. *Creating Tropical Yankees: Social Science Textbooks and U.S. Ideological Control in Puerto Rico, 1898–1908.* New York: Routledge.

Santiago-Valles, Kelvin A. 1994. *"Subject Peoples" and Colonial Discourses: Economic Transformation and Social Disorder in Puerto Rico, 1898–1947.* Albany: State University of New York Press.

Sellen, Jeff. 1999. "The Scramble for Africa." Accessed September 15, 2004. <http://www.wsu.edu:8080/~dee/MODAFRCA/ SCRAMBLE.HTM>

CHAPTER 9

John Dewey, W. E. B. Du Bois, and Alain Locke

A Case Study in White Ignorance and Intellectual Segregation

Frank Margonis

Soldier and President Theodore Roosevelt was stridently committed to an international order that Charles Mills calls "global white supremacy" (Mills 1998, 98, 144). Concerned that England and France had already colonized significant portions of Africa and Asia, Roosevelt was anxious for the United States to stake its claim to the markets of China and Latin America. En route to this aim, the nation embarked upon what Alain Locke called "the flurry of imperialism of 1898," that is, the United States sought to secure strategic real estate by imposing its military might upon Hawaii, Cuba, and the Philippines (Locke 1992, 30). For Roosevelt, conquest of other nations was partly a matter of attaining a regional military hegemony, but it was also a matter of pushing the nation to a higher level. In Roosevelt's view, the traits that made the United States great, the vigor and ambition of the "American race," were forged through conquest, so Roosevelt devoted four volumes of his writings to documenting the process whereby European Americans claimed the West by killing Indian tribes and seizing their land (Roosevelt 1995). For Roosevelt, this history of genocide was something to be cherished, cultivated, and sought in the future. Military conquest brought wealth to the nation as it created the optimal conditions for unifying and elevating a diverse citizenry within the nation.

The exploits that Roosevelt sought to make central to American lore and practice have—as Mills has so significantly shown—been edited out of the debates over the character of justice among white philosophers

(Mills 1997, 18–19). John Dewey, perhaps the most noted European American philosopher of the progressive era, chose not to write about the imperialism of 1898, and indeed, he writes as though the racial dramas foremost in Roosevelt's mind did not exist. For instance, Dewey's retrospective essay on the life of Theodore Roosevelt focuses primarily upon describing a man larger than life, a political personage who could grab the public's attention with the very audacity of his acts (Dewey 1976–1983, mw.11.143).[1] Even though Dewey criticizes President Roosevelt for neglecting economic inequalities, he says nothing regarding Roosevelt's racism, imperialism, or doctrine of manifest destiny. Cornel West and Paul Taylor call attention to a much more serious omission in Dewey's social commentaries: the neglect of lynching and violence against African Americans and his unwillingness to take a stand on federal antilynching legislation (Taylor 2004, 232). While W. E. B. Du Bois, as editor of the *Crisis*, was doing everything within his power to call national attention to events such as the race riots in East Saint Louis, Dewey shows almost no acknowledgment of the phenomena and no awareness of the systematic role that racial violence played in exploiting African American labor in the South and denying African Americans economic opportunities in the North.[2] These silences are structured silences, characteristic silences: the epistemology of ignorance that Mills rightly condemns.

Seeking to make sense of the profound role that race has played in shaping U.S. foreign and domestic policy and practice, on the one hand, and the virtual absence of race in white philosophers' discussions of American democracy, on the other hand, Mills argues that we must recognize the dominant group's unwillingness to attend to and understand historic and ongoing acts of racial subjugation. Racial segregation and the resulting concentration of poverty are not—like the breakdown of communities or the existence of class stratification—routinely discussed by white philosophers as basic obstacles to democracy, because dominant group members have long participated in an epistemology of ignorance.[3] Part of this is due to the positionality of white philosophers as members of white communities; in Mills's (1998) words,

> Communities systematically privileged by an unjust social order will as a rule be less sensitive to its inequities, and this insensitivity will interfere with their "attainment of knowledge." Such communities will not usually experience these injustices directly; they will have a vested interest in the system's perpetuation and thus be prone to evasion, bad faith, and self-deception about its true character. (141–42)

Insulated from experiencing racial injustices and benefitting from them, white philosophers, like much of white society in general, perpetuate their ignorance of the sociological realities of race by adopting a variety of strategies, including "averting one's eyes from certain uncomfortable factual and moral truths, ignoring the evidence, [and] being blind to things they should see" (Mills 2003, 231). When Dewey, a founding member of the National Association for the Advancement of Colored People (NAACP), ignored the steady reports of racial violence in the organization's premier publication, it appears to be a case of averting one's gaze.

However, Dewey's silences on matters of race must be considered in relation to the many cases where he did take strong stands against racial reasoning and racial policies. Indeed, he is hailed by George Hutchinson as a "philosopher of decolonization" who worked to deconstruct racial categories (1995, 60; also see Pappas 2002). Hutchinson (1995) summarizes the antiracist elements of pragmatism, saying,

> Pragmatism's emphasis on process, its embrace of pluralism, its insistence that truths and morals are produced through historically specific practices, its liberating acceptance of epistemological uncertainty, helped undermine Victorian beliefs that supported, among other things, "scientific" racism, imperialism, and Anglo-American ethnocentrism. (33)

Dewey fiercely opposed the crass racial reasoning that led to intelligence testing and vocational tracking in schools as well as the wholesale justifications of undemocratic institutions. He argued that racial categories have no basis in biology, that they are largely creations of ignorance fueled by political, economic, and social motivations (mw.13.242, 13.289). In Hutchinson's view, Dewey's deconstruction of racial categories laid the groundwork for the development of Harlem Renaissance authors and the emergence of the "New Negro." Alain Locke and other African American pragmatists found in Dewey's philosophy the tools they needed both to undercut racial reasoning and to fashion a new vision of African American identity (Hutchinson 1995, 30; also see Fraser 1998).

This portrait of a courageous theorist boldly undercutting the racial reasoning of his own group stands in some tension with Cornel West's (1989, 83) disclosure of Dewey's cautious political nature and the many times Dewey did not speak out on issues of race. I hope we can better understand both the processes of the epistemology of ignorance and the steps European American philosophers, such as myself, need to take to overcome that ignorance if we investigate the ways in which Dewey neglected to consider race in both foreign and domestic policy. In contrast to Roosevelt, who sought to incite further imperialism by glorifying the conquests of Indian tribes, Dewey erased race and violence from his version of the frontier narrative, and in the process, his and his readers' awareness of racial patterns shaping the nation was diminished. Dewey's sanitized story of the nation's development prepared the way for racially blind understandings of the U.S. role in the world and democracy at home. By comparing Dewey's understanding of the U.S. role in World War I to that of his contemporaries, W. E. B. Du Bois and Alain Locke, we can see the degree to which Dewey remained unprepared to understand the ways in which U.S. foreign policy was partly devoted to extending the power of white nations over colonized countries. In domestic policy, Dewey's discussions of "cultural pluralism" exhibited a remarkable—yet common—obliviousness to the social processes of racial segregation that explained what Du Bois called the "color line"—processes that posed the greatest threat to democracy in the minds of Du Bois and Locke. In short, Dewey's opposition to racism—while of undoubted value— nonetheless stayed safely within the parameters of white racial solidarity.

Dewey's Silence on the History and Future of U.S. Colonialism

As a public intellectual, dubbed by one commentator as the conscience of his generation (Commager 1950, 100), Dewey took vocal stands on countless public issues, yet he did not enter the extremely important early twentieth-century debate over the aggressiveness of U.S. foreign policy. In contrast, Roosevelt, in both deed and word, staked out a loud pro-imperialist stance, while Du Bois and Locke used their respective forums to sharply denounce the rush by European nations and the United States to carve out spheres of influence throughout the world, often by coercing those nations populated by people of color. While Du Bois and Locke were well prepared to see the avaricious side of American imperialism, Dewey—as Mills would predict—seemed both unwilling and unable to understand the truly aggressive acts of U.S. foreign policy.

Dewey's struggles in understanding U.S. foreign policy may well be traced to his participation in the white community's epistemology of ignorance. One of the key philosophical strategies for maintaining the epistemology of ignorance is—in Mills's analysis—a tendency to abstract away from social realities. White philosophers often translate an understanding of sociological reality into a language that is infused with democratic principles so the reader receives a description of the U.S. polity that is a hybrid of sociological facts and optimistic normative judgments (Mills 1998, 110; 1997, 76). By comparing Roosevelt's and Dewey's accounts of the nation's genesis, we can see this process of abstraction, glorification, and forgetting in operation. Dewey's very portraits of frontier life and the ways in which this rugged existence forged a nation with a new democratic ethos—in Cornel West's words, a nation that stood "at the beginning of time and before open space"—offer us a vision of an intrinsically democratic United States while we are expected to forget the multiple acts of genocide and theft that were part of this process (West 1989, 92).

For Roosevelt, the history and future of U.S. colonial exploits were central to the American story. As a foremost spokesperson for white racial formation, Roosevelt argued that the American race had reached the highest level of human achievement due to the grueling process of claiming the continent from Indian tribes. To his mind, it was the frontiersman's daily battles with tribal peoples that forged the greatest qualities of strength, cunning, and endurance. And he looked to continued imperialism as a means of maintaining the strenuous life needed to lift the race to an even higher level (Gerstle 2001, 17, 21–22, 24, 26–27).

Dewey shared with Roosevelt the tendency to trace the fundamental traits of the nation to the frontier, but Dewey's accounts of the frontier edited out any claims about forging a higher race through battle. Indeed, Dewey went to great lengths to erase race and violence from Roosevelt's narrative. The expansionism that demonstrated to Roosevelt the superior genes of European Americans was reconceived to be a matter of culture and habit learned on the frontier. Dewey followed Fredrick Jackson Turner, who argued that the repeated process of settling first the East Coast, then the Midwest, and then the West had made expansionism and an orientation to future opportunities absolutely basic to the so-called American character. In Turner's words, the "incessant expansion" learned through decades on the frontier ensured that "American energy will continually demand a wider field of exercise" (Turner 1920, 37).

In Dewey's work, Turner's culturalist interpretation of U.S. imperialistic tendencies was given a distinctively moral and democratic twist. Dewey commonly discusses the impact of the frontier upon the American personality, arguing that nonpretentiousness, egalitarian sentiments, and a willingness to assume the initiative are traits Americans learned on the frontier. These accounts operate as a form of erasure, since the killing of Indigenous peoples (as well as the racism forged in the process) is almost entirely neglected in the name of lauding the traits European Americans gained through settling the wilderness.[4] Dewey's repeated references to the "free land,""the "wealth of unused territory," or the nation's "period of natural and unconscious expansion geographically, the taking up of land, the discovering of resources," allude to a narrative in which European Americans appear not as conquerors but as explorers (Dewey, mw.15.151, 155; Dewey 1981–1990, lw.11.249–50; also see West 1989, 92–93). European American citizens are granted a sort of symbolic redemption by being portrayed as the world's pioneers in forging a democratic ethos. In an essay entitled "Freedom," Dewey offered a representative statement, where the processes of colonization are largely portrayed in terms of the way they prepared American people to assertively pursue better lives and create a superior society:

> With free land, a sparse and scattered population, largely rural, and a continent to subdue, there was room for everyone—not merely physical room, but room for energy and personal initiative, room to carve out a career, seemingly boundless opportunity for all who had the vigor, wit, and industry to take advantage of it. The frontier constantly beckoned onwards. While the frontier was geographical and called for physical movement, it was more than that. It was economic and moral. It proclaimed in effect that America is opportunity; it held out the promise of the reward of success to all individuals who put forth the individual effort which would bring success. This freedom of opportunity more than political freedom created the real "American dream." Even after conditions changed and changed radically, it left its enduring impress in the distinctively American idea of freedom of opportunity for all alike, unhampered by differences in status, birth and family antecedents, and finally, in name at least, of race and sex. (lw.11.249–50)

By suggesting that the principle of equal opportunity was forged on the frontier, Dewey implies that this principle is indeed the structuring principle in U.S. society, creating, in Mills's words, a slippage from "the normative to the descriptive, thus covertly representing as an already achieved reality what is present only in the ideal" (1998, 110). When Dewey says that equal opportunity is accepted "in name" with regard to sex and race, it is implied that these are two anomalous domains where the logic of equal opportunity will, in time, become the operative principle. As with Roosevelt, Dewey's story of the American frontier produced a citizenry and a nation whose moral qualities prepared them to lead the world, and indeed, this is what we find in Dewey's attitudes once World War I is upon the nation.

It is this tendency to view the United States in ideal terms that will explain Dewey's rather problematic support of President Woodrow Wilson's argument that the country should enter World War I to make the world "safe for democracy." Dewey's defense of U.S. entry into the war focused less on the political and economic factors that brought the war about than upon the desirability of the ideal of democracy and its extension to large parts of the world. Asserting the exceptional traits of the United States, Dewey argued that the nation had tested fundamental concepts, such as the idea of *e pluribus unum,* and could offer the world a vision of international government based on the experience of the nation (lw.11.71–72). Insisting that "conceptions of a world federation, a concert of nations, a supreme tribunal, a league of nations to enforce peace, are peculiarly American contributions," Dewey said, "leaders of other nations may regard them as iridescent dreams; we know better, for we have actually tried them" (lw.11.71). Dewey's confidence in American ideals stemmed from an understanding of the United States that was remarkably optimistic, for in his description pluralism appears as an accomplished fact, since the country is

> truly interracial and international in our own internal constitution. The very peoples and races who are taught in the Old World that they have an instinctive and ineradicable antipathy to one another live here side by side, in comity, often in hearty amity. We have become a peace-loving nation both because there are no strong Powers close to our borders and because the diversified elements of our people have meant hope, opportunity, release of virile powers from subjection to dread, for use in companionship and unconstrained rivalries. Our uncoerced life has been at liberty to direct itself into channels of toleration, a general spirit of live and let live. (lw.11.71–72)

This description of a tolerant interracial America governed by a belief in equal opportunity was, of course, in tension with many aspects of U.S. society—such as the racial subordination and economic exploitation of African Americans in the South and the forcible placement of Indigenous peoples on reservations—but Dewey's European American interlocutors did not criticize him for these oversights.

The tendencies toward idealization that one finds in Dewey's work are not as prominent in the perspectives of either Du Bois or Locke. Perhaps because of their personal experiences with racism, the collective knowledge of African American communities, and both men's extensive historical study of European imperialism, neither shared Dewey's tendencies to build democratic principles into their interpretations of U.S. society. In comparison to Dewey, Mills would say that Du Bois and Locke occupied an epistemologically privileged perspective, for they were brought into continual contact with the ways in which the promises of the nation were violated (Mills 1998, 110). Indeed, both men developed far more sophisticated understandings of the social realities of U.S. democracy and the nation's relation to the rest of the world than had Dewey. For Locke, Dewey's exceptionalist belief in the accomplishments of the United States was itself a modern blindness to be understood. He comments:

> Now the reason why we flatter ourselves so much as modern [people and gloat] upon the differences between ourselves and ancient society is simply that we overlook these facts. [We overlook that our race and class practice has scarcely progressed beyond those practices of primitive societies, that we still sequester groups of people on reservations and in ghettos, and that consequently, our society remains disorganized.] We

> overlook these facts for a certain very definite reason, a reason which I
> will cite as a very natural one [:] because modern society has developed
> an instinct for insulating itself, that is to say, for ignoring social facts.
> (Locke 1992, 52)

And indeed Dewey does seem to maintain his U.S. exceptionalism by not
knowing very much about the state of racial relationships in his own society. Moreover, Dewey appeared unprepared to see the racial patterns
in his own nation's foreign policy.

Both Locke and Du Bois had engaged in rigorous studies of the historical development of the United States in relation to the period of European expansionism, and even though both men have been criticized
for being too idealistic and too enamored with European culture, they
did not share Dewey's illusions suggesting that the frontier was the site
where a democratic ethos was forged. Throughout his writings, Du Bois
is continually reminding the reader that the process of claiming the frontier was a matter of conquest. For instance, in relating a trip to rural
Georgia after Reconstruction, he reminds us of the sights of Indian wars
and slave revolts as if the countryside itself symbolized the struggles that
had transpired there (Du Bois 1944, 29, 70, 71, 76). For Du Bois, the conquest of North America was one substory in an era of colonialism:

> Indeed, the characteristic of our age is the contact of European civiliza-
> tion with the world's undeveloped peoples. . . . War, murder, slavery, ex-
> termination, and debauchery—this has again and again been the result
> of carrying civilization and the blessed gospel to the isles of the sear and
> the heathen without the law. (1944, 99)

Since neither Du Bois nor Locke had edited the racial violence out of
their understanding of U.S. history, their assessment of the country's priorities and war aims was far more critical than Dewey's. Believing that the
United States was forged in an international movement that pitted Europeans against people of color, Du Bois and Locke expected to see a
racial dynamic at play both in the motivations that led to the war and in
U.S. response to the warring nations.

In the view of both Du Bois and Locke, World War I was an imperialistic war where European nations were fighting over their access to the
riches of nations populated by people of color (Locke 1992, 30–32, xl).
Du Bois says, in "World War and the Color Line," "The present war in Europe is one of the great disasters due to race and color prejudice, . . . the
wild quest for imperial expansion among colored races between Germany, England, and France primarily, and Belgium, Italy, Russia and Aus-
tria-Hungary in lesser degree." Du Bois's analysis shows that he—unlike
Dewey—had been keeping close track of the ways in which European

powers and now settler states such as the United States were busy carving out domains of plunder among countries populated by people of color:

> The colonies which England and France own and Germany covets are largely in tropical and semitropical lands and inhabited by black, brown and yellow peoples. In such colonies there is a chance to confiscate land, work the natives at low wages, make large profits and open wide markets for cheap European manufactures. Asia, Africa, the South Sea Islands, the West Indies, Mexico and Central America, and much of South America have long been designated by the white worlds as fit field for this kind of commercial exploitation, for the benefit of Europe and with little regard for the welfare of the natives. One has only to remember the forced labor in South Africa, the outrages in Congo, the cocoa slavery in Portuguese Africa, the land monopoly and peonage of Mexico, the exploitation of Chinese coolies and the rubber horror of the Amazon to realize what white imperialism is doing today in well-known cases, not to mention thousands of less-known instances. (Du Bois 1972, 245–46; also see Du Bois 1970, 251)

With European nations vying for competitive positions, Locke argued, the United States was pursuing a strategy of aligning itself with Great Britain:

> America is substantially not only a supporter but an ally in this joint European policy of race empire. Not only in the flurry of imperialism of 1898 but ever since, there has been an adoption of this policy in American thought and American statesmanship, not essentially as a practice of empire but in the growing sense of ethnic unity and affiliation with the group of peoples who propose not only to dominate the universe but to keep that dominance in their hands. (Locke 1992, 30–31)

Locke argued that many U.S. political leaders sought access to international spoils of empire by developing an alliance with the militarily strong and colonially established Great Britain. Given these perspectives, it is understandable that neither Du Bois nor Locke expected World War I or the treaty at Versailles to produce a more democratic international order.

Dewey, in contrast, was surprised and deeply disappointed when the resolution of World War I was not a step toward international democracy (Bullert 1983). When the League of Nations did not realize his hopes, he blamed it on the nationalism and imperialism of European nations, but even at this point of despair, he did not consider the possibility that the United States was itself pursuing an imperialist agenda. Nor did he consider Locke's suggestion that the United States was complicit in a white supremacist arrangement with European powers to divide the global spheres of influence. Even though Dewey felt he had definitely misunderstood

World War I and U.S. participation in it, this blunder did not lead him to abandon the idealistic way of thinking that shaped his work.

Both Du Bois and Locke developed their understandings of the United States in the world economy by paying much greater attention than Dewey to specific historical and sociological realities. Not being burdened with an exceptionalist story of the founding of the United States and its distinctively democratic character, both men were able to see clear racial patterns in U.S. foreign policy that Dewey never appeared to grasp (even in later years when he became critical of U.S. imperialism). If philosophers are to contribute to the development of a more democratic world, then we might do better than Dewey by grounding our theories in a more definite and racially informed sense of the international economy.

Ignorance of Segregation, Cultural Pluralism, and White Racial Formation

The idealism that guided Dewey's foreign policy perspectives likewise shaped his domestic arguments on behalf of democracy. With the tragic aspects of colonialism erased from his narrative of the country's history, Dewey articulated a vision of democracy called "The Great Community," which emphasized the centrality of cross-group social relationships in establishing the context for democratic decision making. Dewey was distinctively aware of the ways in which divisions between European immigrants might prevent the great community from coming into being, but he was entirely unaware of the threat posed to his vision of democracy by the racial segregation of the country. Indeed, the neglect of segregation was the central way in which the epistemology of ignorance became manifest in the political discussions of white political theorists. While Du Bois and Locke expended a significant amount of energy in documenting, describing, and theorizing the undemocratic implications of segregation, white political theorists moved ahead, largely without noticing. Consequently, Dewey and his interlocutors developed a vision of democracy that completely neglected processes of white racial control afoot in the nation; indeed, Dewey was blind to the ways in which his vision of democracy would actually forge and reinforce patterns of white racial formation.

While Roosevelt found the melting pot metaphor of Israel Zangwill's famous play exhilarating, many white philosophers feared its assimilationism and sought a conception of national unity that would allow greater respect for diverse cultural, linguistic, and national traditions. Horace Kallen set the terms for much of this discussion by proposing a conception of cultural pluralism. He argued that different ethnic enclaves ought to be allowed to pursue their own culture, language, and values in their own neighborhood institutions as long as they accepted general processes of democratic decision making when it came to issues regarding the city, state, or nation (Kallen 1956, 100). Kallen considered this a federation of cultures, "a democracy of nationalities, cooperating voluntarily and autonomously through common institutions in the enterprise of self-realization through the perfection of men according to their kind" (Kallen 1924, 124). He likened it to an orchestra:

> As in an orchestra, every type of instrument has its specific tonality, founded in its substance and form; as every type has its appropriate theme and melody in the whole symphony, so in society each ethnic group is the natural instrument, its spirit and culture are its theme and melody, and the harmony and dissonances and discords of them all make the symphony of civilization, with this difference: a musical symphony is written before it is played; in the symphony of civilization the playing is the writing. (Kallen 1915, 220)

Although Dewey appreciated Kallen's defense of groups' cultural integrity, he was a bit concerned that Kallen had not dealt sufficiently with the issue of national unity. He wrote in a letter to Kallen saying, "I quite agree with your symphony idea, but upon condition we really get a symphony and not a lot of different instruments playing simultaneously" (Menand 2001, 400). While Dewey agreed with Kallen's criticisms of assimilation to British norms, he did want a reciprocal process of assimilation of different groups to each other: "I find that many who talk the loudest about the need of a supreme and unified Americanism of spirit really mean some special code or tradition to which they happen to be attached. They have some pet tradition which they would impose upon all." Consequently, Dewey argued for a perspective where each group

> shall surrender into a common fund of wisdom and experience what it especially has to contribute. All of these surrenders and contributions taken together create the national spirit of America. The dangerous thing is for each factor to isolate itself, to try to live off its past, and then to attempt to impose itself upon other elements, or, at least, to keep itself intact and thus refuse to accept what other cultures have to offer, so as thereby to be transmuted into authentic Americanism. (Dewey mw.10.205)

It was in the name of developing a process whereby groups could share knowledge across groups that Dewey developed his conception of democracy and the Great Community. Distinctively, Dewey argued that a democratic society is one where there are high levels of communication within groups and across groups (lw.2.326–27). Given his fear of the ethnic parochialism of groups such as the Polish community in Philadelphia,

Dewey's conception of a democratic society was intended to help break down divisions of nation, culture, and language that separated different immigrant groups—especially the "old immigrants," such as the British, and "new immigrants," such as Italians, Russian Jews, and Polish Catholics.

However, neither Dewey's version of the Great Community, nor Kallen's ethnic federation was developed with attention to the distinctive processes of segregation, where African Americans of all economic levels were relegated to specific sections of the city and where the jobs available to African Americans were limited to low-level sectors of the economy, such as the situation documented by Du Bois in Philadelphia (Du Bois 1966). Kallen's defense of ethnic separatism could easily operate as an ideological justification for segregation, and it is probably Locke's focus upon issues of segregation that prevented him from adopting Kallen's position. According to Locke's reasoning, separatism for African Americans would entail that they did not benefit from what the nation had to offer. Modern societies, he argued, "cannot tolerate any great divergence in what we call the essential social conventions"; "they exact that a man who elects, as an individual or [part of] a group, to live in a modern society must adopt, more or less wholesale, the fundamental or cardinal principles of that social culture." In the United States, he argued, "they have a very fixed and definite notion of their type, and to enjoy the privileges of such a society means to conform to that type" (Locke 1992, 91; Menand 2001, 397–98). Locke thought that African Americans ought to develop their distinctive voices as well as pride in those voices, and that was what *The New Negro* was devoted to, but African Americans should continue, in their housing and work, to seek assimilation (Locke 1992, 97).

Even though Dewey would have welcomed Locke's defense of assimilation, he—unlike Locke—appeared not to notice that African Americans were not being allowed to assimilate or even to have egalitarian cross-group communication across the color line. Dewey's not noticing seems especially suspicious when we have very little evidence that he was engaged in discussion across the color line (even though he had some contact with Du Bois through the NAACP) (Eldridge 2004, 13). Dewey's idealistic model of democracy involves groups building sympathy for one another as they share institutions and cooperatively solve problems. Segregation posed an obvious threat to this vision, and indeed, Du Bois articulates in clear terms the ways in which segregation prevents the development of sympathy across lines of race. Speaking of the segregation in Southern towns, Du Bois says,

> Now if one notices carefully one will see that between these two worlds, despite much physical contact and daily intermingling, there is almost no community of intellectual life or point of transference where the

thoughts and feelings of one race can come into direct contact and sympathy with the thoughts and feelings of the other. (Du Bois 1944, 110)

It is a particular complaint of both Du Bois and Locke that there is no exchange between the "aristocracy and leaders of the blacks" and the "best
elements of the whites" (Du Bois 1944, 110).

In places where Dewey discusses ethnic tensions and divisions within
cities, he is not considering the political, economic, and social forces that
ensure racial segregation. Dewey tends to think of ethnic separatism as a
matter of choosing to live and work with those who share one's language,
culture, and national affiliations, and these are clearly not the factors
that maintain the racial segregation of the color line. In *The Philadelphia
Negro*, Du Bois (1966) shows that African Americans of all classes were
relegated to particular sections of the city and particular job categories
(most commonly jobs, such as domestic service, that were in continuity
with the work African Americans performed as slaves). As large numbers
of European immigrants entered the city, they were able to gain access to
white-controlled housing and job markets by identifying with the white
majority, as both old and new immigrants honored the solidarity of skin
color, apparently viewing the barriers of language, culture, and nationality as secondary. Du Bois shows that, over decades, African Americans
were displaced from the jobs where they had gained the greatest success,
such as catering and skilled labor, as the white community turned to
white workers to fill their places. And when African Americans were part
of strong voting coalitions, new white immigrants were often at the fore-
front of violent mobs that attached African Americans to intimidate
them politically (Du Bois 1966, 31, 98, 120, 126–27). White racial solidarity served to overcome the barriers to community that Dewey considered, but—in itself—operated as a much greater threat to community
than the divisions of language and culture that occupied the attention of
Dewey and Kallen.

By concentrating upon the divisions among European immigrants
and ignoring the processes of racial segregation, Dewey contributed to a
significant tendency in white political and social thought. Because they
had erased the legacy of slavery from their understanding of the modern
city, Dewey and Kallen assumed that the tensions between European
groups were paradigmatic of racial divisions in the society, that is, white
philosophers took cases of cultural separatism to be the same as cases of
forced segregation.[5] Just as Dewey's accounts of the frontier edited out the
violent acts of the dominant group, Dewey's and Kallen's writings about
democracy served as a discourse that erased the race riots and forced relo-
cations then occurring in Midwestern and Northern cities, while redefin-
ing the meaning of segregation to be the same as choosing to live with

one's own group and pursue one's own values. The greatest threats to democracy—such as the white mobs that attacked African Americans in East Saint Louis—were defined outside the theory.

Consequently, what Du Bois had labeled the problem of the twentieth century was placed outside of white philosophers' discussions of cultural pluralism. Mills might say that Dewey's democratic theory has a "lexical gap," that because he has not theorized segregation as an obstacle to the realization of democracy, his theory will not enable us to overcome segregation and work toward democracy (Mills 1998, 110). Moreover, Dewey contributed to the epistemology of ignorance by offering a dominant group understanding of U.S. democracy that blurs the distinction between separatism and segregation and implicitly blames the victims of racial violence for their disinterest in contributing to the national good. And lastly, Dewey's overwhelming focus upon developing close relations among European groups, to the exclusion of people of color, could only serve the process of white racial formation by encouraging "whites" of different languages and nations to band together to reserve the most resources for themselves.

Notes Toward Diminishing
White Philosophical Ignorance

Dewey was antiracist, as Hutchinson argues, but his version of antiracism can hardly be offered as a model for European American theorists seeking to emerge from the epistemology of ignorance. The motivations guiding Dewey's antiracism combined an epistemological distrust of racial categories with an awareness that much of the social science of his day was disproving racial generalizations. Morally and politically, Dewey wished to undercut all specious claims to hierarchy en route to establishing the communicative conditions for democracy. This combination of epistemological and moral concerns enabled Dewey to criticize the faulty reasoning underlying racial practices, such as intelligence testing in schools but did not prepare him to see the macroscopic racial patterns in U.S. foreign policy or within U.S. cities. Consequently, Dewey's suspicions of racially based reasoning did not go far enough to enable him to actually chart a democratic course, because his antiracism was not guided by a larger understanding of the patterns of white supremacy.

Dewey's blindness to patterns of white supremacy appears in his unwillingness to differentiate his position from Roosevelt's. Dewey did not break with the guiding values of a U.S. society set on an expansionist foreign policy, nor did he break with the exceptionalist narrative of the United States as a nation that was every day realizing democracy. Dewey erroneously considered the task of developing a nonracist philosophy to be merely a matter of eliminating unwarranted racial generalizations from his theory. Contemporary European American philosophers hoping to work ourselves out of the epistemology of ignorance must do much more than avoid racist generalizations. We must place ourselves historically and sociologically in relation to the racial strategies of white groups and seek to contest those strategies, whether they be international acts of neocolonialism or domestic acts of segregation and exclusion. When the United States attacks yet another nation populated by people of color, with promises of bringing democracy to the region, it is incumbent upon democratic theorists to critically scrutinize such opportunistic references to "democracy." When conservative white groups increase the surveillance of Latinas/os and thus effectively limit the ability of Latina/o citizens and activists to speak publicly and influence government policy, these racial movements are very much a part of democratic theory (Flores and Benmayor 1997). Philosophers who enter debates over the nature of just wars or cosmopolitanism without considering the racial dynamics of international politics and the disproportionate power of European and European-descendant nations, or philosophers who discuss citizenship assuming a free public space in which the possibilities for political participation and cross-group exchange are available to all people on American soil—such philosophers follow Dewey's example in ignoring and obscuring the very real social processes whereby white racial supremacy is extended.

The most basic step away from Dewey's blindness lies in a rejection of the stories of U.S. exceptionalism. Dewey's sensitivity to the racial strategies of the dominant group was blunted by his acceptance of the basic outlines of the narrative of manifest destiny. As Cornel West argues so brilliantly, Dewey was influenced by Ralph Waldo Emerson's faith that the Anglo-Saxons were a chosen people destined to overrun North America, bringing democracy in their wake (West 1989, 28–35). West invites us to see the resonances of Emerson's position in subsequent pragmatist scholars, and Emerson did indeed leave his imprint upon Dewey's thought. Dewey offers a culturalist narrative that rearticulates the basic outlines of the doctrine of manifest destiny. Even though Dewey's antiracism prevents him from thinking that there is a group that is accurately called the Anglo-Saxons, he nonetheless accepts the fundamental story suggesting that the group that colonized the North American continent is distinctively capable of bringing democracy to the rest of the world. Dewey altered Emerson's and Roosevelt's accounts in believing the advance of American citizens had little to do with their genetic makeup, but Dewey did believe Americans were uniquely positioned to further the spread of democracy, as shown by his testimony in favor of entering World War I. Even in its culturalist rearticulation, this is a narrative that is well designed to justify U.S. expansionism. The promise of bringing democracy to other nations has underwritten countless U.S. invasions; most recently, the promise of bringing democracy to the Middle East has been the most basic justification for the invasion of Iraq (LaFeber 1984; Khalidi 2004). This narrative, with its exceptional protagonist, carries forth the arrogance of Emerson's and Roosevelt's white supremacist accounts and needs to be abandoned.

Instead of accepting the traditional exceptionalist narrative, U.S. philosophers would do better to follow the example of Du Bois and work from a historical understanding that is more completely rooted in the factual record—a record that shows gains and losses, winners and losers. Philosophers cannot further the pursuit of democracy in the United States if we, like Dewey, allow stories of an inevitable advance of democracy to obscure our understanding of historical and contemporary acts of racial control; slavery, the taking of Mexican territories, and the exploitation of Chinese laborers continue to undermine democratic possibilities in the present. We might better release ourselves from the claim that exceptionalist narratives make upon us if we compare those stories to the narratives told by groups that suffered acts of colonization. Du Bois used the words "war, murder, slavery, extermination, and debauchery" to cover the same acts that Emerson, Roosevelt, and Dewey considered the march of progress. Bishop Desmond Tutu offers narratives of reconciliation and national rebuilding following the tragic processes of colonization and apartheid suffered by Africans in South Africa (Tutu 1999). Wole Soyinka offers narratives of repayment for the centuries of devastation that Africans have suffered as Europeans preyed upon their continent—stealing humans, land, and resources (Soyinka 1988). Shannon Sullivan offers us an example of what it takes for a European American philosopher to respond meaningfully to such narratives when she argues that white Americans need to pay reparations to African Americans partly to repay a debt and partly so that dominant group members can learn to stop claiming the credit for African American accomplishments (Sullivan 2003).

European American philosophers could perhaps prepare ourselves to break Dewey's silences if we engaged in dialogue concerning the relative merit of divergent historical narratives. When contemporary philosophers are silent concerning the meaning that imperialist wars have for the nature of U.S. democracy, when we do not consider the role racial segregation presently plays in limiting civic and economic opportunities for people of color, and when discussions of justice do not include a consideration of the disproportionate incarceration of men of color then we are continuing Dewey's tradition of silence. When Dewey was silent on matters of colonization and lynching, it indicated his inability to understand and respond to such acts in a way that would further the cause of democracy. Dewey's sanitized version of U.S. history performed the dual function of disconnecting the nation from the patterns of European colonization (for the United States was a new nation that had broken with the old world) while offering a celebrationist account of Dewey's own group, which effectively prevented him from understanding whites as aggressors. Consequently, the imperialism of 1898 did not raise questions for Dewey concerning the nation's white supremacist alliance with Europe (as it did for Locke), nor did the race riots in East Saint Louis warn Dewey that whites were willing to use violent tactics to monopolize jobs (as it did for Du Bois). Dewey was either unable to see racial patterns, underestimated their significance, or was left with an uneasy sense that he had better say nothing, since acts that violated his conception of democracy (such as the race riots in East Saint Louis) had no systematic place in his understanding of his society, hence the silences Paul Taylor exposed and criticized. According to Taylor,

> claiming that there is *nothing I can say* on a matter that manifestly concerns me, if I claim this sincerely, is a way of denying my connection, and, at the same time, of refusing to examine myself closely enough to uncover and find words for the connection. . . . Participating in whiteness-as-invisibility means denying that one has a perspective on or stake in the racial terrain. It means rejecting, or ignoring, the burden of identifying—of conceptualizing, of seeing which words apply to—one's place in a system of social forces and relations. If this is right, then Dewey's embrace of silence is a way of declining to identify his own perspective, his personal perspective, on racial injustice. He never took up the burden of explaining, to himself and others, his connection to white supremacy. And that is a paradigmatically white thing to do. (Taylor 2004, 231–32, emphasis in original)

Following Taylor's analysis, it is the duty of white philosophers to be able to place themselves in relation to the racist acts of their own group and, when appropriate, to show the nondemocratic aspects of the aggressive acts of white leaders, citizens, or philosophers. Mills's concept, "global white supremacy," is designed to enable theorists to conceptualize the ways in which macroscopic actions of white control are combined with day-to-day acts of racial solidarity to maintain a system of white privilege.

If we employ Mills's concept of "global white supremacy," then recent U.S. wars in the Middle East appear to be an extension of the process whereby the nation is struggling with European powers for access to the wealth and labor of the region—the very process criticized by Du Bois and Locke during World War I. Were contemporary philosophers to use the concept of global white supremacy, then they would be directed to see the ways in which U.S. foreign policy obeys the color line while domestic policies reinforce what Massey and Denton refer to as "American Apartheid" (Massey and Denton 1993). Use of a concept such as global white supremacy would probably violate the methodological scruples of many contemporary European American philosophers—as it would have violated Dewey's methodological principles. However, this tension forces us to consider the ways in which methodological commitments may themselves further the epistemology of ignorance. For Dewey, a commitment to scientific conceptions of definition helped maintain his racial ignorance. The same scientific scruples that led Dewey to reject the use of racial words such as "Anglo Saxon" also prohibited the use of structural words such as "bourgeoisie" and the Marxist analysis that went with the word. Consider Dewey's criticism of class analysis:

> Any one habituated to the use of the method of science will view with considerable suspicion the erection of actual human beings into fixed entities called classes, having no overlapping interests and so internally unified and externally separated that they are made the protagonists of history—itself hypothetical. Such an idea of classes is a survival of a rigid logic that once prevailed in the sciences of nature, but that no longer has any place here. (Dewey lw.11.56)

The word "proletariat," like the word "white," offers a theoretical—that is, nonempirical—prediction that a heterogenous group of people will share the same interests and will act in the same way. Instead of relying upon a theory of classes or utilizing a macroscopic theoretical tool such as global white supremacy, Dewey's social analysis tended to focus on the empirical traits of specific situations. While such a methodology has the advantage of avoiding the importation of a theory a priori, it has the disadvantage of allowing the philosopher to miss definite patterns that a theory of class or race may have enabled the theorist to see. When a white philosopher suffering from the epistemology of ignorance utilizes the situation-specific epistemology espoused by Dewey, then he is very likely to build white common sense—as well as white ignorance—into the explanation. Here Mills's concept of a global white supremacy would force a European American philosopher to consider racial patterns that might otherwise be entirely neglected.[6]

Had Dewey considered the operations of a white global supremacy in explaining the outbreak of World War I, his attention would have been directed to a significant range of evidence that he appears to have ignored. Similarly, had Dewey studied *The Philadelphia Negro*, he would have encountered evidence that problematized the way he was thinking of racial separation in the city. Even though Dewey was known in philosophical circles as someone who was committed to building bridges between his own discipline and psychology, sociology, and anthropology, his methods remained far less factually driven than either Du Bois's or Locke's. Du Bois's extensive writings on the international political economy, as well as his empirical studies of cities and rural areas, reveal a scholar who devoted considerable time to understanding his historical circumstance. Du Bois's ability to theorize by starting with a concrete historical context provides eloquent testimony to the value of philosophy that is informed by its own historical location and a factual portrait of what is happening in the larger society and world.

Had Dewey been in meaningful contact with Du Bois and Locke, his rather problematic understandings of World War I and cultural pluralism would have received a much more stringent intellectual test. Even though Dewey was sharply criticized by European American theorists for his stand regarding World War I, the most common criticism was that he had not maintained his idealism (see, e.g., Bourne 1964). Locke and Du Bois would have brought a very different set of lenses to this discussion. And, indeed, it is Dewey's lack of exposure to the works of Du Bois and Locke that is the most alarming lesson to learn from Dewey's racial blindness. It is difficult to find evidence to explain why white U.S. philosophers in the early part of the twentieth century were not studying a monumental figure such as Du Bois or a profound writer such as Locke. Perhaps methodological disagreements with white philosophers prevented the latter from studying Du Bois and Locke. Perhaps Du Bois and Locke were framing questions in ways white philosophers had difficulty understanding. Perhaps white philosophers were afraid to listen attentively to or read carefully the works of authors who might call their own privilege into question.[7] Perhaps Du Bois and Locke were thought to hail from a group that was unlikely to produce profound thought.[8] Perhaps this intellectual segregation embodies the same denial of Black humanity as housing segregation.

Regardless of the explanation, intellectual segregation ensured that Dewey was not exposed to the insight of Du Bois and Locke, and it is clear that the profundity of Dewey's thought suffered in the process. Contemporary European American philosophers should scrutinize their own work to see if they too are suffering from the intellectual mediocrity produced by intellectual segregation. U.S. philosophy has lagged behind the arts in benefiting from cross-race exchange, and a perusal of most European American philosopher's citations will show that we mostly work from a European American cannon and debate the insights of other white philosophers. Consequently, the methodological standards that govern these debates themselves reflect the insularity of the participants. It should be profoundly humbling to acknowledge the truth of Lucius Outlaw's demonstration that instead of engaging the substance of African philosophical views European American scholars spent four decades debating whether Africans have philosophy, because African conceptions of the true, good, and beautiful were not offered in accordance with the methodological principles hammered out by a small group of European American philosophers (Outlaw 1996, 51–73). Just as there is a need for a plurality of ideas, there is a need for a plurality of methods, and European American philosophers must consider the possibility that their tendency to dismiss particular ways of thinking as "not rigorous" is itself a practice that maintains the epistemology of ignorance.

The separatist tendencies that one finds among European American philosophers today were clearly present in the early twentieth century. Dewey, it appears, felt no need to cross the color line in his philosophical endeavors, while both Du Bois and Locke felt a pressing need for cross-race exchange. Both Du Bois and Locke commented upon the existence of intellectual segregation (while, characteristically, Dewey was silent on the topic). Locke argued that "the most unsatisfactory feature of our present stage of race relationships" was that "the most intelligent and representative elements of the two race groups have at so many points got quite out of vital touch with one another" (Locke 1925, 9). In Locke's view, intellectuals have the responsibility to speak meaningfully across racial divisions, and even though he did not say so, he probably mourned the unwillingness of white intellectuals to engage in those discussions.

An often assumed aspect of philosophical methodology is the process whereby a theorist's work is critically discussed and reviewed by the larger intellectual community. Racial segregation within the academy operates to artificially limit membership in the intellectual community and consequently to lower the standards to which theorists will be held. The most potent weapon against the epistemology of ignorance is the development of personal and institutional commitments to diversify the intellectual community so the perspectives of individuals ranging from all groups and all cultural traditions have a place in shaping the nature of the discussion and the insights brought to the table.

Notes

I would like to thank my colleagues Donna Deyhle and Audrey Thompson for their insightful comments on previous drafts of this chapter. I also would like to thank Shannon Sullivan and Nancy Tuana for their extremely helpful comments on two drafts of this chapter.

1. All subsequent references to Dewey's works will be to *The Middle Works, 1899–1924* (mw) and *The Later Works, 1925–1953* (lw). For instance, lw.15.309 means *Later Works*, volume 15, page 309.

2. See Walter White (1996, 2001). Du Bois's fact-finding mission to East Saint Louis produced ample reason to believe that the killing of African American workers was primarily instigated by white workers' resistance to African Americans claiming an increasing number of jobs. See David Levering Lewis (1993, 536–40).

3. As Mills (1997, 77) shows, neither Rawls nor Nozick considers the legacy of slavery in his discussion of democratic theory.

4. Of the many times Dewey speaks of the frontier in his manuscripts, I can find only one reference to violence, in the later work *Liberalism and Social Action*. Here he does say that contemporary violence is related to the frontier, although it is worth noting that even here he does not recognize the racial character of the violence: "It is not surprising in view of our standing dependence upon the use of coercive force that at every time of crisis coercion breaks out into open violence. In this country, with its tradition of violence fostered by frontier conditions and by the conditions under which immigration went on during the greater part of our history, resort to violence is especially recurrent on the part of those who are in power. In times of imminent change, our verbal and sentimental worship of the Constitution, with its guarantees of civil liberties of expression, publication and assemblage, readily goes overboard. Often the officials of the law are the worst offenders, acting as agents of some power that rules the economic life of a community" (lw.11.46).

5. Notice that the word "race" refers to "Irish, German, and Bohemian" peoples in the essay, Dewey, "The School as Social Center," mw.2.86. See also the use of "race" in mw.10.184, mw.15.151, and lw.15.282.

6. Mills (1998, 100) does not argue that a theory of global white supremacy should supplant other explanatory frameworks, just that it should be included among ways of understanding the U.S. polity.

7. Even sympathetic white reviewers of Du Bois's *Darkwater* appear to have had trouble accepting Du Bois's anger. See Marable (1999).

8. Menand (2001, 390–91) notes that when Kallen advocated to his mentors on Locke's behalf, he took pains to say that Locke was unlike others from his group.

References

Bourne, Randolph. 1964. *War and the Intellectuals.* New York: Harper and Row.
Bullert, Gary. 1983. *The Politics of John Dewey.* Buffalo: Prometheus Books.
Commager, Henry Steele. 1950. *The American Mind.* New Haven, CT: Yale University Press.
Dewey, John. 1976–1983. *The Middle Works, 1899–1924.* Edited by Jo Ann Boydston. 15 vols. Carbondale: Southern Illinois University Press.
———. 1981–1990. *The Later Works, 1925–1953.* Edited by Jo Ann Boydston. 17 vols. Carbondale: Southern Illinois University Press.
Du Bois, W. E. B. 1944. *The Souls of Black Folks* New York: Dover.
———. 1966. *The Philadelphia Negro.* Philadelphia: University of Pennsylvania Press.
———. 1970. "The African Roots of the War." In *W. E. B. Du Bois Speaks*, ed. Philip Foner, 244–57. New York: Pathfinder Press.

————. 1972. "World War and the Color Line." In *The Emerging Thought of W. E. B. Du Bois*, ed. Henry Lee Moon, 245–48. New York: Simon and Schuster.

Eldridge, Michael. 2004. "Dewey on Race and Social Change." In *Pragmatism and the Problem of Race*, eds. Bill Lawson and Donald Koch, 11–21. Bloomington: Indiana University Press.

Flores, William, and Rena Benmayor, eds. 1997. *Latino Cultural Citizenship*. Boston: Beacon Press.

Fraser, Nancy. 1998. "Another Pragmatism: Alain Locke, Critical 'Race' Theory, and the Politics of Culture." In *The Revival of Pragmatism*, ed. Morris Dickstein, 157–75. Durham, NC: Duke University Press.

Gerstle, Gary. 2001. *American Crucible: Race and Nation in the Twentieth Century*. Princeton, NJ: Princeton University Press.

Hutchinson, George. 1995. *The Harlem Renaissance in Black and White*. Cambridge, MA: The Belknap Press of Harvard University Press.

Kallen, Horace. 1915. "Democracy versus the Melting Pot." *The Nation* 100: 190–94, 217–20.

————. 1924. *Culture and Democracy in the United States*. New York: Boni and Liveright.

————. 1956. *Cultural Pluralism and the American Idea*. Philadelphia: University of Pennsylvania Press.

Khalidi, Rashid. 2004. *Resurrecting Empire: Western Footprints and America's Perilous Path in the Middle East*. Boston: Beacon Press.

LaFeber, Walter. 1984. *Inevitable Revolutions: The United States in Central America*. New York: Norton.

Lewis, David Levering. 1993. *W. E. B. Du Bois: Biography of a Race*. New York: Henry Holt.

Locke, Alain. 1925. "The New Negro." In *The New Negro*, ed. Alain Locke, 3–16. New York: Simon and Schuster.

————. 1992. *Race Contacts and Interracial Relations*. Washington, DC: Howard University Press.

Marable, Manning. 1999. "Introduction." In *Darkwater: Voices from within the Veil*, ed. W. E. B. Du Bois, v–viii. New York: Dover Press.

Massey, Douglas, and Nancy Denton. 1993. *American Apartheid: Segregation and the Making of the Underclass*. Cambridge, MA: Harvard University Press.

Menand, Louis. 2001. *The Metaphysical Club*. New York: Farrar, Straus and Giroux.

Mills, Charles W. 1997. *The Racial Contract*. Ithaca, NY: Cornell University Press.

————. 1998. *Blackness Visible*. Ithaca, NY: Cornell University Press.

————. 2003. *From Class to Race*. Lanham, MD: Rowman and Littlefield.

Outlaw, Lucius. 1996. *On Race and Philosophy*. New York: Routledge.

Pappas, Gregory Fernando. 2002. "Dewey's Philosophical Approach to Racial Prejudice." In *Philosophers on Race*, ed. Julie Ward and Tommy Lott, 285–97. Oxford: Blackwell.

Roosevelt, Theodore. 1995. *The Winning of the West*. Lincoln: University of Nebraska Press.

Soyinka, Wole. 1988. *The Past Must Address Its Present*. New York: Anson-Phelps Stokes Institute for Afro-American and American Indian Affairs.

Sullivan, Shannon. 2003. "Remembering the Gift: W. E. B. Du Bois on the Unconscious and Economic Operations of Racism." *Transactions of the C. S. Peirce Society* 39:2: 205–25.

Taylor, Paul. 2004. "Silence and Sympathy: Dewey's Whiteness." In *What White Looks Like*, ed. George Yancy, 227–41. New York: Routledge.

Turner, Fredrick Jackson. 1920. *The Frontier in American History*. New York: Henry Holt.

Tutu, Desmond. 1999. *No Future without Forgiveness*. New York: Doubleday.

West, Cornel. 1989. *The American Evasion of Philosophy*. Madison: University of Wisconsin Press.

White, Walter. 1996. *The Fire in the Flint*. Athens: University of Georgia Press.

———. 2001. *Rope and Faggot*. Notre Dame, IN: University of Notre Dame Press.

CHAPTER 10

Social Ordering and the
Systematic Production of Ignorance

Lucius T. Outlaw (Jr.)

When I ponder my lived-through and learned-about experiences of white racial domination and the subordination of racialized African and African-descended persons and peoples in the United States of America, among the many disturbing matters are several that especially enrage me. First, the centuries-long determined efforts expended by settler-colonists-become-imperialist-capitalist white racial supremacists to ensure that successive generations of white children would be nurtured systematically with both knowledge and ignorance to grow into confirmed, practicing racial supremacist white adults. And second, successive generations of children—black, brown, yellow, red, mixed—would be *mis*educated to be racially inferior adults subordinate to white adults and children. This miseducation would involve the deliberate, ethically sanctioned production of ignorance in folks of all races, too often with concomitant dehumanizing notions: of themselves as superior white persons and race, others as inferior races of nonwhite nonpersons—and these doings and consequences were both legal and ethical . . .

The thematic focus that occasioned this chapter, "Ethics and Epistemologies of Ignorance," has been particularly provocative, provoking more probing considerations of what has long troubled me as one of the most pernicious aspects of the White Racial Supremacist structuring of life among races and ethnie in what became the United States of America: namely, that this ordering of life required that *ignorance*, as well as knowledge of various kinds, be socially produced and distributed, and done so *systematically*, across generations. And as must be the case for any institutionalized construction that serves as machinery for the conceptual and social ordering of shared existence, this systematic production

197

and maintenance of ignorance was made *legitimate*: that is, it was made rationally persuasive for, thus acceptable to and valued positively by, sufficient numbers of persons and groups in dominant positions in the racialized hierarchy to provide a sustaining social base to the ordering by a socially distributed, well-endorsed, and broadly and deeply sedimented "common sense," as well as by more formal and authoritative "knowledge," of *reality*. Persons in institutions and organizations ostensibly devoted to the production, legitimation, sanctification, and mediation of what would serve social ordering as forms of authoritative "knowledge"— teachers and administrators, natural philosophers and scientists, ministers and theologians; in schools, institutions of worship and higher learning, and in learned organizations—in fulfilling their roles would devote considerable effort to the elaboration of epistemologies by which to produce and legitimate *ignorance*. That is, lack of knowledge and understanding would be a consequence of the certainties produced by the sanctioned and legitimated knowledge that would render it unnecessary to engage with fully and humanely, with empathy and openness, thus to learn from those races deemed inferior to the Superior White Race.

The more assured and assuring their presumed knowledge and understanding of the inferior races, the more confident were the racial supremacists of their ordering of the social world on behalf of their superordination and the dominating, oppressive control, the managing of social distance, and the avoidance of intimacies with lower races regardless of how close the social and geographical proximities (as with the utilization of Negro slaves in the homes of white slave owners to prepare and serve food, nurture slave owners' children, and care for the well-being of white folks otherwise). The epistemological requirements for knowledge and understanding necessary for the success of White Racial Supremacy were determined fundamentally by the agenda of enslavement and exploitation.

A constitutive factor in this agenda was a hierarchical racial ontology that provided supposed knowledge of the "natural order" of the races according to which the Negro race had its naturally subordinate place. Social, economic, political, and cultural orderings of the races were effected in keeping with this ontology. Accordingly, there was no need to know living persons of supposedly inferior races in their own right and on their own terms, only that they be "known" *by race*, and "known" as such by white folks. Such knowledge produced ignorance. Further, the "knowing" and concomitant ignorance were ordered and valorized by the requirements of ordering political economies and social-cultural lifeworlds in which the enslavement and exploitation of Africans and their descendants (and there were, as well, epistemological and taxonomic criteria for determining racial ancestry and decent, such as the "one-drop" rule[1]) were enforced as the normal way of life.

And with dire consequences for those peoples who were thought of as inferior and whose lives and living conditions were ordered to produce and maintain their inferiority. Alexis de Tocqueville, the otherwise astute observer and analyst of developing democracy in U.S. America, conveyed a serious misreading of the extent of the dire consequences of racialized superordination and subordination for Africans and their descendants in his "The Present and Probable Future Condition of the Three Races That Inhabit the Territory of the United States," in his *Democracy in America*:

> If we reason from what passes in the world, we should almost say that the European is to the other races of mankind what man himself is to the lower animals: he makes them subservient to his use, and when he cannot subdue he destroys them. Oppression has, at one stroke, deprived the descendants of the Africans of almost all the privileges of humanity. The Negro of the United States has lost even the remembrance of his country; the language which his forefathers spoke is never heard around him; he abjured their religion and forgot their customs when he ceased to belong to Africa, without acquiring any claim to European privileges. But he remains half-way between the two communities, isolated between two races; sold by the one, repulsed by the other; finding not a spot in the universe to call by the name of country, except the faint image of a home which the shelter of his master's roof affords.[2]

I say "misreading" because Tocqueville too was impaired by the ignorance-producing assurance with which he observed and assessed racially ordered life in the United States during his travels. As best I have been able to determine *so far*, at no point during his travels and his many intimate social encounters did he engage in face-to-face conversations with Negroes as a source of information for constructing his "knowledge" of one of the three races regarding which he wrote so passionately, often with sarcasm for and condemnation of the genocidal treatment of Native peoples and the enslavement and invidious discrimination enforced on Africans and their descendants. It seems apparent that he too relied on the racially motivated self-justifying "knowledge" of races constructed and legitimated by the formal and informal knowledges of white folks. In so doing he was not compelled, it seems, to consult Negroes for their accounts of realities as they experienced and thus knew them or their knowledge and senses of themselves.

The consequences of his not doing so have been substantial in contributing to the perpetuation of arrogant ignorance. *Democracy in America* has come to be regarded as one of the greatest works of political philosophy on democracy in the United States of America and thus an authoritative source. While I appreciate Tocqueville's (in many ways) masterful efforts and accomplishments in the two-volume work (the first volume was published in 1835, the second in 1840), I continue to be amazed by the extent to which the work, the first volume in particular, maintains its status, given what the author writes in the chapter on ". . . The Three Races . . ." and given Tocqueville's apparent lack of firsthand, respectful, open-minded experiences with Negroes (or with "Indians"). His ignorance was no impediment to his producing what would subsequently be accorded the status of authoritative knowledge and would be put to service in the production of still more ignorance. That is, while Tocqueville took pains to explore in great breadth and depth the unfolding of the historic, in his judgment Providential, project of democratization, it was a project that, to his mind, could not be understood fully and properly except as one effected by an *Anglo*-American *people*, a distinctive race, intraracial differences and complexities notwithstanding. The continuing status of *Democracy in America* as a "classic" work is perpetuated as though it were an account of a project without regard for raciality, not an account of a project in service *only* to a particular race.

Willful silence about Tocqueville's explicit identification of white raciality as a decisive constitutive feature and factor in the U.S. American democratic project served well the perpetuation of racial apartheid in our nation-state while masking and easing the experiences of the vexing existential dilemmas of the massive instabilities and ethical challenges and contradictions generated by racialized enslavement and genocide while pursuing a historic project of democratization guided by the foundational norm of *equality*. The production, mediation, and legitimation of ignorance regarding these challenges and contradictions provided ethical sanctioning for the easing of the experiences of fear and guilt through denial and contorted rationalizations and provided hope for the stabilization and continuation of White Racial Supremacy. Each generation of persons born to be made racially "white," as well as those from Europe who migrated to the United States of America and would, as well, be (or become) "white," had to be socialized into the country's defining and ordering racial realities.

II

Education became a principal means by which to effect the production, mediation, and legitimation of ignorance-sustaining knowledge, via schooling especially, that would achieve this defining and ordering. Very much in keeping with the racialized ontology by which the meaningful and political (economic and cultural) orderings of social worlds were effected, the establishment of schools to inculcate in successive generations the legitimated orderings—that is, to "educate" them—continued the agenda of racial separation and differentiated social provisioning. Schools founded by white folks were to first prepare white children for their various roles, though as white persons, even as children, they were always superior to all who were of a different race. The subsequent establishment of schools for "free" and "freed" Negro men, women, and children, and for the "Indians" who survived the wars of genocide and displacement to the captivities of "reservations," was accomplished with nearly complete accommodation to and endorsement of the hierarchical racialized color lines of segregation in terms of both curricula and demography and in keeping with the principal agenda of schooling: to "civilize" the darker races. For "Indian" children the mission of schooling under the auspices of white folks was devoted to assimilating the children to the worldviews, cultural mores, and forms of behavior and comportment characteristic of Euro-American white people through a process that would have made Plato proud: relocating the children from their natal communities to boarding schools, often at great distances from their homelands and cultures, where, in isolation from the parents and families, they were compelled to forego their dress and language—their entire natal lifeworlds—and to be remade from "savages" into "civilized" young men and women. In the words of Richard Henry Pratt, the founding director of one of the more prominent of these boarding schools, the Carlisle (Pennsylvania) Indian School, the objective was to "Kill the Indian, save the man."[3] Apparently, in the estimation of "knowing" white educators, nothing defining "Indians" was worth saving, worth being the focus of knowledge preservation and knowledge mediation. Such respect for indigenous knowledge would be found only when schooling was under the control of Negroes and Native peoples themselves where there was much, much more to the education of their children that was subversive of the invidious racial ontology and cultural genocide imposed by racist, even well-intentioned white folks.

Schools serving white folks were primary sites for the ethically legitimated production and social distribution of ignorance regarding other races as well as for the production and distribution of the ethically sanctioned knowledge regarding the absolute and relative superiority and inferiority of the white and "colored" races, respectively. These schools became the principal institution through which the terms and agenda of social ordering were mediated to successive generations with determined efforts to preserve the racial hierarchy by educating all who passed through them to the "proper" significance and places of the races. And as the nation-state unfolded into the nineteenth and twentieth centuries, this mission of schooling became all the more acute with massive influxes of new arrivals from southern and eastern Europe. The identity of the nation-state became a matter of no small concern as demographic complexity increased and challenged the political and cultural intraracial hegemony of transatlantic Anglo-Saxon Protestants as the Founders of a new republic by, of, and for a new *white* civilization-in-the-making, a new *American* civilization. According to Samuel Huntington:

> Americans created the term and the concept of Americanization in the late eighteenth century when they also created the term and the concept of immigrant. They saw the need to make Americans of the new arrivals on their shores. . . . The perceived need to Americanize the immigrants generated a major social movement devoted to that end. It produced many different, overlapping, and at times conflicting efforts by local, state, and national governments, private organizations, and businesses, with the public schools playing a central role. . . . The new large industrial corporations needed masses of immigrant workers and established schools at their factories to train immigrants in the English language and American values. In almost every city with a significant immigrant population, the chamber of commerce had an Americanization program. . . . Progressive era businessmen were concerned with the need to educate their immigrant workers in the English language, American culture, and the American private enterprise system, both to increase their productivity and to inoculate them against unionism and socialism. Their special interest overlapped with what was seen as a broad national interest.[4]

What Huntington does not take full and proper note of, however, is that the varied processes of "Americanization" involved more in the way of "overlapping" special and broad national interests than he identified. Of significant concern to the leaders in business, politics, and social life generally were the consolidation and continuation of White Racial Supremacy and racial apartheid. The very meaning and identity of "American" for the overwhelming majority of white individuals and agents of the nation-state and government at all levels were deeply anchored in the long-prevailing hierarchal racial ontology that undergirded racial apartheid and White Supremacy. Schooling served as both an institution of mediation as well as a site of production, confirmation, and validation of the truth and reasonableness of these agendas and thus served particularly well the stabilization and reproduction of the racialized social, cultural, political, and economic realms by structuring and valorizing the very habits that constituted the taken-for-granted, good "common sense" of routine daily life of hierarchical racial apartheid. Knowledge production and knowledge mediation, including ethical knowledge, as practiced within schools, and institutions of higher learning, were thoroughly conditioned by the requirements of this stabilization and reproduction and thus by these same habits. What would and could come to pass for verified, authoritative "knowledge" in virtually every field of inquiry and teaching had to have the imprimatur of *whiteness* in order to be such. In knowledge production, too, the norms structuring hierarchic raciality were at play. Epistemological matters of truth and falsity and validity and fallacy were ordered in keeping with the racial hierarchy of White Supremacy.

III

Was this true for U.S. American academic philosophy as well, many of the practitioners of which have long identified themselves as the authoritative knowers and practitioners of Knowing and keepers of Knowledge?

Yes indeed. Practitioners of academic philosophy have been, and are, well-socialized and formally educated young adults before engaging in the studies and knowledge-producing activities that have come to be recognized as constituting the disciplinary field and profession. We, too, then, in forming our habits, have been nurtured in schools that, until relatively recently, were generally thoroughly segregated racially as well as by socioeconomic class, not infrequently by religious traditions and worldviews, and less frequently by gender. And while formal education and training in academic philosophy continue to be distinguished by the cultivation of disciplined suspension of belief and the taken-for-granted attitude definitive of the normativity of everyday life, I continue to be amazed by the extent to which those suspensions have *not* been applied with critical rigor to the substantial conditioning influences of raciality on the makeup of the "communities of discourse" constituting the discipline: on intellectual agendas and practices, epistemological standards, canons and curricula, and the sociological and demographical compositions of the various communities.[5] Rather, for decades, into years, into centuries, practitioners of academic philosophy have tended to regard their efforts and productions, at their best, as meeting particularly rigorous standards of right reasoning that ensure that inappropriate ad hominem considerations and influences do not affect their reasoning, conclusions, or agendas of reasoning. According to Mandt: "Academic philosophy is Aristotelian in its self-understanding: it defines its enterprise by reference to what it is like when it is flourishing."[6]

However, a closer examination of past contexts and practices of philosophizing in situations regarded by various practitioners as flourishing would reveal, I believe, substantial extents to which the philosophizing was indeed affected by the habits formed over many years in a society ordered by the agendas of racial apartheid and White Racial Supremacy: again, in the canons of figures, texts, and issues; in the ontologies, philosophical anthropologies, and epistemologies undergirding notions of a "proper" philosopher and "proper" philosophizing. As Maurice Mandelbaum has noted:

In all societies the political and economic conditions tend to determine
the classes of people who have the time and the social positions which
make it possible to engage in philosophic thought in full awareness of
the traditions of that thought. Furthermore, at different times the social
structure seems to determine what groups of people, in what occupa-
tions, for the groups in which one finds concerted efforts to deal with
philosophical problems. . . . If this fact had no influence upon the history of philosophy it would be as surprising as if the fact that mediaeval
philosophers were churchmen had no impact upon how they thought
and wrote.[7]

We should not expect otherwise, and should, accordingly, desist
from the bad faith denials of racial influences on philosophizing, past
and present, and from the no less problematic presumptions that no
such influences have been at play. For it has only been during the last
three decades or so that efforts exerted by philosophers of African descent who came of age and entered graduate programs in philosophy
during and after the Civil Rights and Black Power (Anti-War, Second
Wave Women's, and Third World Anti-Imperialist and Anti-Colonial)
Movements and the efforts of women, persons of color, and persons who
were circumscribed and marginalized by invidious judgments of important aspects of their lives and identities such as sexual orientation and
physical abilities that the discipline has been subjected to transformative
critiques that have left it increasingly less Eurocentric and dominated by
white males and much less captive to the continuing inertia of the agendas and practices of racial apartheid and White Racial Supremacy. (For
confirmation of this one need only look closely at, and read carefully,
a few issues of the American Philosophical Association's publication
Newsletters, which incorporates newsletter sections produced by colleagues working through and on behalf of the Association's several diversity committees: the Committee on American Indians in Philosophy;
the Committee on Asian and Asian American Philosophers and Philosophies; the Committee on Blacks in Philosophy; the Committee on His-
panics and Latinos/as; the Committee on the Status of Lesbian, Gay,
Bisexual, and Transgendered People in the Profession; the Committee
on the Status of Women; and the Committee on Inclusiveness.) As well,
during the past two decades, there has been a surge of published articles,
book chapters, and monographs and undocumented production of important, discipline-influencing, unpublished correspondence on paper
and via e-mail by philosophers in these and other discursive communities
who have been devoted to critiquing the discipline and to expanding the
legitimated range and content of philosophical discourse. New subfields
have been created as the philosophy professoriate has become more diverse demographically and intellectually as a small but influential num-

ber of newcomers from "the lower races" and white women have been trained, educated, and hired, and not a few gone on to earn tenure.

However, such persons and their productive efforts and products hardly constitute the heart and soul of academic philosophy, first, because their number is small and almost never reaches critical mass in any one department of philosophy. In significant part this is a consequence of the very small number of persons choosing careers as academics in philosophy from the groups leading the way in producing the "identity politics" transformations of the discipline. In part, it is a consequence of the orientation and related hiring strategies of many departments, namely, endeavoring to have *at least* one—quite often *at most* one—philosopher of color and/or woman philosopher so as not to be guilty of invidious exclusion but while taking pains, in a number of instances, to ensure that the number of the "philosophers of diversity" not reach the tipping point and change the character (as well as the canonical curriculum and agenda, the culture) of a department.

Far from being surprising, such behavior should be expected. For even before the colonies became a federated union of states, the challenges of demographic diversity, involving races and ethnic groups especially, were of deep concern to the greater majority of the settler-colonists for whom their racial character as *white* people—one people, it was widely believed as a result of deliberate and systematic socialization, by virtue of sharing a complex of traits and special, even Divine, dispensations definitive of *whiteness*—was foundational to the forming of the U.S. America nation-state.

Most academic philosophers it seems, until rather recently, have presumed, virtually without questioning, the founding of our nation-state as a venture in which genocide and enslavement were a historically necessary means to the end of making a decidedly Modern civilization that was to be the guiding beacon to the rest of the world. For all the vaunted concern cultivated in the discipline with identifying and specifying "the good life" and, accordingly, the appropriate moral and ethical principles and practices by which an individual (white) person might achieve and live the "good life," at no point during the long history of development of what, with hindsight, has been reconstructed as the history of academic philosophy in the United States were racial apartheid and White Racial Supremacy, nor the consequent genocide, enslavement, and oppression perpetrated against nonwhite peoples, made the focus of widespread moral and ethical critique and condemnation by practitioners of eventually institutionalized, later increasingly professionalized, academic philosophy.

Note, for example, Bruce Kuklick's discussion in the chapter "Philosophy and Politics" in his *A History of Philosophy in America, 1720–2000*.[8] By his account, the dominance of Puritan theological thought in the

New England colonies as the guide for individual ethical life, exemplified in the works of Jonathan Edwards, was displaced during the run-up
to the Revolution by a form of republicanism investing the authority of
government in "the people," a view formulated and articulated by the
publicly engaged intellectuals who would go on to become the guiding
statesmen of the new republic (George Washington, Benjamin Franklin,
Thomas Jefferson, Thomas Paine, Alexander Hamilton, John Adams,
James Madison, and Aaron Burr). These men

> embraced the ideas of the European Enlightenment. They dismissed
> the inherited doctrines of Calvinism, and stressed, albeit prudently, the
> possibility of incremental reform in human life that wise politics could
> achieve. The American leaders were rationalists in their view that any-
> one with the perseverance to examine the world carefully and to reflect
> on this experience could arrive at fundamental truths; these truths
> could not be honestly gainsaid. But "reason" for them was not defined
> as intuition or a priori deliberation but as calculating practicality about
> the present and historical exploration of the past with a view to using
> the results of the exploration in the present.[9]

And while these nation-state Founding intellectuals embraced a view that
the Creator had made (some) humans equal, in important senses, they
were, however, "by no means levelers or radical democrats and defined
'the people' in a limited sense—women, slaves, and Indians hardly
counted."[10] Still, these politically engaged intellectuals, in assuming the
positions of power in the new federal government, produced what Kuklick characterizes as "a watershed in the career of philosophy in America":

> *This* group was politically active and inclined to write about politics.
> Moreover, it believed that political thought was rooted in the actual give
> and take of the political world and close observation of it: past and pre-
> sent experience of politics was central, as was the shrewd assessment
> that defined what was rational. Political theory was not a product of con-
> templation, nor of matching the rules of the polity to biblical truth, nor
> of deducing what ought to be done in the polis from a religiously based
> ethics; political theory rather arose from engaging in politics, from an
> understanding of political behavior.[11]

With the Founding intellectuals, we should conclude, political philosophy was especially pragmatic, devoted to the achievement of what
past and present experience compelled "reasonable" thinkers to conclude was, *in fact*, possible practically, hence politically, not what *ought* to
be done in accordance with abstract principles of Right. However, by the
nineteenth and twentieth centuries, things had changed substantially for
those now regarded by historians of philosophy as the noteworthy

philosophers of U.S. America: "tradition, training, and institutionalization had made philosophic understanding a different order of knowing from that pursued by the students of political theory," persons who were now to be found in new fields in the ascending social sciences. And the canonical philosophers?

> . . . philosophers developed a hierarchical notion of their field of expertise in which the priority became the exertion of a certain form of high mental energy to solve the most general problems of how one knew the world. Once these problems were answered, one might use the results at once to answer questions about moral and religious questions; philosophers believed issues social and political in character were further down on a list of "applied" topics. The social and political were usually of secondary or even tertiary interest; they had little independent status; and substantive conclusions about political life, they believed, could be read off from the conclusions of what became the chief philosophic discipline—the theory of knowledge or epistemology.[12]

And so the discipline came to be structured, the continuation of White Racial Supremacy as a national and local agenda notwithstanding. It was not until the genocide and enslavement were long gone and the oppression beaten back by organized struggles led by the oppressed and courageous white folks who broke with this agenda that substantial changes were forthcoming. Even though, by one account, the devastating Civil War of 1860–1865 was a decisive experience for several persons who were major contributors to the historic developments through which speculative ministers and theologians as custodians of academic philosophy were displaced by more secular, rationalist, Enlightenment thinkers committed to the modern agendas of applying efforts in the developing empirical sciences to the natural and social worlds, hardly any of them would direct their attention to the injustices of the social ordering of racial apartheid and the oppression of nonwhite peoples.[13] Nearly a century would pass before racial apartheid and White Racial Supremacy would come to be widely regarded as unjust, the pivotal moment being the unanimous ruling by the U.S. Supreme Court in 1954 (*Brown v. Board of Education of Topeka, Kansas I*), that racially separate schools are inherently unequal and unjust. No academic philosopher led the way or contributed substantively to the successful making of the case to the Court. The Court's ruling set in motion developments that gradually, then later, after more struggles still and another ruling by the Court (*Brown v. Board of Education of Topeka, Kansas II*), with increasing speed and widespread impact, altered the racial landscape of schooling in the United States and other areas of public life. One very important consequence was the dramatic confrontation of the systematic production of ignorance that, for centuries, had been key to the perpetuation of the social ordering of white supremacist racial apartheid.

The consolidation of the transformations aided by the Court's rulings and prompted by sustained, organized struggles by courageous citizens of many races and ethnie has yet to be fully realized in academic philosophy in the United States of America. The institutionalized, normatively sanctioned, systematic cultivation and mediation of ignorance by exclusion of and/or inattentiveness to especially significant traditions of praxis-related articulate thought by women and men of our nation-state's various racial, ethnic, socioeconomic, and other significant life orientations (sexual, religious) have yet to be fully integrated into the curricula of undergraduate and graduate education in academic philosophy. For example, it is still possible in a number of departments of hilosophy in the United States to earn a Ph.D. in the discipline with a concentration in "American" philosophy without having to complete a comprehensive and critical survey of U.S. American history (or of any other nation-state in the Americas), or complete a more comprehensive survey or mastery of literate, articulate, more or less systematic thought and writing beyond the writings of three or four, sometimes six to eight, white males who continue to be legitimated and mediated as the exemplary and canonical pioneers and carriers of "American Philosophy." Beyond this pernicious concentration, one will be awarded a Ph.D. in philosophy, certified as being especially able in a number of specialties and competencies in the discipline—among them ethics, moral philosophy, social philosophy, political philosophy—without *ever* having to confront, as part of one's education in the discipline, the holocausts of genocide perpetrated against Native Peoples or the enslavement of Africans and their descendants in the making of a "Modern" nation-state dedicated to individual freedom and equality, and without confronting the question of the viability of the claim that the legacies of Western philosophy are manifestations of proper stewardship of Truth, Justice, and Right by exemplary Lovers of Wisdom. Concerns for the right to life of anti-abortionists are much more likely to be explored in ethics courses in these departments than the right to life denied of the Peoples inhabiting this continent when the explorers and settler-colonists from Europe arrived, or the right to freedom and full citizenship denied to Africans and their descendants for more than three centuries.

Such educational practices, where they persist, are in stark contrast to the education of undergraduates and graduate students in a number of other disciplines in the humanities and social sciences in our nation-state's institutions of higher education. For example, a graduate student in English in my home institution, Vanderbilt University (my awareness of which comes by my serving on the dissertation committee of a young woman of African descent who was awarded her Ph.D. during commencement exercises for 2004), must demonstrate competent knowledge of literary traditions (of works and figures) of various peoples in this country and others. Further, the canon of "American" literature is especially diverse with respect to race and ethnicity, gender, and so on. The battle to diversify literary canons to make them more inclusively "multicultural" has largely been won in literature departments, with revised versions now a part of critically reflective, educated disciplinary common sense. In literature departments where this is the case, one cannot get a Ph.D. without demonstrating competent knowledge of the literate, creative accomplishments of persons of many of our country's and the world's peoples.

To the contrary, the notion of an "American philosopher" has been hijacked in service to continuation of centuries' long projects of education for social ordering by white racial dominance and for U.S. hegemony within the Americas. I am convinced that such miseducation in and about "Philosophy" (as well as the related identity construals and U.S. nation-state positioning), wherever sanctioned and provided, is both intellectually bankrupt and morally grotesque. Education of this sort leading to a Ph.D. is especially inappropriate for persons who, on assuming the roles and responsibilities of teacher-scholars, will be producing and mediating what passes for knowledge to young people in this country, among whom, increasingly, will be more and more students who are not racially white. The systematic production of ignorance by privileging the knowledge claims, agendas, strategies and practices, and the social networks of a handful of U.S. American white males and/or the traditions of philosophical thought of European thinkers as the only appropriate instances of philosophizing *proper* ill prepares graduate students for contributing to the work of fulfilling a desire and an aspiration shared by James Baldwin and Richard Rorty, among many others, myself included, that we "achieve our country."[14] Said Baldwin:

> Everything now, we must assume, is in our hands; we have no right to assume otherwise. If we—and now I mean the relatively conscious whites and the relatively conscious blacks, who must, like lovers, insist on, or create, the consciousness of the others—do not falter in our duty now, we may be able, handful that we are, to end the racial nightmare, and achieve our country, and change the history of the world. If we do not now dare everything, the fulfillment of that prophecy, re-created from the Bible in song by a slave, is upon us: *God gave Noah the rainbow sign, No more water, the fire next time!*[15]

What can and should we do to foster education that is less and less devoted or contributing to the production of ignorance in service to

invidious superordination and subordination and more and more devoted to strategies and practices by which to achieve a more just, harmonious, and stable democratic nation-state of citizen women and
men, many of whose identities and life orientations as well as their
work are nurtured by associations conditioned very substantially,
though noninvidiously, by racial, ethnic, gender, sexual, cultural, and
socioeconomic commitments? I am firmly convinced that we need,
among other things, a very substantial reeducation and redirection of
knowledge workers and knowledge work in academic pilosophy that
will correct for the miseducation and continuing misdirection that I
have described. Such important work is already under way, being contributed to by many, including the editors of this collection. I sincerely
hope that the considerations I have offered will be a fair return on
their investment of trust and respect in extending me the invitation to
contribute this chapter. I hope, as well, that responses from readers
will help me become less ignorant and thus a better contributor to the
reeducative and redirecting work that this collection fosters.

Notes

This chapter is a revised version of the March 28, 2004, presentation to the Conference on Ethics and Epistemologies of Ignorance that was organized and
hosted by the Rock Ethics Institute at Penn State University. My very special
thanks to Nancy Tuana and Shannon Sullivan for the invitation to present to the
Conference and to contribute to this published collection of writings growing
out of the Conference and to all others who made both the Conference and this
collection possible.

1. "The rule held that one drop of black blood made a person black. At first
glance, this might seem to fix racial matters in a final shape and settle the problem of determining who's who. Yet it did just the opposite. . . . Seeking to pin
down the essence of race, the one-drop rule actually made that essence unknow-
able, indeed invisible. It jettisoned the perceptible reality of skin tone for the
dream of racial essence; it made the physical metaphysical. It was simply not possible to know whether you were a real white person or an imitation. There was no
way to find out, no way to be sure. The one-drop rule made whiteness imaginary,
pushed one's whiteness back into an indefinitely receding past of unknown an-
cestors. . . . Here we have the structure of American racial thinking at its barest.
We see its failure to give absolute form to the relatively formless, meaning to the
meaningless, or sense to chance." See Scott L. Malcomson, *One Drop of Blood: The
American Misadventure of Race* (New York: Farrar Straus Giroux, 2000), 356. Here,
also, is a poignant example of fashioning and using a method for knowing that
produced ignorance!
2. Alexis de Tocqueville, *Democracy in America*, vol. 1, trans. Henry Reeve
(New York: Vintage Books, 1990), 332.

3. "Carlisle Indian Industrial School History," http://www.home.epix.net/~landis/histry.html.

4. Samuel P. Huntington, *Who Are We? The Challenges to America's National Identity* (New York: Simon & Schuster, 2004), 132–33.

5. "... the conception of contemporary philosophy as a community of discourse makes it possible to explain both its closed, systematic appearance when viewed from without and its lack of coherence and unity of conviction when viewed from within. At the same time, it accounts for how contemporary philosophers can possess intelligible norms for judging the value of philosophical activity and yet be incapable of asserting effective intellectual authority in the face of ... critique." See A. J. Mandt, "The Inevitability of Pluralism: Philosophical Practice and Philosophical Excellence," in *The Institution of Philosophy: A Discipline in Crisis?*, ed. Avner Cohen and Marcelo Dascal, 89–90 (La Salle, IL: Open Court, 1989).

6. Mandt, "The Inevitability of Pluralism: Philosophical Practice and Philosophical Excellence," 84.

7. Maurice Mandelbaum, "History of Ideas, Intellectual History, and the History of Philosophy," in *History and Theory, Beiheft 5: The Historiography of Philosophy, 1965*.

8. (Oxford: Clarendon Press, 2001), 26–37.

9. Bruce Kuklick, *A History of Philosophy in America 1720–2000*, 28. For an especially informed and provocative discussion of these men—and of Adams's wife Abigail, see Joseph J. Ellis, *Founding Brothers: The Revolutionary Generation* (New York: Alfred A. Knopf, 2001), particularly ch. 3, "The Silence," Ellis's discussion of the pact made by the Founders with the leaders of the slave-holding colonies of the South to keep silent in the halls and chambers of the new federal government about both slavery and abolition.

10. Kuklick, *A History of Philosophy in America*, 29.

11. Ibid., 33.

12. Ibid., 35, emphasis in original.

13. See, for example, Louis Menand, *The Metaphysical Club: A Story of Ideas in America* (New York: Farrar, Straus and Giroux, 2001).

14. Richard Rorty, *Achieving Our Country: Leftist Thought in Twentieth-Century America* (Cambridge, MA: Harvard University Press, 1998).

15. James Baldwin, "The Fire Next Time," in *Baldwin: Collected Essays*, 346–47. (New York: The Library of America, 1998), emphasis in original.

CHAPTER 11

The Power of Ignorance

Lorraine Code

In *Daniel Deronda*, George Eliot writes:

> It is a common sentence that Knowledge is power; but who hath duly considered or set forth the power of Ignorance? . . . Of a truth, Knowledge is power, but it is a power reined by scruple, having a conscience of what must be and what may be; whereas Ignorance is a blind giant who, let him but wax unbound, would make it a sport to seize the pillars that hold up the long-wrought fabric of human good, and turn all the places of joy dark as a buried Babylon. (2002 [1876], 202)

This passage is from the prelude to a chapter in which Gwendolen Harlech, a young English woman of leisured affluence, is summoned home to England from a sojourn in the south of France, when her family falls into penury. In her stunned incomprehension of the sudden unavailability of wealth, fine clothes, spacious living quarters, servants, horses—the refinements of a life whose comforts and economic security had been merely the backdrop against which she, unconsciously, had lived—Gwendolen is oblivious to her own class privilege. She evinces a "practical ignorance" of the very fact of privilege, of the day-to-day constraints straitened circumstances entail, and of "other" lives lived daily in just such circumstances. When the complacent luxury of her ignorance is abruptly interrupted, requiring her to face "conditions of this world [which] seemed to her like a hurrying crowd in which she had got astray, no more cared for and protected than a myriad of other girls, in spite of its being a peculiar hardship to her" (Eliot 2002 [1876], 210), she is incredulous. Years of blithe unknowing had obliterated any "conscience of what must be and what may be," leaving her with none of the resources that knowledge tempered with practical wisdom might have

213

supplied, when her pampered prosperity came to a sudden end and her accustomed "places of joy" turned dark.

The covenant a rigidly stratified class system tacitly makes with its privileged members accords them a double advantage, both of an affluence that comes as their unquestioned entitlement and of an ignorance significantly analogous to the racial ignorance generated by Charles W. Mills's *The Racial Contract*. Not only, borrowing Mills's phrases, does it excuse members of Gwendolen's class from any need to understand "the world they themselves have made," but it tacitly permits them, like white signatories to "the racial contract," to exist in an "invented delusional world" sustained by a social-moral-epistemic imaginary of self-deception and "structured blindnesses" (Mills 1997, 18–19). Thus—again citing Eliot—they are protected against intrusion by "the conditions of this world" in which their experiences have not prepared them to deal knowledgeably with "disagreeables . . . wounding to [their] pride . . . irksome to [their] tastes" (Eliot 2002 [1876], 210). With the unevenly distributed advantages it thus affords, the contract, in effect, generates and thrives on a systemic cognitive failure. In so doing it produces an interlocking structure of immoral beliefs generated out of Enlightenment humanism, with its tacit core assumption that "only Europeans were human" (Mills 1997, 27). Its effects are to "naturalize" myriad social-epistemic patterns and practices of inequality and oppression. When such naturalizing permeates an entire social fabric, holding people accountable and culpable for the beliefs it underwrites is a complex process indeed, given the difficulties of determining whether they could have known otherwise.

In its debt to classical social contract theory, read as "both sociopolitical and moral," Mills's racial contract parallels the sexual contract, familiar to feminists from Carol Pateman's (1988) analysis and enacted in the paternalistic cosseting and tutelage Gwendolen receives from the patriarchal figures in Eliot's novel. For Mills, and central to my purposes here, the social contract also "tacitly presupposes an 'epistemological' contract," as do the sexual contract, racial contract, expropriation contract, slavery contract, and colonial contract, of which he also speaks (Mills 1997, 24–25), contracts that naturalize contingent social orders and reconfigure as "natural kinds" both those advantaged and disadvantaged by their hegemonic explanatory power. The "structured blindness" of which Mills speaks—the tacit "agreement to *mis*interpret the world" (18)—serves to filter out empirical evidence that would unsettle or counter any suspicion that these fundamental beliefs might indeed be held together by webs of distortion and error—of epistemically careless, irresponsible knowledge construction. Social, sexual, racial contracts require, construct, and condone an epistemology, sustained by and sustaining an *ecology* of ignorance that comes to be essential to their survival:

a species of utilitarian argument supports and perpetuates that ecological order, often working to occlude or override both moral and epistemic considerations that might unsettle it.[1] In what follows, I read some of the darker effects, the ethico-politically and epistemologically negative dimensions of the power of ignorance, to promote and/or sustain unjust social orders.

Learned woman that she was, when she was writing *Daniel Deronda* in the 1870s, Eliot will undoubtedly have known the writings and other political activities of the British utilitarians, who had been engaged for some time in "the *invention* of the 'third world'," to borrow Deane Curtin's apt phrase (1999, 34, emphasis added).[2] She will also have been familiar with James Mill's (1968 [1817]) *The History of British India*, which stands as a manifesto of the *colonial* power of and, indeed, the (arrogantly presumed) *right* to, ignorance. In his Introduction to the 1968 edition of *The History*, John Kenneth Galbraith ranks it the best available chronicle of the "transplant" of a British super-structural model onto a colonized society (ninth unnumbered page), Himani Bannerji maintains: "the importance of this book in . . . representing India to the West, and also in India itself, is difficult to exaggerate" (1995, 50), and Curtin notes that it became "the standard text for the [East India] company's college at Haileybury" (1999, 35). Here I juxtapose Mill's *History* with *Daniel Deronda*, to read them through structural continuities that they expose between two nineteenth-century patterns of privilege and ignorance, one most visible in private life, the other with more visibly global consequences.

Yet despite the continuities, these texts are strikingly disanalogous in some of the epistemological and moral questions they pose about the range of puzzles generated by the multiple modalities of ignorance. For Gwendolen Harlech is ignorant of her own ignorance of everyday lives that are not hers, and likewise of the radical contingency of the paternalistic-patriarchal beneficence that makes her life possible. James Mill, in contrast, celebrates, takes pride, in his ignorance of daily life in India, claiming it allows him to produce a supremely objective history. Gwendolen Harlech is also ignorant of other options that—albeit with extraordinary efforts—might have been hers; the same cannot so easily be said of James Mill. Thus to anticipate the direction my discussion will take, when issues of culpability figure among the ethical-epistemological questions posed by ignorance exposed, it is not easy to determine how to weigh ignorant ignorance against conscious, self-congratulatory ignorance. This complication takes on a further twist in light of the apparently self-deceptive aspect of Mill's putative self-presentation, in filtering out from his claims to objectivity any thought that his own history and social status might have infiltrated and thus shaped, informed, his historical research. (Mills observes that, under the racial contract, "evasion and

self-deception become the epistemic norm [1997, 97]; Sara Suleri refers
to "a failure of ignorance to comprehend itself [1992, 2].") When culturally sanctioned ignorance blocks the way to knowledgeability, in an ecology of power and privilege where the logical possibilities favored by many
epistemologists pale before the sheer intransigence of practical impossi-
bilities, how are we successor epistemologists to think, cognitively and
morally, about ignorance? Can those who are ignorant of matters such as
these reasonably be charged with straightforward cognitive failure, to be
remedied by empirical counterevidence? Perhaps not. Must one conclude that there can be no ignorance-free place? Perhaps so.

Mill, on Bannerji's reading, offers up "a seamless 'imagining' or construction of India, unaccommodating of complexities which might have
problematized this construction" (1995, 55–56) while discounting any
possibility that Indians might have been capable of defining or representing themselves. Working from a normative conception of "civilization" that he imagined to be beyond the reach of societies marked by,
immersed in, "traditionalism," Mill dismisses, discounts indigenous
records, literature, and archives as sources of knowledge, contending
that the Hindus, when they were "discovered [*sic*] by the nations of modern Europe" were in the very same "state of manners, society, and knowledge" as they were at the Greek invasion of India, led by Alexander the
Great (1968 [1817], 116–19). Thus, he concludes, they clearly had no
history of their own, no record of progress, and therefore no claim to be
studied as a civilized people remotely akin to that pinnacle of human
achievement, an English gentleman who, in his view, "may be taken as a
favorable specimen of civilization, of knowledge, of humanity, of all the
qualities, in short, that make human nature estimable" (Mill 1955
[1819], 60). Feminists will hear echoes of claims that women's lives have
run their unremarkable course outside history.

In writing his *History*, Mill did have access to impressive textual resources in the archives of the English Orientalists (who had also relied, if
more critically than he did, on the concept of "tradition" as an "Othering" device). He was thus positioned, as historians commonly are, to construct a chronicle of life in a distant land from a study of historical
records, albeit principally—and this was his choice—on those compiled
by other Europeans. Yet he found reason to denigrate even the knowledge the Orientalists had produced, with the epistemically startling contention that because "they knew Indian languages, lived there, and
enjoyed the literature . . . they lacked the necessary detachment . . . essential for a judge-historian." He, by contrast—in his own estimation—
was "eminently suitable" *because of* his "lack of direct connections with or
experiences of India." His "imagined India," Bannerji charges, is an apol-
ogy for colonialism, innoculated against the deliverances of local testi-

mony by an ideology that allowed him to determine whether "a country was civilized or barbaric or savage" according to its success in breaking free from the fetters of traditionalism. On this criterion, India came out as "replete with peculiar barbaric traditions" (Bannerji 1995, 57–58). Ironically, Mill's self-congratulatory stance works with a curious double standard for scholarly research. He excuses himself for not knowing "the relevant Indian languages" yet, as Galbraith notes, "he would not have excused any man who essayed to comment on the Greek or Latin poets without a knowledge of Greek or Latin. He discusses the *Mahabarata* under this limitation, exacerbated by the further, more serious one that, at the time, it had not been rendered into English" (1968, fourth unnumbered page). And he is dismissive of the efforts of Sir William Jones, a linguist whose knowledge of Sanskrit made it possible for him to compile a "digest" of Indian laws and thus, according to Curtin, both to resist the imposition of British law on India and to attempt to preserve traditional Indian cultures (Curtin 99, 39). In extensive, erudite footnotes and comments to the 1968 edition of Mill's *History*, H. H. Wilson offers "corrections" to the text that begin to expose "Mill's enormous ignorance of India and his even greater arrogance that his very ignorance was a prerequisite for knowledge" (Bannerji 1995, 58). This manifest arrogance at the basis of Mill's judgments of India seems plainly to count both as epistemically irresponsible and immoral, for arrogance qualifies, on many accounts, as a morally reprehensible stance.

In a subtle, Kantian-based analysis of arrogance as "the deadliest of moral vices," and thence of its capacity to function as an instrument of "sociopolitical arrangements of dominance and subordination," Robin Dillon offers persuasive reasons, beyond any of the personal character flaws it exposes, for judging arrogance, and hence the beliefs on which it draws, as morally blameworthy. While much of her discussion is of individually displayed or practiced arrogance, the larger social effects she acknowledges throughout the essay bear directly on the breed of arrogance that drives Mill's assessment of his own epistemic and thence colonial policy-informing ignorance. In the dismissive contempt, the disdain for others where arrogance typically makes itself known, it ranks as one of "the vices that violate our duty to respect human beings as such," Dillon proposes (2004, 192–93). Indeed, she concludes that arrogance incorporates an "improper valuing of . . . one's capacity for autonomous rational agency, which stands as the chief obstacle to morality" (209): if she is right, and her argument is persuasive, then it is a serious cognitive failure indeed. And although there is a certain incongruity in evoking Kantian-derived values to counter a utilitarian position, the complexity of this issue requires an assemblage of conceptual resources that do not accord undue respect to the boundaries of specific philosophical schools of thought.[3]

Mill's *History,* then, is emblematic of a politics of unknowing that effectively shaped nineteenth-century British colonial theory and practice,
condoning ignorance about colonized peoples, places, and environ-
ments in the name of self-deceptive, often coercive, paternalistic assumptions about a universal human nature, needs, practices, values, and
customs, reinforced by imagining the colony as *terra nullius*: an incongruous image for so ancient a culture as India, but one Mill was able to
craft by creating "an empty historical-cultural slate for India inscribed
with barbaric traditions" (Bannerji 1995, 58). (For Mill, Curtin notes,
"colonies are not countries because they have no productive capital of
their own" (Curtin 1999, 36).) On a macrocosmic level, Mill's ignorance
points toward intriguing analogies with Gwendolen's: a female member
of the colonizing classes living at home, ignorant (and perhaps also arrogantly so) of the lives of those, both at home and abroad, whose labors
made her leisure possible. Nor, according to Mill, would there be any
reason for her to attempt to know differently from the gentlemen of her
circle, for in his view the interests of "almost all" women will be "involved
either in that of their fathers or in that of their husbands" (1955 [1819],
73–74). Thus in a different register his ignorance exposes a striking para-
dox in the triumphalist narrative of progress that infused British colonial
fervor, where liberal political philosophy, generated out of conditions
specific to Europe during the Industrial Revolution (and still at the beginning of the twenty-first century invoked in the affluent West to fuel
emancipatory social movements), assumes a hegemonic, coercive de-
meanor when it is superimposed upon a traditional, collectivist society.

This imagined template for generic progress *as such* does not travel
as well as its global pretensions suggest. Putatively universal, transcultural
practices betray both their local specificity and their tacit reliance on a
radical ignorance of and disregard for cultural particularity—indeed,
their contempt for that very idea—when they move to superimpose a
capitalist, scientific, instrumental rationality born of historical-material
conditions specific to one (presumptively white) part of the world, upon
a people living in radically different circumstances, "deeply embedded in
a place and in subsistence methods of production." Curtin aptly suggests
that for Mill, progress meant moving toward a society with "an economically rational capitalist middle class." It precluded his evincing any respect for traditional social structures "based on subsistence agriculture
that did not produce rent (1999, 38–39). Charles Mills's (1997) claim
that "whites will . . . be unable to understand the world they themselves
have made" bears, a fortiori, on the "global cognitive dysfunction" evident in James Mill's reading of India as it informed policies and practices
instrumental to "the invention of the 'third world'."

These texts, across their local specificities, reveal how the proposal of starting ethical or epistemological inquiry from behind a veil of ignorance can be complicit in advancing a range of microcosmic and macrocosmic colonizing moves: can, unwittingly, contribute to the production of immoral, socially-politically oppressive beliefs and actions. In the interests of preserving an imagined objectivity, the veil conceals and thus condones an ongoing ignorance of *its own* positionality vis-à-vis people variously Othered by the norms of a liberal-empirical ethical-epistemological imaginary (cf. Card 1991). Although in *epistemophilic* societies (= societies in love with knowledge) it is tantamount to an act of heresy to criticize a methodological device designed, in the name of objectivity, to erase every taint of vested interest from inquiry, the very difficulty of mounting such a critique exposes the limitations of an objectivist epistemology of disinterested, individually "owned" knowledge when it moves from a formal, universalist mode to analyses of specific lives, materialities, politics, power, and ignorance. It points to the impotence of the epistemologies of mastery single-handedly to address the questions ignorance poses and to the insensitivity of their conceptual apparatus to the nuances and particularities of situated, local politics of knowledge and ignorance. To my mind, then, these problems call for revision at the level of the instituted imaginary that holds epistemic communities in place, complete with their conceptions of entitlement, and of hierarchical epistemic and social positioning. It points, just as forcibly, to the pertinence of epistemic responsibility to projects of inquiry more complex than simple observations of medium-size material objects: a point of view for which people, singly and collectively—indeed, singly *because* collectively—are *responsible* for what and how they know, on an understanding of responsibility that is as epistemological as it is ethical and political (see Code, 1987, forthcoming).

Modalities of Ignorance

I see this chapter as primarily diagnostic: as an examination of certain modalities of ignorance that shaped the governing imaginary of the English-speaking white Western world at a turning point in its history, when the sense of supreme rightness that shaped the social-political imaginary of Britain as a colonizing nation at the time of the Industrial Revolution combined with a reformist utilitarianism to generate a *need* for colonies to serve the material needs of a newly powerful middle class,[4] and when "four or five fraternities of men," according to James Mill, would be charged with forming a representative government whose interests would be congruent with those of the "community at large" (1955 [1819], 81–82). Into this period James Mill's illustrious son, John Stuart, inserted his treatise on *The Subjection of Women* which, despite or because of its radical subject matter, gained scant recognition in comparison with the rest of his opus. Nor in the treatise itself did he seriously doubt that, however their educational, economic, and other options might be enhanced, women of his—and Gwendolen Harlech's—social class would continue to adorn the lives of men. As Michèle Le Dœuff proposes, it took Harriet Taylor to expose and oppose Mill's persistent, naturalistic conception of "a single destiny for woman: dependence on a man for bread" (Le Dœuff 2003, 204). It is she—Taylor—who, as Le Dœuff reads her, refuses to endorse any suggestion that there could be a fixed human nature imagined by extrapolating from the lives he (Mill) knew; Taylor contrasts moral knowledge with the sciences of nature, insisting that moral knowledge must go "beyond all classifications." Le Dœuff, with characteristic irony, calls this "a bold idea at a time when philosophical anthropology was flourishing like a fictionalized botany of humanity" (2003, 203, citing Taylor 1951, 276). The fictions endemic in James Mill's work provide a fine example.

In taking these two figures, one fictional, one historical, as emblematic for thinking about ignorance as it figures also in today's world, I may seem to portray it as both *individual* and a *malady* and thus in this knowledge-as-information-venerating culture to imagine it amenable to individual "cure." But my purpose in citing "individual" examples is to illustrate a larger point about how epistemic subjects are positioned within and contribute to perpetuating, systemic structures of ignorance in ongoing, reciprocal processes: Polycarp Ikuenobe, referring to an African colonial context, speaks of culturally induced ignorance in which "migrated social structures" destructive of precolonial indigenous structures "have induced some amount of moral ignorance, which have made people unable to know right from wrong" (1998, 112). The idea is richly persuasive, as it is also in Londa Schiebinger's reading, in quite a different setting, where she invokes the provocative idea of "agnotology"—"the study of culturally-induced ignorances" for understanding the consequences of social-political struggle that resulted in the "*non-transfer* of important bodies of [botanical] knowledge from the New World into Europe" (2004, 237, emphasis in original). Her pivotal example is of an exotic plant, the "peacock flower," effectively used as an abortifacient by Amerindian slave women to abort infants who would otherwise have been born into bondage. The paternalistically driven sexual politics that fueled a conspiracy of ignorance against importing such knowledge into Europe imposes a structuring of right and wrong on societies "at home" that exposes another facet of the subsumption of women's interests, and indeed their bodies, under those of their husbands or, indirectly, their fathers. Acknowledging that such ignorance is culturally produced or socially-culturally pervasive neither excuses nor exculpates its particular, individual episodes, even though it may offer a partial explanation and open new sites of analysis. Nonetheless, the *S*-knows-that-*p* epistemology, of which I have been consistently critical, holds a straightforward ignorance/knowledge opposition in place, together with an equally straightforward assumption that knowledge achieved can erase ignorance with one stroke. Singly asserted propositions are like that: open to counterassertion that annuls their claims. In fact, integral to the structure of mainstream epistemology is this either/or (either knowledge or ignorance) structure that is too crude to engage well with the complexities—the ecological questions and the responsibility imperatives, both epistemic and moral— invoked by ignorance.

With Gwendolen Harlech and James Mill I have examined two local, negative modalities of ignorance as Eliot imagines it, but not to condemn ignorance as always wicked, culpable, akin to evil. There is more to be said about ignorance as a mixed, even in some circumstances a positive, strategically judicious mode. My interest here, however, is in how, in performing the power of which Eliot writes, ignorance articulates with certain *vulnerabilities*: Gwendolen Harlech's to the naturalized-female material and intellectual dependency of "her own" situation, the dependency of a woman who knew nothing of nascent movements to counter the subjection of women, and James Mill's contribution to naturalizing the *vulnerability* of precolonial India to the exploitation from which it became "British" India. Gwendolen's ignorance close to home finds a counterpart in Mill's in the faraway colonies. Thus my interest is in how ignorance works to reify sexual, racial, and colonial contracts in diverse, differently situated lives and vulnerabilities.

The utilitarian-derived imperatives of the empiricism of the day are of a piece with a line of thought that was to grow into the positivist empiricism whose effects in spawning and nurturing the epistemologies of mastery feminist and other postcolonial projects have sought to understand and to counter. (James Mill characterized his method "as that of a 'positive science'," Bannerji writes [1995, 55].) Striking among its effects is that it conceals the everyday experiences, ignorance, and vulnerability of knowing subjects behind a barrier much less ephemeral than a veil: a rigid barrier of presumed and prescribed sameness. There, race, class, and other specificities drop out—and are kept out—of sight in an epistemology that itself virtually becomes *terra nullius* while condoning an imaginary of (tradition-steeped) races and of women, as Other, as themselves *terra nullius* in their putatively mysterious lack of reason and their "natural incomprehensibility": beliefs ultimately exposed as immoral for their founding contribution to social-political arrangements of dominance and subordination.

Although I enter this inquiry from a feminist position, my focus so far has been on certain modalities of ignorance that permeate a late-nineteenth-century imaginary of coloniality (James Mill) and class (Gwendolen Harlech). I have not yet confronted the (willed or otherwise) oblivion to the structural effects of patriarchy—of the interweaving of *gender*, class, and colonial politics—that variously shape both of these epistemic and moral lives. And this is the challenge: to engage with the multiple manifestations of the powers of ignorance as it pervades an instituted social-epistemic imaginary that naturalizes and sustains diverse, mutually reinforcing oppressions. I have discussed Gwendolen Harlech's oblivion to her own class position and its privileges, noting analogies and disanalogies with James Mill's prideful ignorance of the lives and situations of the colonized people of India. Class and colonial-racial ignorance have occupied my analysis. Yet the politics of ignorance everywhere sustains and is sustained by *gendered* patterns of incredulity and unearned-unwarranted epistemic privilege that are intricated with, constitutive of, and constituted within a politics of difference exemplified in my analyses of class and race. Perhaps most notable among these intrications, for the purposes of this chapter, is how the trope of femininity functions, in Orientalist narratives, "to shroud the East in a 'female' mystery," as Sara Suleri puts it. In the rhetoric of English India, she reads the "feminization of the colonized subcontinent . . . [as] the most sustained metaphor" common to ethnographic, historical, and literary inquiry (1992, 16). In its manner of drawing together caste, race, and gender, feminization serves to contain the peoples of India within a rhetorical space where they are symbolically invisible, and thus their interests and customs need not be taken any more seriously into account in their compliant subjection to the (paternalistic) colonizer than English women's interests at home or in the colonized country need be acknowledged as potentially distinct from those of male providers. Suleri's observation that "the 'femininity' of the 'Indian intellect' accounts for its opacity" (1992, 19) suggests that it is scarcely surprising for Mill to evince as little cultural sympathy for the particularities of Indian civilization and tradition as he does for the specificities of the lives of women of the colonizing culture, or that he should assert "a man who is duly qualified may obtain more knowledge of India in one year, in his closet in England, than he could obtain during the course of the longest life, by the use of his eyes and ears in India" (1968 [1817], 13, cited in Suleri 1992, 176). He would need take no more care to understand the effects of the subjection of English women than to understand the minutiae of Indian civilization and culture.

In modalities of ignorance and oppression such as these, the gendered facets of Gwendolen Harlech's and James Mill's ignorance evoke provocative conceptual affinities with Le Dœuff's exposure, in *The Sex of Knowing*, of women's relegation to the castoffs, the leftovers of sanctioned, publicly credentialed knowledge. Le Dœuff shows how sexed/gendered epistemic hierarchies were maintained in Europe, historically, through what amounts to a communally manifested, willed ignorance about who women are, what they are able and allowed to know, and how they can be in the material and social world, an imaginary that women—such as Gwendolen—are prone to ingesting: her French counterparts were confined to knowledge that "must relate to God and to France" (2003, 26).[5] Particularly useful for my thoughts here is Le Dœuff's practice of working within an imaginary, of showing through immanent critique how implicitly "sexed" social-political-epistemic patterns weave through events, texts, subjectivities to engender the exclusionary practices they enjoin, and her celebration of the power to disrupt those patterns, evident in certain landmark refusals to remain contained within their boundaries.

Taking a position that may, at first glance, seem antithetical to George Eliot's, Le Dœuff maintains that knowledge "is not power, but resistance to domination . . . sustained by the ignorance of the dominated." In fact, she argues, "as access to knowledge increases in this world, power decreases . . . [whereas] ignorance of the range of our sufferings leaves us vulnerable to suffering"; adding acerbically, "just as ignorance of marriage is what allows such an institution to persist: no one with any foreknowledge of married life would have any part of it" (2003, 40, 39). Gwendolen Harlech's "disastrous marriage to a moral monster . . . through which she had naively and egotistically hoped to attain freedom and power," as Deborah Heller describes it, exemplifies the point. It is less in consequence of a neglected responsibility to *know* that Gwendolen Harlech is prompted to enter into such an arrangement than of her upbringing in a segment of English society where her breed of narcissism, together with an "insular self-satisfaction" (Heller 1990, 84),[6] not unlike a private version of James Mill's more public arrogance, are the social-cultural norm for a woman of her station.

Many of these passages in Le Dœuff's text are informed by her readings of little-known (cast-off?) seventeenth-century French philosopher Gabrielle Suchon who, in her two-volume *Traité de la morale et de la politique* (1693), meditates on ignorance and knowledge and offers innovative strategies for women to refuse their position as mere gleaners from the discards, the leftovers of male knowledge. Most striking is her recommendation that women refuse their exclusion from masculine knowledge through practices of an autodacticism that is neither "second best" nor merely a project for solitary, isolated selves. Women, according to Suchon, "know nothing about definition, categorization, description, argumentation, and everything that serves to perfect reason and discourse, and it seems that the aim is to keep them in ignorance by depriving them of everything that might nourish their intelligence." Le Dœuff commends Suchon for having achieved so clear an understanding of women's oppression by ignorance, from a situation within that very oppression: for proposing innovations to annul their "Robinson Crusoe-like isolation" (2003, 36)—innovations so radical that members of "the first sex would never imagine [them]" (54). She urges women to develop societies of learning where in collaborative work they will break the boundaries of closed, exclusive knowledge.

The dominant imaginary whose effects are to "en*gender*" social-political prohibitions of knowing and to nourish the ignorance that promotes those ends resembles Cornelius Castoriadis's *instituted social imaginary*, "a *world* of social imaginary significations whose instauration as well as incredible *coherence* goes unimaginably beyond everything that 'one or many individuals' could ever produce" (1991, 62, emphasis in original). To it, he opposes the *instituting* imaginary: the critical-creative activity in which a society exhibits a capacity to put itself in question in the ability of (some of) its members to act from a collective recognition that the society is incongruous with itself, with scant reason for self-satisfaction (Castoriadis 1994). In Le Dœuff's reading, Suchon's imaginatively initiated counterpossibilities attest to just such a capacity. They interrogate the social structure in order to destabilize its pretensions to integrity, "naturalness," and "wholeness." But such interrogations are not about admonishing isolated, individual knowers, showing them the errors of their ways. Although, as I hope to have shown, such "individuals" can serve an emblematic purpose as the vehicle that carries the argument forward, countering such entrenched, culturally sanctioned ignorance cannot be an *individual* project.

Because an instituted social imaginary so effectively sustains a self-assured *rightness*, it may seem impossible even to imagine how an opening could be made for a "new" conceptual frame to find a point of entry. For this reason, Suchon's insights are truly remarkable. Doxastic shock, ontological shock such as Le Dœuff's wry, outrageous juxtapositions of observation and incredulity achieve, suggest how cracks can be opened in otherwise apparently impervious, seamless structures. Such a shock, one supposes, would be a common male response, in Suchon's time, to encountering learned women educated by their own endeavors in defiance of the naturalized "sex of knowing": women doubly shocking for having imagined such possibilities within a society of "closed" knowledge and having brought those imaginings to fruition through cooperative projects. But not even doxastic shock is ubiquitously or uniformly effective, nor can it take the form of the one-off corrections that simple/single "mistakes" invite. Acknowledgment, if it comes, will be gradual, multilayered, persistent, and patient, for webs of belief that hold an entire imaginary together have to be slowly untangled, piece by piece, in a hermeneutics of practice/praxis where it would be implausible to imagine that straightforward true/false—"truth confronting falsity"—could serve as well as many epistemologists have hoped to "correct" simple individual empirical errors and the damaging moral-political beliefs they generate. Socially embedded ignorance readily *prevails* (hence its power, of which Eliot speaks); it adjusts and expands to overwhelm knowledge-in-the-making. It holds tenaciously against nonconformist individual testimony, especially from the margins, is intransigently entrenched, sedimented, ossified, requiring more than mere empirical counterexamples to dislodge it. It claims the power to discount "aberration" from its dogmatic certainty: indeed, ironically, socially sanctioned ignorance often carries an air of certainty even more stubborn than knowledge. Writing of Plato's *Laws*, Le Dœuff observes: "What is described as ignorance is, in reality, the possible conflict with beliefs concocted by those at the top or an affective detachment from them" (2003, 66). Suchon's bold innovation had fallen into obscurity among the cast-offs, until Le Dœuff unearthed it.

Excavations such as these can, with sustained effort, serve as catalysts for the conceptual change that a renewed and renewing *instituting* imaginary requires.

The imperatives such epistemic events generate are simultaneously *ecological* and ethical (moral) in the *responsibilities* they invoke, in a complex ontology of truth where there probably cannot be one true story, one *true* way of knowing sex, class, race—yet the specificities of the analysis require an explanatory story *grounded* in the detail of place—the nineteenth-century British class system and sexual politics; nineteenth-century myths of civilization, colonialism, and tradition—where entrenched and interlocking injustices, social *ethos*, and *habitus*, are painstakingly exposed (genealogy is patient, meticulous, gray) and where the outcome is rarely like the effect of flicking an on-off switch. Careful, often fragile, collectively initiated change is the only possibility: rarely linear, constantly yearning backward to blissful ignorance (as in Gwendolen Harlech's comfortable life, in the glories of British colonial supremacy). Appeal can rarely be just to "the facts," nor only to the present "facts," since they themselves are shaped and sustained by the processes that have produced the very imaginary under pressure. Like the hard-won civil liberties Le Dœuff discusses, freedom from constraints in knowledge has to be "recreated continuously," a creation she deems "impossible unless the history of . . . [their] difficult construction is taught" (2003, 180). Such historical inquiry, informed by the sophisticated politics of difference feminists, critical race theorists, and other postcolonial thinkers have crafted, can work to expose the contingency of the tacit naturalizing processes on which sexual and colonial oppressions rely to demonstrate that things could and should be different.

For a woman of Gwendolen's station, ignorance cannot be diagnosed as culpable with the old "she should have known better" charge, since the claim is vacuous; a hollow "should" when she *could not* have known otherwise, in a strong sense of "could." I follow Michel Foucault in recognizing the impediments to knowing what is not "within the true" (1972, 224), thus within the knowable, within the conceptual framework held in place by an intransigent hegemonic discourse, an instituted social imaginary.[7] Nor is there an innocent position from which "we" could level charges of culpability, for often, in the "normal"course of events, we cannot, by definition, know of the ignorance from which *we* speak, and yet there was Gabrielle Suchon. People—more often collectively than singly—do "come to know," for example, that *terra nullius* as a piece of epistemological ignorance performs gross moral-political violence, as do James Mill's images of India, which is to say that colonialism undergoes radical modifications, can even be destabilized, if not always for the good. Patriarchal, class, and racial consciousness are more available in the early twenty-first century than they were for Gwendolen Harlech; feminists have ensured that the sex of knowing can mutate from male to *epicene* (a literary term Le Dœuff deploys as a more refined way of saying "unisex") and have brought it about that women in some situations now have access to much more than the cast-offs of male knowledge and lives. Le Dœuff may find justification in these developments for having called the final section of her book *Bonne espérance*—which we have translated "an epistemology of hope." But because so often we cannot know the ignorance from which we speak, "we," whoever we are, have constantly to be vigilant, for we are always vulnerable to the power of ignorance, as Eliot puts it, "to seize the pillars that hold up the long-wrought fabric of human good." Does it all, then, yield a counsel of despair? Who can say? What it does, I think, is refocus epistemological inquiry away from unrealistic hopes for ubiquitous certainty, incontestably moral believing and knowing, and an overblown veneration of homogeneous autonomy toward acknowledging the pervasiveness of ambiguity and human vulnerability, where the task is to learn how to work well within the responsibilities they engender.

Implications

In this chapter I have offered a meditation on knowledge and ignorance in the form of a mini-genealogy centered around two emblematic examples as a way into thinking more productively about the power and the imperatives and prohibitions that knowledge and ignorance, singly and together, invoke. Striking in the process, from an epistemological point of view, is a marked asymmetry between knowledge and ignorance: ignorance is not the symmetrical, negative counterpart of knowledge in the way evil seems to be the negative counterpart of good, even though in each pair, one polarity does/can obliterate the other. There are, for example, bodies of knowledge, but it is less easy to imagine bodies of ignorance, even though we allow, somewhat vaguely, that there are vast tracts/areas of ignorance, of unknowns by definition beyond "our" ken. Ignorance is often ignorant of itself (Gwendolen Harlech is no anomaly in this regard), whereas knowledge, it would seem, can more readily know itself. (It is tempting to think that Sartrean existentialists might see areas of ignorance as the supreme ontological *lack*.) But one reason epistemic responsibility is so difficult a concept to insert into received epistemological discourse has to do with a thought like this: the idea of ignorance brings real human knowers and their capacities and responsibilities squarely into the picture: there could perhaps be an epistemology without a knowing subject—or so Karl Popper hoped (1972)—but it is even less plausible than the Popperian formulation to think of an epistemology of ignorance without ignorant subject(s). It is implausible to imagine how to postulate ignorance in the absence of human creatures embodying, living, constructing possibilities of not-knowing. Hence, imperatives of epistemic responsibility become urgently salient when the focus shifts from knowledge as a putatively unqualified good (a thought that also comes under pressure in this analysis) toward ignorance which, at least in common parlance, is usually attributable, and thus more directly implicated in issues of culpability, responsibility, blame. Ignorance often seems to be *somebody's*, in situations where it is opened to analysis, with the consequence that charting attributions of responsibility and/or culpability is a complex process, given that in so many instances they are more communal, more social than individual, and given the force of culturally induced ignorance. Nonetheless, for all its difficulties, I take epistemic responsibility as the crucial regulative concept and the place where epistemology and ethics of ignorance merge—cross—even though this merging will not achieve a congruence that would have them melding seamlessly into one another.

Because it is fundamentally oxymoronic, then, at least on orthodox readings of epistemology as an inquiry into conditions for the possibility of knowledge, the normative dimensions of an epistemology of ignorance are ambiguous, contradictory/paradoxical. It is because it is not and cannot be a normative inquiry—at least not a priori and possibly not even a posteriori—that it is best conceived as a genealogical inquiry into the power relations and structures of power that sustain, condone, or condemn ignorance. But in its diagnostic dimensions, it is an inquiry with a stronger descriptive-empirical and social-historical component than epistemology in an authorized sense would countenance. From my point of view, this component is the source of its strength.

Notes

An earlier version of this essay was published in *Philosophical Papers* 33, 3 (2004).

1. For an extended elaboration of the pertinence of ecology discourse to issues such as these, see Code (2006).

2. The title of Curtin's chapter 2 is "The British Utilitarians and the Invention of the 'Third World'."

3. Charles Mills persuasively suggests: "The terms of the Racial Contract set the parameters for white morality as a whole, so that competing Lockean and Kantian contractarian theories of natural rights and duties, or later anticontractarian theories such as nineteenth-century utilitarianism, are all limited by its stipulations" (1997, 17).

4. Cornelius Castoriadis observes that "the dominant social imaginary (*imaginaire social*) of our epoch" claims the assent of the social majority through sustained processes of nurturing citizens throughout their lives to ingest an unquestioned relationship to an "ensemble of needs" whose satisfaction becomes a lifelong project, even though he affirms, provocatively (for the Western world), "there are no natural needs"—only the needs capitalism creates, that it alone can satisfy" (1981, 12).

5. Here Le Dœuff is citing Monseigneur Dupanloup, *La Femme Studieuse* (Paris: C. Guignol, 1869).

6. Heller contrasts the British hypocrisy from which these traits emerge with the "idealism and wider culture and sympathy characteristic of the best elements of the Jewish section" of the novel, which is not the subject of my discussion here.

7. Foucault writes: "Mendel spoke the truth, but he was not *dans le vrai* (within the true) of contemporary biological discourse" (1972, 224).

References

Bannerji, Himani. 1995. "Beyond the Ruling Category to What Actually Happens: Notes on James Mill's Historiography in *The History of British India*". In *Knowledge, Experience, and Ruling Relations: Studies in the Social Organization of Knowledge*, ed. Marie Campbell and Ann Manicom. Toronto: University of Toronto Press.

Card, Claudia. 1991. "Removing Veils of Ignorance." *Journal of Social Philosophy* 22:1: 155–61.

Castoriadis, Cornelius. 1981. "From Ecology to Autonomy". *Thesis Eleven* 3.

———. 1991. "Individual, Society, Rationality, History." In *Philosophy, Politics, Autonomy: Essays in Political Philosophy*, ed. David Ames. New York: Oxford University Press.

———. 1994. "Radical Imagination and the Social Instituting Imaginary." In *Rethinking Imagination: Culture and Creativity*, ed. Gillian Robinson and John Rundell. London: Routledge.

Code, Lorraine. 1987. *Epistemic Responsibility*. Hanover, NH: University Press of New England.

———. 2006. *Ecological Thinking: The Politics of Epistemic Location*. New York: Oxford University Press.

Curtin, Deane. 1999. *Chinnagounder's Challenge: The Question of Ecological Citizenship*. Bloomington: Indiana University Press.

Dillon, Robin S. 2004. "Kant on Arrogance and Self-Respect." In *Setting the Moral Compass: Essays by Women Philosophers*, ed. Cheshire Calhoun. New York: Oxford University Press.

Eliot, George. 2002 [1876]. *Daniel Deronda*. New York: Random House Modern Library.

Foucault, Michel. 1972. "The Discourse on Language." Translated by Rupert Swyer. Published as an appendix to *The Archaeology of Knowledge*. New York: Pantheon Books.

Galbraith, John Kenneth. 1968. "Introduction." In *The History of British India*, vols. 1 and 2. New York: Chelsea House.

Heller, Deborah. 1990. "Jews and Women in George Eliot's *Daniel Deronda*." In *Jewish Presences in English Literature*, ed. Deborah Heller and Derek Cohen. Montreal: McGill-Queens University Press.

Ikuenobe, Polycarp. 1998. "Colonialism in Africa, Culturally Induced Moral Ignorance, and the Scope of Responsibility." *Journal for the Theory of Social Behaviour* 28:2: 109–28.

Le Dœuff, Michèle. 2003. *The Sex of Knowing*. Translated by Kathryn Hamer and Lorraine Code. New York: Routledge.

Mill, James. 1955 [1819]. *An Essay on Government*. Edited and with an Introduction by Currin V. Shields. New York: Bobbs-Merrill.

———. 1968 [1817]. *The History of British India*, vols. 1 and 2. New York: Chelsea House.

Mill, John Stuart. 1970 [1869]. "The Subjection of Women." In *John Stuart Mill and Harriet Taylor Mill: Essays on Sex Equality*, ed. Alice S. Rossi. Chicago: University of Chicago Press.

Mills, Charles W. 1997. *The Racial Contract*. Ithaca, NY: Cornell University Press.

Pateman, Carol. 1988. *The Sexual Contract*. Stanford, CA: Stanford University Press.

Popper, Karl. 1972. "Epistemology without a Knowing Subject." In *Objective Knowledge*. Oxford: Clarendon Press.

Schiebinger, Londa. 2004. "Feminist History of Colonial Science." *Hypatia: A Journal of Feminist Philosophy* 19:1: 233–54.

Suleri, Sara. 1992. *The Rhetoric of English India*. Chicago: University of Chicago Press.

Taylor, Harriet. 1951. "An Early Essay." In *John Stuart Mill and Harriet Taylor: Their Correspondence and Subsequent Marriage*, ed. F. A. Hayek. Chicago: University of Chicago Press.

CHAPTER 12

On Needing Not to Know and Forgetting What One Never Knew

The Epistemology of Ignorance in Fanon's Critique of Sartre

Robert Bernasconi

Aristotle called the knowledge that accompanies action *phronesis*, which is usually translated as "practical wisdom" or "prudence" (Aristotle 1947, 1140a 24–114ob 30). The one who habitually possesses this knowledge is the *phronimos*. The *phronimos* does not follow pregiven directives but is distinguished from the other participants in a given situation by being the one who sees what action that situation calls for. To see the situation for what it is and to act are, for the *phronimos*, one and the same: no act of will intervenes. The situation compels the response, but the *phronimos* never knows if he or she got it right, not even afterward: what provisionally looks to have been successful might subsequently prove to have been disastrous. That is why, as the Greeks well knew, only the historian or the poet as storyteller, from a vantage point created in part by temporal distance, can tell whether a given agent is a *phronimos*. They do so by constructing a narrative that shows someone to have acted well, that is, as the situation demanded. However, there is always a danger in trying to construct these narratives prematurely, especially if the narrative in question is that of the philosophy of history, understood teleologically.

The mark of philosophical ethics in our time, after the widespread loss of the consensus formed by religion, is that we lack pregiven directives, hence the rebirth of interest in *phronesis* within contemporary ethics. However, in contrast to the Greeks, who focused on the knowledge of the agent but who were impressed by this knowledge precisely because of a pervasive sense of the obscurity of situations and outcomes, philosophers today highlight the agent's ignorance. For example, Sartre, early in the posthumously published second volume of his *Critique of Dialectical Reason*, contrasts the knowledge that an officer studying the art of war in the military academy might have to the lack of knowledge from which the combatants at the time of the action suffer (Sartre 1985, 17, 1991, 9). The combatants "know and do not know what they are doing." They *decide*, Sartre says, because they are ignorant: "were one to know, the *act of will* would be redundant: the thing would be done automatically" (Sartre 1985, 19, 1991, 10). In keeping with modernity's heightened sense of the agent's ignorance, such that, on Sartre's account, action is a transcended ignorance, an act of will is called for, as it was not in Aristotle. Since its discovery, the will has been seen as a somewhat mysterious faculty. It often operates blindly, and within modernity there is an overriding suspicion that one never knows for sure what moves it.

In what follows I will focus on Sartre's own ignorance, especially as it relates to black experience, as Fanon exposed it in *Black Skin, White Masks*. In "Black Orpheus," Sartre made the mistake of locating the black agents he was addressing within a narrative. In so doing, he claimed he had more knowledge than they did, even though they knew the situation, as he did not, from the inside. His claim was unwarranted because he did not occupy a vantage point, such as that provided by temporal distance, that would allow him to supply a meaning to what was going on around him, as the poets of old had done. Quite simply, he had forgotten his own ignorance and he had forgotten too that pervasive sense of ignorance that often accompanies action. The agent's knowledge of a situation is as much defined by the blind spots as by what is visible, and to rush in prematurely and define the meaning of action distorts that aspect of it. To say this is not to deny the significance of "Black Orpheus" within the history of the negritude movement, something Fanon never sought to deny. However, I want here to establish its significance for an understanding of the epistemology of ignorance, a significance that Fanon's phrase—"the European knows and does not know"—clearly brings out (Fanon 1952, 161, 1982, 199). As I have explored elsewhere, Fanon's book has attracted a growing number of white commentators who have been eager to use it as a basis for discussions of blackness, but who have not used it to the same degree as a basis for discussing whiteness, although it also has a great deal to contribute to that issue as well.[1] What is today called race theory still has a great deal to learn from Fanon's critique of Sartre's "Black Orpheus," as Sartre himself learned from it, if I am right in thinking of his discussion of ignorance in the second volume of the *Critique of Dialectical Reason* as informed by Fanon.

In the central chapter of *Black Skin, White Masks*, Fanon confronts Sartre's attempt in "Black Orpheus" to locate the negritude movement within a dialectic as a passing phase between white supremacy and "the realization of the human in a raceless society" (Sartre 1948, xli, 2001, 137). Sartre does so by announcing a dialectic according to which white racism is the first term, the negritude movement understood as an antiracist racism is the second term, and a raceless society is the conclusion. Fanon, who had been searching for a way of negotiating his identity in a racist society, declares that Sartre had robbed him of his last chance; at the moment when he had tried to reclaim his negritude, Sartre had snatched it from him (Fanon 1952, 106–107, 1982, 133). The dialectic "shatters my non-reflective position" (Fanon 1952, 109, 1982, 135). The culmination of Fanon's response to Sartre are these lines:

> Jean-Paul Sartre, in this work, has destroyed black enthusiasm. In opposition to historical becoming, there had always been the unforeseeable. I needed to lose myself completely in negritude. One day, perhaps, in the depths of that unhappy romanticism. . . . In any case, I needed not to know. (Fanon 1952, 109, 1982, 135)

Fanon does not say that Sartre was wrong and that he, Fanon, was right. Fanon says that he needed not to know, or, more precisely, "En tout cas *j'avais besoin* d'ignorer." What Fanon needed to be oblivious of were, he tells us, the essences and determinations of the being of consciousness: "Consciousness, when committed to experience, does not know and must not know the essences and determination of its being" (Fanon 1952, 108, 1982, 134, translation modified). And yet none of this would have mattered if Fanon had not suspected that Sartre was right in what he said. That is the basis on which Fanon could complain that his illusion had been shattered by Sartre (Fanon 1952, 109, 1982, 135). When Fanon explains that Sartre had destroyed his black enthusiasm, this sounds like a severe criticism, but Fanon is only marking a change. He tells us in the introduction to *Black Skin, White Masks* that he no longer trusts enthusiasm. The passage is worth quoting at length:

> This book should have been written three years ago. . . . But these truths were a fire in me then. Now I can tell them without being burned. These truths do not have to be hurled in men's faces. They are not intended to ignite enthusiasm. I do not trust enthusiasm. Every time it has burst out somewhere, it has brought fire, famine, misery. . . . And contempt for man. Enthusiasm is the weapon of choice of the impotent. (Fanon 1952, 6–7, 1982, 9, translation modified)

So when Fanon says that Sartre destroyed black enthusiasm, its loss was not the problem. He now sees this enthusiasm as itself a problem, a sign of impotence. But this alters everything: the situation no longer remains the same.

To be sure, there is a problem with the knowledge that Sartre brings, but one has to be clear what the problem is. Fanon previously saw only the unforeseeable, that is, he acted not knowing how things would turn out. However, the dialectic, as Sartre presents it, is a narrative of historical becoming and allegedly takes away the uncertainty. Indeed, Sartre, in "Black Orpheus," extends the narrative beyond the battle between blacks and whites that Fanon in his impotence and rage wanted to join. Sartre's dialectic leads beyond race to a raceless society and, indeed, to a classless society, but there was nothing new in saying that: some negritude poets were saying the same thing, and Sartre cites them in "Black Orpheus" (Sartre 1948, xl–xlii, 2001, 137–38). Furthermore, in chapter 6 of *Black Skin, White Masks*, after a long quote from Aimé Césaire, Fanon writes, "One can understand why Sartre views the adoption of a Marxist position by Black poets as the logical conclusion of Negrohood" (Fanon 1952, 159, 1982, 197). Fanon himself does not object to this goal of a raceless society, as is clear from the conclusion to *Black Skin, White Masks*, which is decisively future oriented and clearly against all forms of identity rooted in the past. Belief in this future is the spur for action. However, Fanon also sees with stunning clarity that for action to be possible, it must be rooted not so much in knowledge of the situation but in the experience of it, a being immersed in the situation that occludes seeing all sides. Sartre knew about the needs and the suffering of blacks in an intellectual way, but by saying what he said he showed that he did not really know it. That is why Fanon calls Sartre's "Black Orpheus" an event in the intellectualization of black existence (Fanon 1952, 108, 1982, 135). The intellectualization of black existence is in this context a bad form of ignorance.

However, through Sartre's misunderstanding, through his ignorance, Fanon discovers something about his own situation. Indeed, to that extent Sartre could be said to be part of his situation. In chapter 6, after the remark about understanding why Sartre adopted the Marxist position of some black poets, Fanon replays part of the narrative of chapter 5: "I catch myself hating the Negro. But then I recognize that I am a Negro." He rejects both of the obvious ways out of the conflict, that of paying no attention to his skin and that of insisting on it. The situation itself is neurotic. That is, the kind of society in which we live is such that to respond to the situation leads to a choice of "an unhealthy, conflicted solution, fed on fantasies, hostile, inhuman" (Fanon 1952, 159, 1982, 197). To respond to the situation in the terms given, black and white, leads to enthusiasm. He rejects the two terms that, he says "are equally unacceptable and across a particular human reaches out for the universal." This reference to the universal should not evoke thoughts of color blindness. Indeed, at this point Fanon renews the effort to discover the white man in himself and kill him. This can even take the form of literally killing white men, as is already suggested by the quote from Césaire that follows immediately. Fanon crosses the bridge from fighting out of despair, where one is as likely to hurt one's own people as those who oppress one, to fighting to create a new humanity. This is one of the clearest indications that even here he was moving from diagnosis to strategy, albeit the full statement of the solution awaited *The Wretched of the Earth* (Bernasconi 2001, 17–19).

Because Fanon lived in a society in which black and white were each locked, enclosed, sealed in their race, he could not without bad faith choose to disregard race, to simply renounce it unilaterally. Sartre does not ask him to do so at once, but he tells him that by embracing his black identity, he will pass beyond negritude and free both blacks and whites for a new humanity. That is, what he chooses under the description of reclaiming his negritude can also be described, as Sartre and Césaire did describe it, as choosing a society without races. The problem is that Fanon did not yet know it under that description. More precisely, he thought that by reclaiming his negritude, he had chosen the absolute, but Sartre tells him that he had chosen only the relative, that is, a stage in a dialectic. Sartre thereby took the meaning of Fanon's act from him and assigned it to history, except that Sartre himself provided the master narrative and in so doing retained his position as master. Hence, Fanon legitimately describes Sartre not just as a Hegelian but as "a born Hegelian" (Fanon 1952, 108, 1982, 133). Sartre located negritude in a dialectical history that has white racism for its first term. Despite its liberatory intent, it is in a certain sense a philosophy of white history, a white philosophy of history.

Fanon's response to Sartre is the response of an existentialist to a Hegelian or dialectical account. That is, Fanon is here more Sartrean than Sartre, insofar as Sartre had abandoned the phenomenology of action by imposing a narrative on an agent, a narrative that the agent, acting from ignorance, does not recognize. What Fanon seems to have had in mind is the distinction from the *Phenomenology of Spirit* between natural consciousness, which understands itself as free, and absolute consciousness, which recognizes the necessity governing the dialectic. That is why it is a mistake to think that Fanon's objection was that Sartre looked beyond the conditions that spawned the negritude movement to a time after it. This was something Fanon himself did so incessantly. Indeed, one of the ways to secure disalienation lay in refusing to take present realities as definitive (Fanon 1952, 183, 1982, 226). Sartre concedes the point in a remark that might even have been occasioned by Fanon's critique when, again in the second volume of the *Critique of Dialectical Reason*, he writes: "Does anyone imagine that you could die or sell your soul for *the relative*?" (Sartre 1985, 40, 1991, 30).

At the time Fanon wrote *Black Skin, White Masks* there were significant differences between his position and Sartre's position, as Fanon seems to have known it at that time. Fanon endorses the Sartrean framework of facticity and transcendence, that is, the framework of a solidarity with Being through which one surpasses Being (Fanon 1952, 186, 1982, 229), but he experiences the weight of the social constraints on freedom differently from the way Sartre presented them in *Being and Nothingness.* The situation is such that the facticity of race presents itself differently to blacks than to whites. This means that the application to black experience of an ontology based on the white experience of the body proved fallacious. According to Fanon, black consciousness is immanent to itself and is not a potentiality, because black consciousness is not a lack but adheres to itself (Fanon 1952, 109, 1982, 135). However, Fanon was more concerned with the way Sartre said what he said, the position he occupied, and the fact that he, a white man, was the one saying it. When blacks discuss race among themselves, differences and disagreements emerge that reflect the ambiguity of the situation. When Sartre, who Fanon expressly acknowledges as "a friend of the colored peoples" (Fanon 1952, 108, 1982, 133), says what Césaire had already said, it takes on another meaning because it reinscribes the white gaze, undoing precisely what it affirms. Sartre was not altogether wrong, but he was wrong to say it as he said it because he was white. Epistemologists do not always acknowledge the significance of the social identity of the speaker in assessing knowledge claims, but here is a case in point when they should.

Sartre undermines his own narrative by giving away the plot too early: Fanon points out that the story, as Sartre tells it, relies on the characters not knowing what they are doing. But Fanon is able to remake himself and take on another absolute, that of humanity, albeit his belief in it is tempered by the inhumanity of whites (Fanon 1952, 187, 1982, 231). Fanon does not adopt the Marxist position of a historical becoming that Sartre passes on secondhand from Césaire, but he comes to accept that race is not an absolute, even though that is how society presents it. However, Fanon learns about his race, his blackness, from experience as he negotiates for himself the contradiction of his own existence. Sartre, of course, had not and could not experience blackness in this sense. Fanon, who had already complained about Sartre forgetting that consciousness needed to lose itself in the night of the absolute, said it again in another more direct and personal way: "Jean-Paul Sartre had forgotten that the Negro suffers in his body quite differently than the White" (Fanon 1952, 112, 1982, 138). This is not merely "an individual failure of judgment," as one commentator has recently called it (Krucks 2001, 103). If Sartre had not been white, then he could not have forgotten how the black suffers in his or her body. A black person could not forget it.

Sartre's knowledge of this suffering is a memory of what he has been told, but the black person's knowledge is like *phronesis* in this regard: *phronesis*, as Aristotle explains, is not learned, nor can it be forgotten (Aristotle 1947, 1140b 28–30). That Sartre forgot the difference between black and white experience of the body suggests that if he knew at all, it was only intellectually: he did not really know. The difference between what one can and cannot forget is emphasized by Fanon. After saying that Jean-Paul Sartre has forgotten that the Negro suffers in his body differently from the white, he begins the next paragraph by saying that "one has forgotten the constancy of my love." Because he is that constancy of love, what Sartre told him does not change the direction of history.

The fundamental issues raised by Fanon's criticisms of Sartre are by no means peculiar to this encounter. One might think of Frederick Douglass berating the Garrisonians, with whom he had earlier been allied, for being prepared to accept a compromise with slavery. Douglass was afraid that the Garrisonians would dissolve the Union and leave slavery intact in the South (Douglass 1950, 416). He responded by drawing a disinction between white reasons and black reasons. White reasons are met if slavery is kept at a distance, so one can no longer be judged responsible for it:

> Instead of walking straight up to the giant wrong and demanding its utter overthrow, we are talking of limiting it, circumscribing it, surrounding it with free States, and leaving it to die of inward decay. (Douglass 1950, 367–68)

This was unacceptable to what Douglass called black reasons. White reasons do not know these black reasons because they were based on the solidarity that would not allow one black to suffer while others went free (Douglass 1950, 414; also see Bernasconi 1991, 1291–96). Douglass, of course, knew white reasons and shared them because he had to live in both worlds, but he assessed them differently because he knew what whites did not know.

One sees something similar when, in Robert Penn Warren's *Who Speaks for the Negro?*, Ralph Ellison addressed Hannah Arendt's "Reflections on Little Rock" from 1957. Arendt had criticized the NAACP and the parents of the young African American students for putting children on the front line of the struggle for civil rights. Ellison complained in response, "She has absolutely no conception of what goes on in the minds of Negro parents when they send their kids through those lines of hostile people" (Warren 1965, 344). In her essay Arendt had begun by asking, "What would I do if I were a Negro mother?" Her answer went entirely contrary to what these mothers had done. She then asked, "What would I do if I were a White mother in the South?" Her answer was that she could have done the same as the white mothers of Little Rock. It was the same answer in both cases: to try to prevent one's child from being dragged into a political battle. Arendt also took it upon herself to advise blacks on their strategies. She was worried that those she called law-abiding citizens had left the streets to the mob rather than see the Little Rock nine safely to school, but rather than castigate them or express outrage that in a poll of Virginians only 21 percent said that they would feel bound to obey laws integrating the schools, she argued against limiting governmental intervention. She did not ask for moderation from whites, but she called for "caution and moderation rather than impatience and ill-advised measures" from African Americans (see Bernasconi 1996, 3–24). What makes this example so telling is that Hannah Arendt, who had suffered persecution as a Jew and who had had to negotiate the trials of being a woman in academia at a time when there were very few of them, was not able to recognize the need to listen to African Americans before pontificating to them on how they should conduct their struggle and what their order of priorities should be. That whites and blacks had very different political priorities was well known at that time and had already been introduced into the philosophical literature by Alfred Schutz. In an essay entitled "Equality and the Meaning of the Social World," Schutz cited from Gunnar Myrdal's classic work *An American Dilemma* evidence that if one asked African Americans to prioritize the changes that needed to be made within society, they came up with a parallel list to that which whites constructed (Myrdal 1949, 60–61). The only difference was that their list was in inverse order! Changing the marriage laws was the top priority for whites, including Arendt, but the least important issue for blacks, which is hardly surprising for anyone with personal experience of life in a segregated society (Schutz 1964, 266). Arendt ignored their testimony.

Throughout the history of philosophy there have been philosophers who have made a point of marking the limits of legitimate knowledge claims. However, the urgent task of establishing the extent and depth of the white man's ignorance of how the targets of racism suffer—just as the targets of sexism do—is still largely ignored by white philosophers in their attempts to contribute to race theory. Fanon's critique of Sartre, like Douglass's of Garrison and Ellison's of Arendt, shows how even some of the best-intentioned whites failed. The stories of their failures serve as an appropriate warning.

Notes

1. R. Bernasconi, "The European Knows and He Does Not Know: Fanon's Response to Sartre," in *Frantz Fanon's "Black Skin, White Masks,"* ed. Max Silverman (Manchester: Manchester University Press, 2005), 100–11.

References

Arendt, H. 1959. "Reflections on Little Rock." *Dissent* 6:1: 45–51.

Aristotle. 1947. *Nicomachean Ethics.* Translated by H. Rackham. London: William Heinemann.

Bernasconi, R. 1991. "The Constitution of the People: Frederick Douglas and the Dred Scott Decision." *Cardozo Law Review* 13:4: 1281–96.

———. 1996. "The Double Face of the Political and the Social." *Research in Phenomenology* 16: 3–24.

———. 2001. "Eliminating the Cycle of Violence: The Place of a Dying Colonialism within Fanon's Revolutionary Thought." *Philosophia Africana* 4:2: 17–25.

———. 2002. "The Assumption of Negritude: Aimé Césaire, Frantz Fanon, and the Vicious Circle of Racial Politics." *Parallax* 23: 68–83.

Douglass, F. 1950. *Pre-Civil War Decade: The Life and Writings of Frederick Douglass,* vol. 2. Edited by Philip S. Foner. New York: International Publishers.

Fanon, F. 1952. *Peau noire, masques blancs.* Paris: Seuil.

———. 1961. *Les damnés de la terre.* Paris: François Maspero.

———. 1982. *Black Skin, White Masks.* Translated by C. L. Markmann. New York: Grove Weidenfeld.

———. 1991. *The Wretched of the Earth.* Translated by C. Farrington. New York: Grove Weidenfeld.

Krucks, S. 2001. *Retrieving Experience: Subjectivity and Recognition in Feminist Politics.* Ithaca, NY: Cornell University Press.

Myrdal, G. 1949. *An American Dilemma.* New York: Harper and Brothers.

Sartre, J-P. 1948. "Orphée Noir." In *Anthologie de la nouvelle poésie nègre et malgache de langue francaise,* ed. L. Senghor, ix–xiv. Paris: Presses Universitaires de France.

———. 1985. *Critique de la raison dialectique: Vol. 2: L'intelligibilité de l'Histoire.* Paris: Gallimard.

———. 1991. *Critique of Dialectical Reason: Vol 2: The Intelligibility of History.* Translated by Quintin Hoare. London: Verso.

———. 2001. "Black Orpheus." Translated by J. MacCombie. In *Race,* ed. R. Bernasconi, 115–42. Oxford: Blackwell.

Schutz, A. 1964. *Studies in the Meaning of the Social World: Collected Philosophical Papers,* vol. 2. The Hague, The Netherlands: Martinus Nijhoff.

Warren, R. P. 1965. *Who Speaks for the Negro?* New York: Random House.

CHAPTER 13

On the Absence of Biology in Philosophical Considerations of Race

Stephanie Malia Fullerton

A focus on the ethical and epistemological implications of ignorance asks us to interrogate absences in our knowledge for what they are, how they arise, and what they may mean for our appreciation and understanding of the knowledge we currently hold. In this context, it is perhaps surprising to suggest that those actively engaged in the investigation of "race" as a key organizing principle of human relations have ignored the significance of human biological variation (what shall be called here, in abbreviation, biology) in their analysis of the meaning and salience of the category. After all, most would argue that discussion of race has been focused on biology for far too long, to pernicious and often racist effect. Furthermore, have not the scientists, the ones who are in the best position to investigate and interpret the physiological and genetic evidence relevant to this question, ruled definitively that the individuals and populations that "common sense" assigns to different racial categories are themselves so similar as to be virtually indistinguishable? Are we not all in agreement that any so-called natural basis of racial differentiation is a fiction, such that if we could only get this information out to the public at large, dangerous and misplaced assumptions regarding fundamental distinctions would melt away, taking along with them the social hierarchies upon which they are based? If the biological salience of one's racial identity is ultimately an illusion, then what is there to ignore?

As this chapter will briefly outline, potentially a great deal. For while it is certainly true that science (specifically, the fields of physical anthropology and population genetics) has, in its investigation of genetic relationships among humans, shown clearly that no fixed, innate, biological differences categorically separate individuals understood socially as belonging to different racial groups, this is not the same thing as saying that no biological differences whatsoever exist among such groups. The population genetic investigations that have permitted the robust denial of a typological ontology of race also demonstrate that at nearly every human gene there is variation systematically correlated with geography, such that when the term *race* is based on aspects of geographic origins, racial identity can, and often will, predict genetic differences among groups. That such differences are typically matters of degree rather than kind, that they represent only a very small proportion of the total biological variability observed in the human species, and that their morphological and biomedical significance remain in many cases uncertain does not take away from the fact that such differences are widely recognized *and* the continuing object of scientific and clinical attention. Thus to assert that "there is no biological basis to race" is to ignore both this continuing scientific interest and the social and biomedical implications inherent to such investigation.

Nevertheless, most philosophical accounts of race and ethnicity begin, almost as a matter of course, by refuting the relevance of biology to racial identity or identification.[1] Race is said to be a "biologistic fallacy" (Gates 1997, viii) that lacks "scientifically accessible referents" (Zack 2002, 4), and that "no existing racial classifications correlate in useful ways to gene frequencies, clinical variations, or any significant human biological difference" (Alcoff 2002, 15). Such statements, which are grounded in the authority of objective scientific investigation (albeit rarely via reference to a specific literature), reflect a widespread consensus understanding among philosophers and other critical theorists that "race" is, first and foremost, a social construction, and that indeed any potential natural correlates of the phenomenon can, and in fact must, be discounted in advance of its deconstruction. Obviously such claims sit uneasily in the face of widespread evidence of the ongoing scientific investigation of the relationship between race and biology, and yet, as alluded to earlier, they are not wholly without empirical justification. Population geneticists and physical anthropologists *have* demonstrated that a typological understanding of racial biological difference is unsustainable in the face of data describing patterns of genetic variation within and between human populations. The "no biological basis" mantra has thus propagated throughout much of the philosophic race theory canon, acquiring an epistemological significance disconnected from contemporary scientific investigation and debate.[2]

This unreflexive propagation of a social constructivist understanding of race and racial identity relies on a peculiar form of ignorance, one in which specific features of the empirical record, not to mention pervasive scientific practices, have been systematically overlooked in favor of broad disclaimers relevant to only a narrowly applicable model of human biological difference. Here, scientific findings are simultaneously co-opted and denied, as observations that allow a strategic partition of social (cultural) and biological (natural) domains of inquiry and critique are allowed to take precedence over other, equally well-supported but ultimately far less tidy glimpses of "race" as encountered in biomedical and population genetic settings. While both scientists and philosophers have had much to gain in perpetuating the nature-culture divide in this way, it is also clear that the ignorance required to sustain the dichotomy is epistemically unwarranted and, perhaps most importantly, ethically unjustifiable. Though denying the relevance of biology in critical philosophy of race accounts may permit race to "look and feel differently" (Zack 2002, 8), it also inappropriately and unhelpfully constrains consideration of the phenomenon to the realm of social relations, foreclosing comprehensive consideration of the multifaceted contributions to racial identity operating in contemporary society. Even more importantly, such ignorance leaves the ongoing scientific construction of racial biology immune from evaluation, critique, and correction, opening the way for fresh abuses associated with the biological reification of social categories. In short, there is simply too much at stake to leave biology at the door of race theory.

How Biology Was Written
Out of the Philosophical Critique of Race

Philosophy, as a discipline, is not unique in its acceptance of the "no biological basis to race" message, but the specific genesis of that understanding in philosophic race theory[3] can be convincingly traced to the writings of Kwame Anthony Appiah, beginning with his 1986 article "The Uncompleted Argument: Du Bois and the Illusion of Race" (Appiah 1986). In that article, Appiah used a reading of the current scientific consensus regarding human biological variation to critique W. E. B. Du Bois' failure to fully transcend a biologistic account of racial formation in his speeches and writing. This critique, in turn, informed Appiah's influential attempt to rebut the intellectual rationale for racism by denying the ontological legitimacy of race as a basis for human classification. Though he has since tempered this anti-essentialist position to some degree, granting the significance of racial identity in such a way as to acknowledge the nonillusory nature of race as a sociohistorical phenomenon (Appiah 1996), he has held fast to the claim that races are not real in any tangible biological sense. Arguably, therefore, it is Appiah's account that has done much to legitimate the ongoing ignorance of biology in the critical philosophy of race canon. A brief review of that account, which illustrates the ways in which scientific evidence can and has been used, underlines the strategic role of ignorance in the assertion of an exclusively social constructivist understanding of racial identity.

In "The Uncompleted Argument," for example, Appiah referenced widespread scientific consensus while citing the research findings of a single research group, reported in a single scientific paper: an article by population geneticists Masatoshi Nei and Arun Roychoudhury published several years earlier in the journal *Evolutionary Biology* (Nei and Roychoudhury 1982). The authors, recognized leaders in the field, had previously published on the genetic variation revealed by systematic investigation of blood group and protein (i.e., non-DNA-based) differences within and between human populations. The 1982 report represented their most extensive survey to that point, summarizing results gathered from the wider population genetic literature and encompassing gene frequency data for over 100 separate genetic systems and thirty-six populations (analyzed with respect to membership in five major racial groups: Caucasoid, Negroid, Mongoloid, Amerind, and Oceanian[4]). As a comprehensive analysis of much of the then-publicly available genetic data, it was appropriate to read the report as being representative of current scientific consensus. It is important to recognize, however, that Nei and Roychoudhury were neither the first, nor the only, biologists to summarize and interpret human genetic variation on a global scale.[5] Although he neither explained nor defended his specific choice of research publication, the decision to cite this report clearly reflected a desire to marshal the latest scientific results in support of his argument. This preference for the most recent and comprehensive data is a common feature of accounts that look to scientific observations for ontological justification and support.

Appiah highlighted four major population genetic findings in his review and discussion of the Nei and Roychoudhury (1982) report. Despite their grounding in the latest research, these were noncontroversial observations, already extensively previously documented by prior empirical investigation.[6] First, he noted that genetic variability between the populations of Africa, Europe, or Asia was not much greater than that observed within those populations, citing the observation that only 9 to 11 percent of total genetic variation was attributable to differences among races (Appiah 1986, 21, citing Nei and Roychoudhury 1982, 11). Second, he suggested that there were few, if any, genetic characteristics found in one human population (say England) that were not found in similar proportions in other populations (such as those of Zaire, or China).[7] In other words, as Nei and Roychoudhury noted, "Racial differences . . . are essentially due to gene frequency shift rather than complete gene substitution."[8] Third, he described how two people drawn at random from a single population were almost as likely to differ genetically as two individuals chosen at random from anywhere in the world, making it impossible to accurately predict a person's underlying biological characteristics from an outward assessment of her or his racial identity.[9] Finally, he also cited the observation that the degree of genetic difference between races was not always closely correlated with the degree of morphological (physical) differentiation (Appiah 1986, 31, citing Nei and Roychoudhury 1982, 44). Given these accepted scientific facts, he argued that "race" was of no real meaning to an understanding of human biological difference. Instead, he asserted, "the truth is that there are no races: there is nothing in the world that can do all we ask 'race' to do for us" (35).

These four observations, and the elegant conclusions drawn from them, have been the mainstay of philosophical understanding for nearly twenty years. But note what Appiah did not claim about scientific understandings of racial biology. First, he did not suggest that the ontological reality of race was *scientifically* settled. Indeed, in the very first sentence of his article he noted that "contemporary biologists are not agreed on the question of whether there are any human races" (1986, 21). Nor did he suggest that the interpretation of population variation was straightforward. Though there was enough information about genetic differences to statistically quantify the extent to which variation was partitioned between rather than within specific populations, he allowed that particular scientists were inclined (for a variety of reasons) to regard that proportion as being either very important or not important at all in biological terms.[10] He also acknowledged that the geneticists he cited were those who "believe in human races" (36) but disputed their claim that their data "shows the existence of a biological basis for the classification of human races" (37, note 10). Instead, he argued that the only thing that the work of Nei and Roychoudhury (1982) demonstrated was that "human populations differ in their distribution of genes," refuting the scientists' own interpretation of the observed variation with the objection that any categorical classification of individuals on such a basis was impossible (Appiah 1986, 37, note 10). In other words, for Appiah, the clear overlap in the population distribution of genetic variation meant that no consistent biological criteria were available for drawing robust distinctions among individuals recognized socially as belonging to different racial groups.

Appiah's firm denial of the biological salience of racial classification, in common with subsequent accounts, was informed by the available population genetic data and by a wider scientific understanding that lay assumptions regarding the existence of large, consistent, and deterministic biological differences among major racial groups are misplaced. He called on the latest scientific evidence, which had been collated and analyzed by respected genetic investigators, and accurately represented those findings to his philosophical audience. And yet even as he invoked the authority of the genetic data in his claim that races were not "real," he dismissed the significance of an analytical design that explicitly presupposed the existence of distinguishable biological races and then demonstrated that the genetic differentiation between such groups was "real and generally statistically highly significant" (Nei and Roychoudhury 1982, 41). In doing so, Appiah fundamentally ignored the epistemological basis of the continuing scientific belief in race, a belief that made no sense according to a model of races as discrete taxonomic categories but could have meaning on probabilistic and other empirical grounds.

Appiah acknowledged this slight of hand in his subsequent article "The Conservation of 'Race'" (Appiah 1989) but defended his conclusions both by citing the scientists' own (somewhat puzzling) justification that the words "race" and "population" were used "interchangeably without any social implication" (Nei and Roychoudhury 1982, 4) and with the matter-of-fact statement that "talk of 'race' in evolutionary biology is usually defended as a harmless reflex of old lexical habits" (Appiah 1989, 38). Critical race theorist Ian Haney López has also pointed to the disconcerting ways in which Nei and Roychoudhury invoke race in the presentation of their scientific evidence while simultaneously arguing that talk of biological races should be abandoned (Haney López 1994).[11] However, even as Haney López attributed the scientists' reliance on "race" to "their continued reflexive belief in the existence of the biological races" (14, note 51), he noted the tendency of the scientists to "use 'race' only when discussing large groups popularly considered races, and rarely when discussing smaller groups." Indeed, Nei and Roychoudhury (1982) were quite explicit in the distinction, explaining that their article would "not pay much attention to the genetic differentiation of local populations within races" (2). Therefore, as these acknowledgments make clear, the continuing scientific recognition of race has been readily apparent and yet repeatedly denied in the insistence that biology has no place in the philosophical discussion of race and racial identity.

Where Race and Biology Meet in Contemporary Scientific Discourse

Today, much of the philosophic race theory literature is premised on the belief that there is "no biological basis to race," by which theorists appear to mean that there are no prior ontological types of human persons distinguishable unambiguously on the basis of a set of shared unique genetic or physical characteristics. As described earlier, this conclusion is amply supported by the observations of population geneticists, who have demonstrated that genes vary in a continuous fashion within and among human populations, and that the groups understood socially as races differ more within themselves than they do from one another. Despite this consensus understanding of human genetic variation, however, many scientists, clinicians, and anthropologists continue to employ races as categories of investigation (either implicitly or explicitly) in their research, acknowledging a biological dimension to racial identification that appears inconsistent with the available empirical evidence. This understanding has, for the most part, been ignored by writers such as Appiah, who have preferred to read the contradiction as a lexical difficulty rather than concede the existence of a "scientifically recoverable notion of race" (Appiah 1989, 38). A closer consideration of scientific practices in this area, focusing on the different ways in which race is conceived in biological terms, suggests that the contradiction instead reflects an inherent flexibility in the scientific understanding of population variation, one that leaves open the relationship between race and biology.

Race, according to many historians, philosophers, and science studies theorists, is supposed to have been removed as a valid category of biological investigation when the modern evolutionary synthesis replaced the typological conception of racial biology with a population-based understanding of genetic variation (Stepan 1982; Haraway 1989; Barkan 1992).[12] Recent scholarship, however, which has revisited scientific research in the post-World War II period, has begun to challenge this assessment, demonstrating that racial biological differences were not denied entirely but merely redefined in population-based terms (Gannett 2001, 2004; Reardon 2005).[13] As Gannett (2001) has described, this redefinition was instigated by population biologist Theodosius Dobzhansky, who explicitly conceived of biological races not as permanent, static types of people but rather as "Mendelian [breeding] populations which differ in the frequency of genes" (Gannett 2001, S484, citing Dobzhansky 1951, 611). Importantly, to conceive of races in such terms did not deny their biological reality: such populations were, to Dobzhansky, real and prior to arbitrary human attempts to identify and classify them. The definition of race as literally any genetically distinct group was, however, too broad in many cases to sustain the use of "race" as a separate descriptive term, and most biologists reverted to "population" as an equivalent, politically less charged, way to describe their units of investigation.

Dobzhansky's definition, which continues to be operationally relevant today, not only kept a place for biology in scientific conceptions of race, it left room for an important flexibility with respect to the interpretation of patterns of genetic variation, recognizing as it did that "racial differences are different orders of magnitude, ranging from differences among neighboring villages to differences among continents" (Gannett 2001, S485). Under this conception, scientists could disavow a typological understanding of race while remaining empirically invested in describing

and explaining genetic similarities and differences among groups of individuals understood to constitute biologically meaningful breeding populations.[14] In practice, of course, what exactly constitutes a "breeding
population" in this context is far from clear. In the absence of direct measures of mating behavior, evidence of sufficient (i.e., statistically distinguishable) genetic differences between samples of individuals collected
from distinct populations (separated by geography, language, or other
cultural characteristics) is often taken as indirect evidence of barriers to
genetic exchange or gene flow. Such definition leaves open the degree of
internal genetic coherence expected of any specific population sample,
so that individuals sampled from a broad range of geographic locations,
or belonging to the same socially ascribed racial or ethnic group, can be
regarded as a breeding population for purposes of comparison, even if
the individuals so designated may not actually constitute a "true" biological population of randomly mating individuals.[15]

In practice, the choice of individuals to include in a population sample depends largely on the objectives of the specific population genetic
investigation in question, but has traditionally taken one of two forms.
Studies aimed at identifying population relationships and inferring from
these aspects of human evolutionary history (e.g., Chen et al. 2000;
Karafet et al. 2002; Rosenberg et al. 2002) most often begin with samples
of individuals gathered from multiple discrete locales (often several such
groups drawn from the same broad geographic region, with sampling extended to other regions, depending on the scope of the investigation),
each of which is assumed to represent a sample of a locally bounded
breeding population.[16] Genetic variation within each population sample
is then identified, and similarities and differences among samples are
summarized statistically as measures of genetic distance in such a way as
to demonstrate that some populations are more closely related genetically than others. This form of investigation allows breeding populations
to be characterized and related populations to be clustered and distinguished from other population groups. An alternative analytical aim is to
identify genetic diversity more sparsely, usually at a global scale (e.g., Siffert et al. 1999; Gabriel et al. 2002; Marth et al. 2004). Such investigations
typically begin with samples drawn from groups of individuals currently
living on separate continents,[17] or with recent ancestry traceable to individuals who lived in widely separated geographic locales (e.g., individuals
with distinct socially ascribed racial identity). In this case, barriers to random mating are assumed a priori and the emphasis is less on distin-
guishing breeding populations per se (or local relations between them)
than on characterizing the range of genetic diversity present in the
species as a whole.[18]

To be clear, although from a formal philosophical standpoint the most appropriate empirical question to ask about the biological basis of race might be "whether there are human populations, or collections of human populations, that are races" (Gannett 2004, 327), in a biological sense, geneticists and other biologists rarely, if ever, ask this question. Instead, a form of racial biological differentiation is more often taken for granted—either by treating groups of populations that cluster on some (often arbitrary) measure of genetic identity as coherent analytical categories or in structuring global population sampling to compare single sample exemplars of broad geographic regions (typically continents) against one another. In either case, the aim of population genetic investigation is rarely to objectively confirm or deny the biological reality of groups recognized as races on sociocultural grounds but rather to describe how groups so defined (or the individuals contained within them) are similar or different genetically. Invariably, most such studies, such as the one by Nei and Roychoudhury (1982) cited by Appiah, identify small but statistically replicable differences among such groups, differences that affirm a contingent biological distinctiveness,[19] even as they undermine a typological racial ontology.

It is precisely this socially mediated and contingent designation of particular groups as races that Appiah and related philosophers have found so problematic in their review of prevailing population genetic investigation. If races are to count as real ontological entities, then they should be bounded in space and time and exist prior to the perceptive practices of scientists and clinicians. That they do not is a reflection both of the natural history of the human species, especially the recency of our shared evolutionary ancestry, as well as the conceptual and empirical difficulties inherent to deciding precisely what counts as either a population or a race. In other words, the biological investigation of race is, to a very large degree, bound up in the social construction of race, and from this point of view it makes little sense to look to science for an independent denial (or, alternatively, ratification) of its objective reality. Of course, many scientists working on human genetic variation do not recognize this, and debate continues to rage, most recently in the wake of the completion of the Human Genome Project, regarding whether, and to what extent, individuals and groups understood socially as belonging to different racial categories can be expected to differ genetically (Wadman 2004). The prominent reemergence of the race question in human biology, which has been viewed by some as the natural outgrowth of the availability of new forms of genetic evidence, is in fact better related to the arrival on the scene of molecular geneticists with an interest in studying the genetic basis of common disease in populations but little prior training in population genetic assumptions or methodology.[20]

Putting Biology Back into the
Philosophical Discussion of Race

Philosophers and other critical theorists interested in understanding and dismantling racist discourses and ideology have accepted, largely at face value, empirically grounded arguments regarding the lack of a biological basis to race while ignoring the persistent use of races as categories of biological investigation. Perhaps because they are not philosophers, most scientists making claims in this area failed to acknowledge that the race concept their data allowed them to reject was the narrow, typological one, in which all members of one race are understood to share genetic characteristics that differ completely from those found in other races. The rejection of this biological basis of race was a rejection of just one model of racial difference, however, and not a repudiation of the existence of biological (genetic) distinctions among groups of individuals understood socially as constituting different races. These differences, which in a population-based conception of race have long been recognized as matters of degree rather than kind, are nevertheless empirically verifiable properties of such groups and, to a large extent, permit inferences of biological distinctiveness that would not be possible if race really were the biological "illusion" it is sometimes claimed to be.

The assertion of "no scientifically recoverable notion of race" by Appiah and downstream theorists therefore fails to account for a widespread operational understanding of race present in many population genetic accounts, an understanding that has been explained as "lexical habit" and subsequently ignored. Ignorance can, of course, arise from an unconscious failure to recognize what is otherwise available to inspection, or it can instead mark a deliberate refusal to acknowledge a state of affairs of which one is consciously aware. In this case, it is clear that the ignorance of race's biological dimension stems not from an inadequate or incomplete consideration of scientific consensus, or from an accidental misreading of a specific population genetic investigation, but from a deliberate decision to deny the salience of scientific practices at odds with the preferred empirical conclusion. For example, it was not that Appiah was unaware that groups recognized socially as races could be distinguished at a genetic level. Rather, he regarded taking such differences as a basis for believing in their prior ontological reality as semantically and philosophically unjustified. Such strategic ignorance is productive for particular philosophical purposes, allowing the a priori dismissal of realist (naturalistic) accounts of race before getting down to the business of what matters most, namely, the political and historical perpetuation of real, but not "really real," sociocultural conglomerations.

Unfortunately, the antirealist rationale for ignoring biology in philo-sophical considerations of race, namely that "once the biology of race is put to rest, 'race' will look and feel differently to people of all races" (Zack 2002, 8), appears to place much (most?) of the blame for racism on inappropriate assumptions regarding racial biological distinctions. Yet to locate racism in beliefs about biological difference seems to make the mistake that Fields has described as transforming "the act of a subject into an attribute of the object" (Fields 2001, 48) and leaves the antiracist project vulnerable in the face of evidence suggesting that underlying ge-netic and external morphological differences can be identified. If such differences are "real," does that render racist practices inevitable and in-controvertible? Surely not. The irony, however, is that in claiming that bi-ological differences must be denied as a precondition for combating racism, this line of reasoning epistemologically privileges what it other-wise seeks to deny. The insistence that race has no biological basis there-fore places biological "facts" about race outside the realm of critique and denies the philosophical analysis of the biological and social coconstitu-tion of racial identity.

However such systematic ignorance was first sanctioned, or whatever the rationale for its continued propagation, philosophic race theory's re-liance on the irrelevance of biology to race and racial identity is ill advised and ethically unsustainable. This is because many of the genetic differ-ences that coincide with different sociocultural identities have material consequences for those who inherit them. These consequences are, first and foremost, bound up in the genetic determination of the overt mor-phological characteristics that figure so prominently in the perceptual practices inherent to racial embodiment and recognition (Outlaw Jr. 1996; Alcoff 2002). They also extend much more widely to encompass predisposition to (or, conversely, protection from) particular acute (O'Brien and Nelson 2004) and chronic (Abate and Chandalia 2003; Freedman 2003; Schaefer et al. 2003) pathological conditions, metabolic responses to drugs (El Rouby et al. 2004; Kim, Johnson, and Derendorf 2004) and other environmental [including toxic (Bolt, Roos, and Thier 2003)] agents, and propensities to specific behaviors such as anxiety, de-pression (Lin 2001), or addiction (Russo et al. 2004). Even genetic differ-ences that are understood to have no direct effect on physiology, such as those used by scientists to indirectly "map" genotype-phenotype relation-ships (Consortium 2003), those interrogated in the matching of forensic specimens (Jobling and Gill 2004), and those traced in the course of identifying ancestral relationships among individuals (Shriver and Kittles 2004), can be tremendously consequential to the individuals whose genes are the objects of inquiry and social and scientific ordering (Elliott and

Brodwin 2002; Nelson 2004). Thus to ignore these differences is to ignore a whole domain of lived experience and to risk the perpetuation of unjust practices that either inappropriately racialize the biological consequences of specific genetic predispositions or deny the inclusive consideration of genetic diversity in clinical and scientific contexts.

For example, a large (and growing) number of genetic variants have been identified with measurable effects on the ability to metabolize (i.e., break down chemically) a range of pharmaceutical compounds prescribed routinely in the course of biomedical treatment (Goldstein, Tate, and Sisodiya 2003). Inherited variability in drug metabolism is important, because it can sometimes lead to serious, unanticipated health effects: either a lack of clinical benefit, because the drug clears the body before its effects are manifest, or an unintended adverse buildup of a toxic side effect, owing to the failure of the drug to be broken down in a timely manner. Moreover, approximately two-thirds of such variants have been observed to vary in frequency from one population to another, sometimes to an appreciable degree (Goldstein and Hirschhorn 2004), leading to calls to consider racial self-identification in the course of drug prescription and treatment (Holden 2003). Using race as a proxy indicator of otherwise hard-to-anticipate biochemical responsiveness appears to make good clinical sense and can be ethically justified, particularly in those cases when prescribing the wrong medicine might lead to great discomfort or even be life threatening. But applied inappropriately, racial profiling in a clinical context can also foreclose treatment options, denying otherwise biochemically suitable individuals access to appropriate drugs under the erroneous assumption that an incompatibility common to some members of a socially recognized category is shared by all members absolutely (Lee 2003).

It is wrong, however, to see the philosophical problem of racial profiling in the medical arena as a problem of biological difference and clinical ascertainment alone. The fact that individuals linked socially to particular racial identities may metabolize drugs to different extents would not be a difficulty if the drugs available for prescription were designed with the global range of diverse metabolic responses in mind. More commonly, however, drugs are designed and tested on very narrow cohorts, typically white, middle-class, U.S.-based research subjects with adequate health insurance and regular access to medical care, who may conform to the ideal downstream prescription drug consumer but do not otherwise provide a generalizable base from which to make assessments about the biological side effects, or environmental codeterminants, of drug response in diverse social groups. In such a drug development milieu, commercial common sense and economic expediency trump justice-based arguments for inclusiveness and comprehensive assessment, so that an individual physician is forced by lack of knowledge, or lack of options, to use race-based criteria in diagnosis and treatment. This current, unsatisfactory state of affairs is only likely to be exacerbated by the burgeoning enthusiasm for the development of racially targeted medicines, such as the new African American-specific drug for heart failure, BiDil (Bloche 2004).

That philosophical descriptions of race and racial identity should pay attention to these, and related developments, is clear. Important questions can, and should, be asked about how the clinical instantiation of race orders particular bodies as diseased or well, predisposed or immune, treatable or irresponsive, and how such designations may impact understandings of collective and individual well-being and belonging. Equally relevant, and pressing, questions should be asked about the ways in which genetic measures of identity can, and are, being used in the scientific ratification of ancestry or the forensic certification of guilt or innocence. This does not mean privileging biological knowledge for its own sake but rather extending philosophical analysis to encompass the varying means by which emerging scientific and technical discourses surrounding biological difference extend the visual registry (Alcoff 2002) of racial embodiment. Simultaneously, philosophers and other race theorists must engage critically with scientific and clinical practices themselves in an effort to encourage more reflexive forms of empirical investigation (Gannett 2004) and with the aim of circumventing interpretations that foreclose, rather than expand, the emancipatory potential of biological and genetic information.

In conclusion, leaving biology at the door of the critical philosophy of race perpetuates a problematic schism between biological and social domains of understanding, denying the complicated amalgam, of inheritance and phenotype, culture and history, that acts simultaneously and coconstitutively in the genesis of racial identity and meaning. This schism not only limits the epistemological terrain of philosophical inquiry, it leaves geneticists and other scientists free to construct accounts of similarity and difference on wholly biological terms. Yet scientific knowledge of human population variation is shaped continuously by sociocultural considerations, and what scientists understand today about the relationship of genetic variation to racial identity will not be precisely the same as what scientists understand tomorrow. In other words, it is just as inappropriate to unreflexively invoke scientific authority in the claim that race *does* have an objective (i.e., empirically verifiable) biological basis as it is in the claim that it does not. Instead, race theorists must recognize the ways in which biological knowledge in this area both shapes, and is shaped by, sociocultural understanding and must engage critically with that knowledge production as it occurs. To not do so is to miss dangers inherent to current empiricist projects and by inaction to allow scientific racism to gain a renewed foot-hold in contemporary discussions and debates.

Notes

Thanks to Anne Buchanan, Lisa Gannett, Michael Montoya, Alondra Nelson, Mark Shriver, Shannon Sullivan, Nancy Tuana, Ken Weiss, and several anonymous reviewers for comments and helpful discussion. S. M. F. was supported by a Ruth L. Kirschstein Postdoctoral Fellowship from the Ethical, Legal, and Social Implications Program of the National Human Genome Research Institute (HG002629).

1. The critique here is restricted to philosophical treatments that explore phenomenological, social, or political manifestations of racial identity, not those involved in the interrogation of competing scientific conceptions of race (i.e., the work of philosophers of biology).

2. An important exception may be found in the work of Lucius L. Outlaw Jr. (Outlaw Jr. 1996). Outlaw advocates for a philosophical recognition of races as *social-natural kinds* (7), which he describes as "groupings of biologically and socially evolving living beings who are also part of socially conditioned natural histories" (12) that are knowable "visibly as well beneath the outer configurations that first meet our culturally socialized senses" (4).

3. This discussion is aimed at describing how the "no biological basis" message became established specifically in philosophy, as opposed to broader arenas. Key scientific papers outlining the empirical case against a typological conception of race were publicly important much earlier (see note 5). An interesting question—which will not be taken up here—is why it took several decades for an established scientific consensus to manifest itself as relevant to philosophical consideration.

4. Nei and Roychoudhury explicitly conceive of these racial groups as representing "five major geographic areas on earth" (1982, 2).

5. Data relevant to this question have been available since at least the time of the UNESCO Statements on Race, of 1950 and 1952 (UNESCO 1952), if not earlier (i.e., the population distribution of various blood group systems was extensively studied prior to World War II). The two scientific publications most often credited with bringing the relevant scientific data to wider public scrutiny are the paper by Frank Livingstone, "On the Nonexistence of Human Races" (Livingstone 1962) and the paper by Richard Lewontin, "The Apportionment of Human Diversity" (Lewontin 1972).

6. Moreover, though the kinds of genetic markers available for investigation have changed dramatically in the last thirty years, these general observations about human genetic variation, properly caveated, continue to withstand the test of time. For a recent comprehensive review, see Kittles and Weiss (2003).

7. See Appiah (1986, 22). A specific statement to this effect in Nei and Roychoudhury (1982) was not cited.

8. See Nei and Roychoudhury (1982, 41). They follow this statement with a small caveat: "Of course, many human races or racial groups have their own unique alleles [genetic variants] at some protein and blood group loci.... However, these unique alleles generally exist in low frequency."

9. See Appiah (1986, 31). For this claim, Appiah drew on estimates of average variation for particular sample subsets provided by Nei and Roychoudhury (1982).

He acknowledged (see note 10), however, that the values he chose for his example made the genetic differences among racial groups look particularly small.

10. He then went on in his own critique to adopt the vantage point of those disinclined to regard the differentiation as meaningful.

11. While Haney López seems to think that Nei and Roychoudhury (1982) advocate abandoning race talk (12, note 46), I could find no statement to this effect in their *Evolutionary Biology* report.

12. These interpretations have been explicitly affirmed in the 1998 adoption of a social constructivist definition of race by the American Anthropological Association (http://www.aaanet.org/stmts/racepp.htm). But note the role of disciplinarity: a corresponding statement on race by the American Association of Physical Anthropologists, adopted in 1996, is decidedly biological in tenor (http://www.physanth.org/positions/race.html).

13. See Reardon (2005), chapter 2, "Post-World War II Expert Discourses on Race" (17–44), in particular, for a discussion of the tensions and internal contradictions inherent to the UNESCO Statements on Race of 1950 and then 1952.

14. My colleague, Michael Montoya, rightly notes that geneticists and other biologists rarely, if ever, speak of "breeding populations" in explaining their sampling choices. Nevertheless, a wealth of evidence supports the contention that this operational understanding drives many of the scientific practices outlined here.

15. Dobzhansky's definition of a "Mendelian population" as "a reproductive community of sexual and cross-fertilizing individuals which share a common gene pool" (Gannett 2001, S484) is consistent with this practice only if one assumes that such individuals "share a common gene pool" by virtue of shared genealogical relations, that is, they can trace their ancestry to individuals who did, in fact, constitute a breeding population in the not-too-distant past. An interesting complication of such sampling is that individuals who describe themselves as being of "mixed" racial ancestry are often excluded from investigation (unless the effects of population admixture are a specific focus of investigation).

16. Such populations are sometimes described as "indigenous." There are, however, very specific understandings of what constitutes population indigenousness, and hence who should be sampled. For example, I was born in the central Pacific but am of European ancestry and thus would never be included in an investigation of Pacific Islander genetic diversity.

17. Who may, or may not, be sampled from the same narrowly defined geographic location within each continent.

18. Variation identified at this latter scale is more often described using explicitly racial descriptors, for example, "Caucasoid," although of course both types of variation would count as "racial" under Dobzhansky's definition.

19. Contingent on the nature of the individuals and populations sampled, as well as the type and absolute number of genetic markers examined, in the specific survey of genetic variation under consideration.

20. As noted earlier, fundamental observations regarding human biological variation have changed little since the publication of the Nei and Roychoudhury (1982) report.

References

Abate, N., and M. Chandalia. 2003. "The Impact of Ethnicity on Type 2 Diabetes." *Journal of Diabetes and Its Complications* 17:1: 39–58.

Alcoff, Linda Martín. 2002. "Philosophy and Racial Identity." In *Philosophies of Race and Ethnicity*, ed. P. Osborne and S. Sandford, 13–28. London: Continuum.

Appiah, Anthony. 1986. "The Uncompleted Argument: Du Bois and the Illusion of Race." In *"Race," Writing, and Difference*, ed. H. L. Gates Jr., 21–37. Chicago: University of Chicago Press.

Appiah, K. Anthony. 1996. "Race, Culture, and Identity: Misunderstood Connections." In *Color Conscious: The Political Morality of Race*, ed. K. A. Appiah and A. Gutmann, 30–105. Princeton, NJ: Princeton University Press.

Appiah, Kwame Anthony. 1989. "The Conservation of 'Race'." *Black American Literature Forum* 23:1: 37–60.

Barkan, Elazar. 1992. *The Retreat of Scientific Racism*. Cambridge: Cambridge University Press.

Bloche, M. G. 2004. "Race-Based Therapeutics." *New England Journal of Medicine* 351:20: 2035–37.

Bolt, H. M., P. H. Roos, and R. Thier. 2003. "The Cytochrome P-450 Isoenzyme CYP2E1 in the Biological Processing of Industrial Chemicals: Consequences for Occupational and Environmental Medicine." *International Archives of Occupational and Environmental Health* 76:3: 174–85.

Chen, Y. S., A. Olckers, T. G. Schurr, A. M. Kogelnik, K. Huoponen, and D. C. Wallace. 2000. "MtDNA Variation in the South African Kung and Khwe and Their Genetic Relationships to Other African Populations." *American Journal of Human Genetics* 66:4: 1362–83.

Consortium, International HapMap. 2003. "The International HapMap Project." *Nature* 426:6968: 789–96.

Elliott, Carl, and Paul Brodwin. 2002. "Identity and Genetic Ancestry Tracing." *British Medical Journal* 325:7378: 1469–71.

El Rouby, S., C. A. Mestres, F. M. LaDuca, and M. L. Zucker. 2004. "Racial and Ethnic Differences in Warfarin Response." *The Journal of Heart Valve Disease* 13:1: 15–21.

Fields, Barbara J. 2001. "Whiteness, Racism, and Identity." *International Labor and Working-Class History* 60 (Fall): 48–56.

Freedman, B. I. 2003. "Susceptibility Genes for Hypertension and Renal Failure." *Journal of the American Society of Nephrology* 14 (7 Suppl 2): S192–94.

Gabriel, S. B., S. F. Schaffner, H. Nguyen, J. M. Moore, J. Roy, B. Blumenstiel, J. Higgins, M. DeFelice, A. Lochner, M. Faggart, S. N. Liu-Cordero, C. Rotimi, A. Adeyemo, R. Cooper, R. Ward, E. S. Lander, M. J. Daly, and D. Altshuler. 2002. "The Structure of Haplotype Blocks in the Human Genome." *Science* 296:5576: 2225–29.

Gannett, Lisa. 2001. "Racism and Human Genome Diversity Research: The Ethical Limits of 'Population Thinking'." *Philosophy of Science* 68:3: S479–92.

———. 2004. "The Biological Reification of Race." *British Journal for the Philosophy of Science* 55:2: 323–45.

Gates, E. Nathaniel. 1997. "Volume Introduction." In *Cultural and Literary Critiques of the Concepts of "Race,"* ed. E. N. Gates, vii–viii. New York: Garland.

Goldstein, D. B., and J. N. Hirschhorn. 2004. "In Genetic Control of Disease, Does 'Race' Matter?" *Nature Genetics* 36:12: 1243–44.

Goldstein, D. B., S. K. Tate, and S. M. Sisodiya. 2003. "Pharmacogenetics Goes Genomic." *Nature Reviews. Genetics* 4:12: 937–47.

Haney López, Ian F. 1994. "The Social Construction of Race: Some Observations on Illusion, Fabrication, and Choice." *Harvard Civil Rights-Civil Liberties Law Review* 29:1: 1–62.

Haraway, Donna. 1989. *Primate Visions.* New York: Routledge.

Holden, C. 2003. "Race and Medicine." *Science* 302:5645: 594–96.

Jobling, M. A., and P. Gill. 2004. "Encoded Evidence: DNA in Forensic Analysis." *Nature Reviews. Genetics* 5:10: 739–51.

Karafet, T. M., L. P. Osipova, M. A. Gubina, O. L. Posukh, S. L. Zegura, and M. F. Hammer. 2002. "High Levels of Y-Chromosome Differentiation among Native Siberian Populations and the Genetic Signature of a Boreal Hunter-Gatherer Way of Life. *Human Biology* 74:6: 761–89.

Kim, K., J. A. Johnson, and H. Derendorf. 2004. "Differences in Drug Pharmacokinetics between East Asians and Caucasians and the Role of Genetic Polymorphisms." *The Journal of Clinical Pharmacology* 44:10: 1083–1105.

Kittles, Rick A., and Kenneth M. Weiss. 2003. "Race, Ancestry, and Genes: Implications for Defining Disease Risk." *Annual Reviews in Genomics and Human Genetics* 4: 33–67.

Lee, S. S. 2003. "Race, Distributive Justice and the Promise of Pharmacogenomics: Ethical Considerations." *American Journal of Pharmacogenomics* 3:6: 385–92.

Lewontin, Richard C. 1972. "The Apportionment of Human Diversity." *Evolutionary Biology* 6: 381–98.

Lin, K. M. 2001. "Biological Differences in Depression and Anxiety across Races and Ethnic Groups." *Journal of Clinical Psychiatry* 62 (Suppl 13): 13–19, discussion 20–21.

Livingstone, Frank B. 1962. "On the Nonexistence of Human Races." *Current Anthropology* 3:3: 279–81.

Marth, G. T., E. Czabarka, J. Murvai, and S. T. Sherry. 2004. "The Allele Frequency Spectrum in Genome-Wide Human Variation Data Reveals Signals of Differential Demographic History in Three Large World Populations." *Genetics* 166:1: 351–72.

Nei, Masathoshi, and Arun K. Roychoudhury. 1982. "Genetic Relationship and Evolution of Human Races." *Evolutionary Biology* 14: 1–59.

Nelson, Alondra. 2004. "'I Bought My First Ghanaian Flag Last Year': Genetic Heredity Tracing, Diasporic Subjectivity, and the Pursuit of African Ancestry." Unpublished paper presented at the Society for the Social Study of Science, Ecole des Mines, Paris, France, August 28.

O'Brien, S. J., and G. W. Nelson. 2004. "Human Genes That Limit AIDS." *Nature Genetics* 36:6: 565–74.

Outlaw Jr., Lucius T. 1996. *On Race and Philosophy.* New York: Routledge.

Ozeki, Ruth L. 1999. *My Year of Meats.* New York: Penguin Books.

Reardon, Jenny. 2005. *Race to the Finish: Identity and Governance in an Age of Genomics*. Princeton, NJ: Princeton University Press.

Rosenberg, N. A., J. K. Pritchard, J. L. Weber, H. M. Cann, K. K. Kidd, L. A. Zhivotovsky, and M. W. Feldman. 2002. "Genetic Structure of Human Populations." *Science* 298:5602: 2381–85.

Russo, D., V. Purohit, L. Foudin, and M. Salin. 2004. "Workshop on Alcohol Use and Health Disparities 2002: A Call to Arms." *Alcohol* 32:1: 37–43.

Schaefer, B. M., V. Caracciolo, W. H. Frishman, and P. Charney. 2003. "Gender, Ethnicity, and Genes in Cardiovascular Disease. Part 2: Implications for Pharmacotherapy." *Heart Disease* 5:3: 202–14.

Shriver, M. D., and R. A. Kittles. 2004. "Genetic Ancestry and the Search for Personalized Genetic Histories." *Nature Reviews. Genetics* 5:8: 611–18.

Siffert, W., P. Forster, K. H. Jockel, D. A. Mvere, B. Brinkmann, C. Naber, R. Crookes, P. Heyns, A. Du, J. T. Epplen, J. Fridey, B. I. Freedman, N. Muller, D. Stolke, A. M. Sharma, K. al Moutaery, H. Grosse-Wilde, B. Buerbaum, T. Ehrlich, H. R. Ahmad, B. Horsthemke, E. D. Du Toit, A. Tiilikainen, J. Ge, Y. Wang, D. Rosskopf et al. 1999. "Worldwide Ethnic Distribution of the G Protein Beta3 Subunit 825T Allele and Its Association with Obesity in Caucasian, Chinese, and Black African Individuals." *Journal of the American Society of Nephrology* 10:9: 1921–30.

Stepan, Nancy Leys. 1982. *The Idea of Race in Science*. Hamden, CT: Archon Books.

UNESCO. 1952. *The Race Concept: Results of an Inquiry: The Race Question and Modern Thought*. Paris: United Nations Educational, Scientific, and Cultural Organization.

Wadman, M. 2004. "Geneticists Struggle Towards Consensus on Place for 'Race'." *Nature* 431:7012: 1026.

Zack, Naomi. 2002. *Philosophy of Science and Race*. New York: Routledge.

CONTRIBUTORS

Linda Martín Alcoff is a professor of philosophy, women's studies, and political science and currently the director of women's studies at Syracuse University. Her books and anthologies include *Feminist Epistemologies* (1993), *Real Knowing: New Versions of the Coherence Theory* (1996), *Epistemology: The Big Questions* (1998), *Thinking From the Underside of History* (2000), *Singing in the Fire: Tales of Women in Philosophy* (2003), and *Visible Identities: Race, Gender, and the Self* (2006). She has written over fifty articles on topics concerning Foucault, sexual violence, the politics of knowledge, Latino/a identity, and gender and race identity.

Alison Bailey is an associate professor of philosophy and the director of the women's and gender studies program at Illinois State University. Her philosophical interests are largely motivated by issues of social justice. She has published on issues of feminist peace politics, race privilege and resistance, and moral responsibility for hate crimes. She is currently coediting with Jacquline Zita a special volume of *Hypatia* on race, reproduction, and the regulation of gendered bodies. She is an enthusiastic practitioner of Iyengar yoga.

Robert Bernasconi has been Moss Professor of Philosophy at the University of Memphis since 1988. He is the author of two books on Heidegger and numerous articles on continental philosophy and social thought. In the area of race theory, in addition to publishing a number of essays, he has edited *Race* and, with Tommy Lott, *The Idea of Race*. He also has been heavily involved in trying to make important documents from the history of racial thought more readily available. He has recently completed, with Kristie Dotson, a three-volume set of nineteenth-century American essays under the title *Race, Hybridity, and Miscegenation.*

Lorraine Code is Distinguished Research Professor of Philosophy at York University in Toronto, Canada. In addition to numerous articles and chapters in books and four coedited books, she has published *Epistemic Responsibility* (1987), *What Can She Know?: Feminist Theory and the Construction of Knowledge* (1991), and *Rhetorical Spaces: Essays on (Gendered) Locations* (1995). She is general editor of the Routledge *Encyclopedia of Feminist Theories* (2000), editor of *Feminist Interpretations of Hans-Georg Gadamer* (2003), and with Kathryn Hamer has translated Michèle Le Doeuff's (1998) *Le Sexe du savoir* as *The Sex of Knowing* (2003). Her most recent book, *Ecological Thinking: The Politics of Epistemic Location*, was published in 2006. She is currently working on questions generated by the new epistemologies of ignorance, on knowing across differences, and on developing a moral epistemology sensitive to vulnerability.

Harvey Cormier is an associate professor of philosophy at Stony Brook University. He has published articles on film, Nietzsche, and American philosophy, and he is the author of a book on William James's pragmatism, called *The Truth Is What Works* (2000). Forthcoming essays will discuss Josiah Royce's view of logic, William James's overlooked arguments concerning race, and connections between the ideas of "race" and "species" in evolutionary psychology.

Stephanie Malia Fullerton is an assistant professor of medical history and ethics at the University of Washington School of Medicine. Trained first in human population genetics, her current research focuses on epistemological, ethical, and historical phenomena underlying contemporary scientists' understandings of genetic variation and its relation to disease predisposition and health. Her contribution was composed while completing postdoctoral training in the ethical, legal, and social implications (ELSI) of human genetics research in the Department of Anthropology and Rock Ethics Institute, Pennsylvania State University.

Sarah Lucia Hoagland is a professor of philosophy and women's studies at Northeastern Illinois University, Chicago. She is author of *Lesbian Ethics* (1988) and coeditor of *For Lesbians Only*, with Julia Penelope (1988), and of *Re-reading the Canon: Feminist Interpretations of Mary Daly*, with Marilyn Frye (2000). She is a collective member of the Institute of Lesbian Studies in Chicago, a staff member of the Escuela Popular Norteña, and a research associate of the Philosophy Interpretation and Culture Center, Binghamton University. This is the fourth in a series of papers on epistemology.

Frank Margonis is an associate professor in the Department of Education, Culture, and Society at the University of Utah. He has published works in political theory, educational policy, and the philosophy of pedagogy. His most recent work focuses on using Heidegger's and Merleau-Ponty's conceptions of "being-with" to develop relational approaches to pedagogy.

Charles W. Mills is Distinguished Professor of Philosophy at the University of Illinois, Chicago. He works in the general area of radical political theory and is the author of three books: *The Racial Contract* (1997), *Blackness Visible: Essays on Philosophy and Race* (1998), and *From Class to Race: Essays in White Marxism and Black Radicalism* (2003). His current projects include a book of Caribbean essays, *Radical Theory, Caribbean Reality: Race, Class, and Social Domination*, and a joint book with Carole Pateman, tentatively titled *Contract and Domination*.

Lucius T. Outlaw (Jr.), formerly T. Wistar Brown Professor of Philosophy at Haverford College (Pennsylvania), is a professor of philosophy and African American studies and an associate provost for undergraduate education, at Vanderbilt University. (Outlaw also has been a member of the faculties of Fisk University and Morgan State University; a visiting professor at Spelman College, Howard University, and Hamilton College; and for the 1996–98 academic years, the David S. Nelson Professor of Boston College.) He teaches, researches, and writes about African philosophy, African American philosophy, Marx, critical social theory, social and political philosophy, and the history of philosophy in the "West." Born in Starkville, Mississippi, he is a graduate of Fisk University (BA, philosophy, 1967, magna cum laude, Phi Beta Kappa) and of the Graduate School of Arts and Sciences of Boston College (Ph.D., philosophy, 1972). His essays have been published in *Philosophical Forum, Journal of Social Philosophy, Man and World, Graduate Faculty Philosophy Journal,* and *The Journal of Ethics*, as well as in a number of anthologies. A collection of several of his essays, *On Race and Philosophy*, was published in 1996. Another book, *Critical Social Theory in the Interests of Black Folk*, was published in 2005.

Elizabeth V. Spelman is a professor of philosophy and the Barbara Richmond 1940 Professor in the Humanities at Smith College. Her most recent book is *Repair: The Impulse to Restore in a Fragile World* (2002). A new project exploring various meanings of abundance is in progress.

Shannon Sullivan is head of the philosophy department and an associate professor of philosophy and women's studies at Penn State University. Her articles on feminist philosophy, critical race theory, American pragmatism, and continental philosophy have appeared in such journals as *Hypatia, Philosophy Today, Radical Philosophy,* and *Transactions of the C. S. Peirce Society*. She is the author of *Living Across and Through Skins: Transactional Bodies, Pragmatism ,and Feminism* (2001) and *Revealing Whiteness: The*

Unconscious Habits of Racial Privilege (2006). With Nancy Tuana, she has guest edited a special issue of *Hypatia* on "Feminist Epistemologies of Ignorance" (2006).

Paul C. Taylor received his BA in philosophy from Morehouse College and his Ph.D. in philosophy from Rutgers University. He has authored numerous publications in the areas of aesthetics, race theory, Africana philosophy, and social philosophy, including the book *Race: A Philosophical Introduction* (2004). Taylor teaches in the department of philosophy at Temple University, and he is a fellow at the New America Foundation in Washington, DC.

Nancy Tuana is the DuPont/Class of 1949 Professor of Philosophy, Humanities, and Women's Studies and director of the Rock Ethics Institute at Pennsylvania State University. Her research and teaching specialties include feminist science studies, with particular attention to the intersection of ethical and epistemological issues in science, feminist theory, philosophy and sexuality, and environmental ethics. Her books include *Engendering Rationalities* (2001), *Feminism and Science* (1989), *The Less Noble Sex: Scientific, Religious, and Philosophical Conceptions of Woman's Nature* (1993), *Revealing Male Bodies* (2002), and *Women and the History of Philosophy* (1992). She is series editor of the Penn State Press series *ReReading the Canon* and coeditor of the Stanford Encyclopedia's entries on feminist philosophy.

INDEX

263

Orwell, George, 60–62, 64–65, 69, 74
Other: exoticization of, in Puerto
  Rican colonial oppression, 159–60;
  logic of resistance and role of, 107,
  115n.13; Mill's concept of, 216–19;
  in Spanish colonialism, 97–98, 100,
  113n.2, 114n.5
Outlaw, Lucius T. (Jr.), 7, 191–92,
  197–210, 251, 254n.2

P

Panama Canal, 156
Pan-American Exposition, 159
Passel, Jeffrey, 136
Pateman, Carol, 214–15
patriarchy: Freud's discussion of, 105;
  modalities of ignorance and,
  220–26; strategic ignorance and,
  87–88
Peirce, Charles, 65
perception: boomerang perception
  concept, 107; Horkheimer on ignorance and, 54–56; white ignorance
  and, 23–24
Petras, John W., 14
Phenomenology of Spirit, The, 235–36
Philadelphia Negro, The, 185, 190–91
Philippines, U. S. occupation of,
  156–60, 173–74
philosophical canon: African influence in, 203–4; biology of race in,
  241–53; epistemology and, 14–17;
  production of ignorance and,
  204–10; racial issues in, 6–35
phronesis, Aristotle's concept of, 231,
  237
*Pilgrimages/Peregrinajes: Theorizing
  Coalition against Multiple Oppressions*,
  82–84
Piper, Adrian, 150n.2
Plato, 8; on knowledge, 59–60, 64–65
political activism: Emerson's discussion of, 70–71; pragmatist view of,
  66–74; production of ignorance/
  knowledge and, 163–67; role of
  faith in, 145–50

Politics of Reality, The, 2–3
Poma de Ayala, Guaman, 113n.2
Popper, Karl, 227
population genetics, race theory and,
  242–53
Porter, Eduardo, 136
postmodernism: ideology and, 64–65;
  pragmatism and, 65–66
Powell, Colin, 141, 148–49
power relations: ignorance and,
  203–28; logic of oppression and,
  109–10, 115n.14
practical racialism, 140–41
pragmatism: colonialism and, 175–76;
  Horkheimer's discussion of, 54–56;
  ignorance and, 4; Rorty-West debate concerning, 65–73
Price, Joshua, 111
Prince, Mary, 106
Proctor, Robert, 3
progressivism, pragmatism and,
  67–68, 70
public policy, ignorance promoted in,
  95–97
"publics," Dewey's concept of,
  138–41
Puerto Rico: commonwealth status
  of, 166–67, 171n.7; ignorance concerning, 156–58; independence
  movement in, 165–67, 170n.6;
  "Porto Rico" created in, 157–60,
  163–65; reciprocity with U.S. in,
  168–70; resistance to colonialism
  in, 163–67; U.S. colonialism in, 6,
  155–57; white ignorance and
  colonial oppression in, 153–70
Puritan theology, influence in philosophy of, 205–6
purity: split-separation logic of, 82–84,
  92n.7; strategic ignorance and,
  87–91; white ignorance and, 85–91
Putnam, Robert, 147

Q

Quijano, Anibal, 101
Quine, W. V., 14, 54, 60, 65

Sartre, Jean-Paul, 8, 108; Fanon's
    critique of, 231–38
Savage, Kirk, 30
"savage" concept, white ignorance
    and, 26–28
Schaefer, B. M., 251
Scheler, Max, 14
Schiebinger, Londa, 3, 220
Schlick, Moritz, 52–53
Schmitt, Frederick F., 15
school integration, production of
    ignorance and, 207–8
School of the Americas, 148
Schutz, Alfred, 238
science. *See also* biology: colonialism
    and role of, 97, 160–63; neglect of
    ignorance in, 3; racial issues in
    context of, 8, 138–41, 190–92,
    242–53, 254nn.2; 4; white igno-
    rance and, 20–21
Scully, Judith, 95–96
segregation, white racial formation
    and, 182–86
self-deception, managing ignorance
    with, 121–30
"Self-Reliance," 70
Sellen, Jeff, 156
Sen, Amartya, 137
separatism: logic of oppression and,
    105–8; relationality and, 112–13;
    segregation as, 184–86
sexism, science of female sexuality
    and, 3
Sex of Knowing, The, 223
Shapiro, Thomas, 31
Sharpton, Al, 61
Shriver, M.D., 251
Siffert, W. P., 248
situated knowledge, Code's discussion
    of, 40–43
slavery: Founding intellectuals' silence
    on, 206–10, 211n.9; historical era-
    sure of, 30–31, 182–86, 208–10;
    logic of resistance and, 102–8; oblit-
    eration of testimony concerning,
    32–35, 106; post-Civil War reconcili-

ationism and invisibility of, 129–30,
    131n.9–10
Smith, Dorothy, 99
Smith, Rogers M., 17
social constructivism, racial identity
    and, 242–53, 255n.12
social contract theory: power of igno-
    rance and, 214–15; strategic igno-
    rance and, 78–91
Social Epistemology (book), 14
Social Epistemology (journal), 14
social good: ideology as threat to,
    62–65; pragmatist view of, 66–73;
    racialized distribution of, 140–41;
    white ignorance and, 21–23
social ignorance: faith and, 147–50;
    Haitian policies in context of,
    140–43; optimism and, 146–47;
    racial identity and, 136–50; systemic
    critique of, 6, 145–46
Socializing Epistemology, 14
social order, production of ignorance
    and, 197–210
social sciences, racial issues and white
    ignorance in, 33–35
social trust, political activism and,
    147–49
sociology of knowledge, epistemology
    and, 14–17
Souls of Black Folk, The, 18
Soyinka, Wole, 188
Spain, Puerto Rican colonization and,
    155–57, 161–63
Spanish-American War, 155–57
Spanish language, preservation in
    colonial Puerto Rico of, 161, 170n.4
Spelman, Elizabeth V., 5, 109, 119–30;
    boomerang perception concept of,
    107
Spindel, Carol, 91n.2
split-separation logic, multiple oppres-
    sions and, 82–84
Stalin, Josef, 72
standpoint theory: epistemology of
    ignorance and, 4; evolution of,
    14–15

Made in the USA
San Bernardino, CA
01 September 2013